Where the Wild Coffee Grows

By the same author

*Darjeeling: The Colorful History and Precarious
Fate of the World's Greatest Tea*

Spain: Recipes and Traditions

Morocco: A Culinary Journey with Recipes

Rice, Pasta, Couscous: The Heart of the Mediterranean Kitchen

*La Paella: Deliciously Authentic Rice Dishes from
Spain's Mediterranean Coast*

Where the Wild Coffee Grows

The Untold Story of Coffee from the Cloud Forests of Ethiopia to Your Cup

JEFF KOEHLER

B L O O M S B U R Y

NEW YORK · LONDON · OXFORD · NEW DELHI · SYDNEY

Bloomsbury USA
An imprint of Bloomsbury Publishing Plc

1385 Broadway	50 Bedford Square
New York	London
NY 10018	WC1B 3DP
USA	UK

www.bloomsbury.com

BLOOMSBURY and the Diana logo are trademarks of Bloomsbury Publishing Plc

First published 2017

© Jeff Koehler, 2017

Photographs © Jeff Koehler, 2017

No responsibility for loss caused to any individual or organization acting on or refraining from action as a result of the material in this publication can be accepted by Bloomsbury or the author.

ISBN: HB: 978-1-63286-509-0
         ePub: 978-1- 63286-511-3

Library of Congress Cataloging-in-Publication Data is available.

2 4 6 8 10 9 7 5 3 1

Typeset by Westchester Publishing Services
Printed and bound in the U.S.A. by Berryville Graphics Inc., Berryville, Virginia

To find out more about our authors and books visit www.bloomsbury.com. Here you will find extracts, author interviews, details of forthcoming events, and the option to sign up for our newsletters.

Bloomsbury books may be purchased for business or promotional use. For information on bulk purchases please contact Macmillan Corporate and Premium Sales Department at specialmarkets@macmillan.com.

For my maternal grandparents, Joe and Ione, who taught me to begin each day with a scalding pot of coffee, and in memory of my paternal ones, Bob and Edith, whose stories of Ethiopia inspired me to go to see the country myself for the first time twenty years ago.

As well, for a dozen friends who remind me that life's most memorable moments tend to be quiet ones and usually happen over (good) coffee.

Contents

Contents

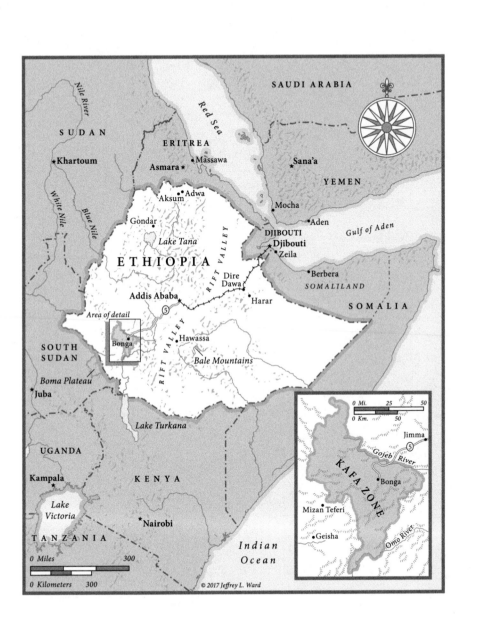

© 2017 Jeffrey L. Ward

Notes on Spelling, Names, and Abbreviations

SPELLING

The transliteration of words from Amharic, Arabic, and Kafinoonoo are phonetic and generally lack standardized spelling. Differences tend to be minor but numerous—from Kafa (Kaffa, Keffa, Kefa), Mocha (al-Makha, Mokka, Mokha), and Shawa (Shewa, Shoa) to the more than a dozen ways to spell Muhammad. I have kept the spelling of the original when quoting, but elsewhere followed the form that seems to me to be the most widely accepted. For Arabic words, I have left off macrons and subscript dots.

ETHIOPIAN NAMES

In Ethiopia, a second name is the father's first name rather than the family name. For Ethiopians, then, I have used both names on first occurrence in a chapter, and the first rather than second name thereafter.

ABYSSINIA

Abyssinia is often used as a synonym for Ethiopia and was popular usage in Europe in the past. Historically, it refers to the ancient kingdom on the central plateau, while Ethiopia more succinctly means the modern empire created by Menelik II at the closing of the nineteenth century. To avoid confusion, I have used Ethiopia throughout, except when quoting.

ABBREVIATIONS

AFS	Agro-Forestry System
CATIE	Centro Agronómico Tropical de Investigación y Enseñanza (Tropical Agricultural Research and Higher Education Center)
CBD	coffee berry disease
CIRAD	Centre de Coopération Internationale en Recherche Agronomique pour le Développement (Center for International Cooperation in Agricultural Research for Development)
FAO	United Nation's Food and Agriculture Organization
HT or HdT	Híbrido de Timor or Timor hybrid, a spontaneous hybrid between Arabica and Robusta
IRD	Institut de Recherche pour le Développement (Research Institute for Development)
JARC	Jimma Agricultural Research Center
NABU	Nature and Biodiversity Conservation Union, a German conservation charity
NGO	nongovernmental organization
ORSTOM	Office de la Recherche Scientifique et Technique Outre-Mer (Office of Scientific and Technical Research Overseas), precursor to IRD
PFM	Participatory Forest Management
SCAA	Specialty Coffee Association of America
VOC	Verenigde Oostindische Compagnie (Dutch East India Company)
UNESCO	United Nations Educational, Scientific and Cultural Organization
USDA	United States Department of Agriculture
WCR	World Coffee Research

Coffee Is Our Bread

A sking for an after-lunch coffee at the popular Kofi Laande Hoteelo—aka Coffeeland—in Kafa's regional capital of Bonga is not as simple as placing an order at Starbucks and stepping over to the pickup counter. And the woman preparing it is certainly far more than what that chain calls a barista. Sitting on a low stool in the corner of the restaurant-bar, she had sorted, cleaned, and then roasted the green coffee beans on a wide, lipless metal disk over a brazier of embers, moving them around with a hooked piece of metal until deep, glossy brown. Once they had cooled, she pounded the fragrant beans with a steel rod in a wooden mortar made from a hollowed log. Curling a piece of woven mat in her palm, she funneled the grounds into the narrow neck of the bulbous terra-cotta coffeepot called a jebena that was simmering on a brazier beside her.

Two dozen handleless demitasse cups with slightly flared lips crowded a low round table in front of her. On the cement floor beneath it, she had fanned out reedy grasses and arranged a handful of yellow and red blossoms. Nature, she said, had to be present, and the greens and flowers had come from the forest, where the spirits live. Wisps of smoke curled up from a smoldering dish of waxen incense, a blend of myrrh and local frankincense that recalled gloomy ancient churches and brought Orthodox sacredness into the preparations, too.

Preparing and drinking coffee is so stylized in Ethiopia that the process is known as a coffee ceremony, a slow ritual with requisite tools and a dozen unvarying steps. This was the shortened version.

It was a Friday, one of the week's two fasting days, and lunch after a morning deep inside the cloud-shrouded forests of southwestern Ethiopia consisted of dollops of a dozen different legumes and vegetables atop spongy injera flatbread. The rattan blinds of Coffeeland had been rolled up, filling the room with glare and gusts of breeze that heralded another lashing sweep of unseasonable rain.

The isolated highlands of Kafa are a mosaic of deep valleys, dense forests, and hamlets of subsistence farmers. Nearly every home is surrounded by enset trees and a garden of field peas, fava and haricot beans, cabbage, and onions. Those living around the forest gather long pepper, dig for wild cardamom, and hang rudimentary cylindrical hives high in trees for honey to make murky, home-fermented *tej*. Coffee, though, is the cash crop. Eighty-five percent of Kafa's people rely directly or indirectly on coffee for their livelihood, including lowlanders. In the highlands, it is close to 100 percent.[1] Locals forage for it in the wild and grow it in their gardens, buy it, sell it, hoard it until prices go up, and, in the meantime, drink numerous cups of it a day. Even toddlers sip the drink. "When kids start walking, talking, and touching everything, they simultaneously start taking sips of coffee," as one Kafa resident put it.

Ethiopia scarcely receives more than a sentence or two in the histories of coffee, and Kafa—the place that arguably gave everywhere outside Ethiopia its name for the drink—rarely gets any mention at all. Kafa is home to the world's original coffee culture, yet remains virtually unknown.

The long-held, and often still-believed, narrative that Arabica coffee—the most prevalent and superior of the two main species of coffee cultivated today—came from Arabia is wrong. It came from the southwestern cloud forests a few hundred miles from Addis Ababa. Finding coffee's origin story requires a journey into those forests. Not only did the Arabica coffee plant originate here, but so did coffee drinking. Historians generally credit Arabs or Sufi monks with developing and refining the brewing process, or even inventing it. Yet those living in and around the forests where coffee grew wild undoubtedly were the first to prepare it.

Part of the reason for attributing this to the Arabs is that there was no early written evidence of coffee being drunk in Kafa. The local language had no script until the 1990s (or by the time Starbucks had already opened its first thousand outlets). Stories of coffee's discovery and how the people here gradually came to brew the drink were told over the generations but not written down. With the area difficult to reach and the long-unwelcoming attitude of rulers in Ethiopia and also in Kafa itself, Western travelers didn't make it to the area until the mid-nineteenth century. The coffee forests remained virtually unvisited by Westerners until the 1930s.

Kafa's obscurity is all that much more surprising because it was one of the richest kingdoms in the Horn of Africa. Bonga was the starting point of a trio of important ancient trade routes that connected the interior of Ethiopia with the coast, and along them traveled caravans with slaves, ivory, musk, and dried coffee pods. For five centuries an unbroken line of god-kings ruled Kafa, until it was nearly wiped out as Ethiopia forcibly absorbed the medieval kingdom into an expanding empire. At the end of the nineteenth century Kafa was home to one million people. Within two decades its population had fallen by up to 90 percent.[2] The story of the lengthy reign, and fall, of the Kingdom of Kafa and its indigenous coffee culture is untold.

The jebena gurgled. The woman lifted the blackened pot off the embers and set it near her feet, tilted forward slightly, to allow the grounds to settle before pouring.

Coffee is one the world's most traded commodities and is the livelihood of some 125 million people across the globe.

The first outsider to claim that the original source was Kafa—the eighteenth-century Scottish traveler James Bruce—had his travelogue mocked for its far-fetched tales of Ethiopia. Not until the 1960s, nearly two centuries later, did scientists say with any level of certainty that Arabica originated and grew wild in the southwestern highlands. These montane rain forests are the mother source of the world's most spectacular cultivated coffees, grown from Kenya to Guatemala, Brazil, and Jamaica's Blue Mountains. (Yet, somewhat perversely, even here the coffee goes by an official name that means "from Arabia.")

In 2016, more than twelve billion pounds of Arabica was produced around the globe, enough to brew more than five hundred billion six-ounce cups of coffee. Latin America grows the vast majority of it. Yet that region's coffee is in trouble. With an extraordinary lack of genetic diversity, cultivated Arabica is unable to withstand or adapt to increasing threats. Diseases and a changing climate are battering production. A fungus known as coffee leaf rust has sent Latin America's coffee industry into a tailspin and left families hungry, communities desperate, and futures uncertain. In El Salvador, one the many countries dependent on its coffee crop, the 2015–16 harvest was down 80 percent from just four years before. Plummeting coffee yields have led to a surge of unaccompanied minors fleeing Central America for the United States and is impacting one of the most divisive issue in American politics today, illegal immigration.

From instant Sanka to a southern-Italian espresso so short that there is just enough liquid to dissolve a spoonful of sugar, perhaps no other substance holds sway over the human experience like coffee. For the past five centuries it has been a driver of great thoughts, a mother of inspiration, a provider of energy behind many of mankind's greatest inventions. We wake to it, confab over it, reinvigorate with it, attempt to quit it only to return again. "If it is not indispensable to man's happiness," wrote one mid-twentieth-century coffee expert, "it certainly contributes a good deal to it."[3] Few would argue the conceit, and many would take it further. For some it is an obsession, for others an identity.

Ethiopia is one of the world's largest producers of coffee. Yet it exports less than half of what it grows. To put that another way, it consumes more than half its own production. No other country comes even close to that. Coffee is not just the national drink but its staple. *Buna dabo naw* goes a popular expression: "Coffee is our bread." Nowhere is that more true than in Kafa.

The woman lifted the jebena and poured out the coffee into a half dozen small cups in a single, smooth motion. As the pot had no filter, a gentle, continuous pour is key to keeping grounds inside the pot.

It had taken her an hour to prepare, making even the most elaborate manual pour-over coffee in a hipster joint in Brooklyn seem as easy as pressing the button on a Nespresso machine. In a couple of slurps it was gone.

The coffee was powerful and as viscous as a well-pulled espresso, with notes of citruses and of red berries from drying the coffee fruits on rudimentary bamboo beds in the sun. The beans had been gathered in the dense forests outside Bonga from scrawny, moss-covered trees, and unlike the bright, clean flavors of most Ethiopian coffees served in high-end specialty cafés in San Francisco, Oslo, and Seoul, wild coffee has an unevenness to it from the mismatched ripeness of the picked fruits—a wini-ness from overripe ones came through—and dusty aromas of the woods that it never shakes. Yet sipping coffee that carries with it such an earthy imprint is thrilling.

At the back of the throat came that familiar tingle, the sensation that energy, clarity, and excitement were close behind.

"Another?" the woman asked, taking back the empty cup.

Even though it was already the fourth of the day and not yet two o'clock, yes. It wouldn't be the last coffee of the day. There would be one or two more—and probably another insomnia-plagued night from such unaccustomed levels of caffeine.

From smallholders in Antigua Guatemala to ones on the central highlands below Mount Kenya, from a bearded barista at Intelligentsia in Chicago wearing a flat-brim cap to dockworkers in Palermo before their morning shift or someone picking up a Skinny Cinnamon Dolce Latte in a Starbucks drive-through, each cup of their Arabica is linked to the undergrowth of Ethiopia's coffee forests.

But the forests around Kafa are not just important because they are the origin of a drink that means so much to so many. They are important because deep in their shady understory lies a key to saving the faltering coffee industry. They hold not just the past but also the future of coffee.

PART ONE

In the Forest

CHAPTER I

Sown by the Birds

tartan of paths wove through the weedy expanses at the edge of the hamlet. Banana-like enset trees, with peeling trunks and sword-shaped leaves standing erect as quills, clustered around each of the two dozen squat huts. The wattle-and-daub walls had long settled and cracked, and the conical tukuls sat slightly askew. They had no chimneys, and morning cook smoke rose like steam through the thatched roofs. Among snatches of conversations and the soft domestic clank of pots came the muted jingle of a brass cowbell.

Woldegiorgis Shawo crossed the bottom of his hamlet, cut into the quiet shade, and entered the Mankira Forest. The thin path disappeared as soon as he began winding down the slope. Fit and still strong at seventy-five, he walked with a quick, rolling gait, his shoulders thrown back, his knees coming up high as he stepped though the tangles of thistles and thorns and long grasses that covered the ground.

The damp forest was hushed but not still. Twitching movement above revealed a troop of black-and-white colobus monkeys with potbellies, bored expressions, and long tails that dangled like shaggy white lichen. Lanky branches arched overhead among cords of lianas, while yellow epiphytic orchids cascaded down dull tree trunks veined limpid emerald by leafy climbers. A ray of sunlight pierced the tunnel of foliage, catching the taut grid of a spider's web and illuminating tiny, star-shaped topaz flowers that tattooed the sodden leaf litter. From the canopy above came the deep whoosh of a silvery-cheeked hornbill taking flight. *Wa-wa-wa-wa-wa*, it brayed like an agitated goat.

After twenty minutes or so, Woldegiorgis stopped. Through a fissure in the branches appeared a young man in an oversize cable-knit sweater and jacket, the sleeves thickly rolled past the elbow. He reached up, doubled over a spry branch, and began stripping off the fruits, spinning the deep red berries between thumb and fingers to separate them from the short stem. It was the end of October, and the gathering of wild coffee was just beginning in Kafa's highland rain forests.

Wreathed in tender ferns, the smooth grayish-brown trunks were slender as forearms and forked and had long, drooping branches. Festoons of silvery-green moss hung from twigs like unkempt beards. The shiny dark-green coffee leaves—oval and ribbed, with fine, tapering ends—were sparse.

A trio of barefoot teenage girls materialized through the quiet lattice of woodsy green. The middle one, perhaps fourteen years old, stepped out last. Broken sunlight streaked her face with its shy smile, downcast eyes, and tight necklace strung with a single red bead that at first appeared to be a ripe coffee fruit. A small woven basket hung from an arm of each holding cherries, as the fruits are called.

Wild coffee trees grow spontaneously under the towering, broad-leafed canopy. They are neither cultivated nor maintained. Nor do the trees have a defined owner. Instead, a complex system of ancestral entitlements govern who is allowed to gather the ripe coffee berries and precisely from where in the forest. With a fluttering wave of his hand, Woldegiorgis indicated the sweep of the generous ten hectares (twenty-five acres) where the hereditary right for him to collect coffee had been passed down for generations. The forest has no boundary markers, but he knew his plot to the bush by the fall of the land and its natural features—the cuff of a certain hillock, a cluster of shrubs gathered in a hollow, a stream that forms part of its border.

The four pickers returned to stripping the fruits off the branches, working steadily and quietly, slipping, on occasion, into song, sung low and to themselves. Many of trees had few berries, and some none at all. The young man scaled a sturdy tree to get a group of higher fruits.

The cherries that brew the best cup are the supple ruby ones. But in the cloud-smothered rain forest wild coffee ripens asynchronously, and the pickers took pale fruits that were only beginning to blush, yellow ones, and even some still green, dropping them all in their baskets. It was an effort to return to this isolated spot, but it was also risky to leave any cherries on the branches. There was no guarantee that the ripe fruit would be there when they returned. While Woldegiorgis had the right to the coffee from these trees, and the remoteness ensured few would venture to the spot, access was open.

The main threat, though, Woldegiorgis said, gathering fistfuls of coffee while he spoke, isn't people but the natural world. Heavy rains during the past evenings had knocked down many of the riper cherries. "This," he said, motioning to the crimson coffee fruits scattered around the ground, a result of the fickle weather. "Also animals." As the berries mature, they become more enticing to the baboons and monkeys, certain birds, and rodents that savor their sweet pulp. Woldegiorgis pointed to a branch that had been recently broken by the heavy weight of a baboon trying to get to the ripe fruit.

But animals are also key to the survival of wild coffee, as they sow the seeds around the forest. The white-cheeked turaco and large silvery-cheeked hornbill, known for its distinctive oversize cream-colored casque and bold, noisy call, carry the seeds the farthest.

"This coffee"—Woldegiorgis said, his hand around a lithe trunk—"is *wof zerash*." Sown by the birds.

Kafa is officially a "zone" within Ethiopia's Southern Nations, Nationalities and Peoples' Region, a large state and one of the most culturally and linguistically diverse areas in Africa. Kafa measures some 4,250 square miles, a bit smaller than Connecticut, with an overwhelmingly rural population of 850,000. Its capital, Bonga, by far Kafa's biggest city and, apart from Jimma, in the neighboring region, the largest for hundreds of miles in any direction, is home to just twenty-seven thousand people.

In Bonga, Mesfin Tekle, the leading authority on the forests of Kafa, said, "The legend tells us coffee started in Mankira." Local tradition specifically points to this forest as the birthplace of coffee.[1] Among a grove of trees inside Mankira, Woldegiorgis said, "This is the place."

The Mankira Forest is only fifteen miles from Bonga. Some seven hundred people live around it in four hamlets and a larger, eponymous village. For much of the year they are inaccessible and remain difficult to reach the remainder of it. From Bonga, it is an hour's drive in a Land Cruiser until the truck can go no farther on a washed-out road strewn with rocks and gouged with runoff channels, and another hour on foot down to the Gumi River, losing a thousand feet in elevation.

The Gumi ("dark") marks the boundary of Mankira, and during the lengthy April-to-September rainy season, locally called *yooyo*, the swollen river cuts it off. (The other route, which is generally muddy and boggy, takes three hours to walk, and crosses several rivers, remains a desperate rather than realistic alternative.) In June, the river had been impassable and highly treacherous. Now, during harvest time four months later, and into the short *qaawoo* (dry season), the water should have been calf deep. But *dry season* is a relative term at best. Storms were breaking late at night, flashing across distant hills before arriving with thunderous urgency, pummeling the corrugated-metal roofs in Bonga and sending rivulets of water cascading down the unlit dirt roads. The Gumi was rushing through its ravine in near-full spate and laden with soil from the hills. A pair of Abyssinian horses, small grayish mares, carrying jute sacks of dried coffee from Mankira to be milled in Bonga, plunged to their bellies as they crossed. Two teenage boys prodded the animals through the strong current that pushed them downstream toward the rapids as they made their way to the opposite bank.

After they had crossed, a forester and guide named Alemayu Haile stepped into the water that nearly reached his waist. Stripping down, looping pants, boots, and backpack around his neck, Asaye Alemayehu, a forest guide from Bonga, took up one of the tall sticks left on the bank and walked into the swift magenta-orange water, lurching the fifteen yards across the river over jagged, hidden boulders that lined the riverbed.

From the Gumi it was nearly an hour climb to Gola, the first small hamlet, and then another hour to the village of Mankira itself. The path cleaved through dense forest, quickly gaining elevation. Troops of olive baboons mingled along the edge of the track. A scythe-billed hadada ibis fluttered up from a tree, calling *Haa-haa-haaaa-haa*, as a couple more laden mules came down the hill. Later, half a dozen people, each bearing a piece of living room furniture bound for sale in Bonga, filed passed. Black butterflies spun upward from rain puddles, and inch-wide columns of feisty red ants crossed the track. Along both side were groves of wild coffee. Scattered among their branches were brilliant, waxy yellowish and red coffee fruits that popped out of the leafy greens like berries on Christmas holly.

Unlike maize, carrots, or bananas, which are nearly unrecognizable beside their domesticated relatives, wild coffee fruits look identical to cultivated ones. About the size of a plump blueberry or cranberry, they are slightly elliptical and have a small nipple scar at the tip. Each fruit holds a pair of hard oval pale seeds—the beans. Wrapped in a fine silvery membrane and covered with a parchment, they are embedded in sticky, sugar-rich mucilage and enclosed in a thin layer of pulpy flesh (the mesocarp) and smooth outer skin (the exocarp).

The biggest differences between wild and cultivated coffee are in the trees, their height, the slimness of the trunks—and the amount of fruit they bear.

A fertile patch of well-tended, shade-grown Guatemalan coffee produces annually about 400 to 450 kilograms of green coffee—clean, unroasted coffee beans—per hectare. Colombia's national average is nearly 1,000 kilograms (2,200 pounds), although some farms are producing more than three times that amount. In Kafa, the same-size piece of dense forest might yield as little as 15 kilograms, or 33 pounds, of wild coffee.[2] "In the Kombo Forest if they get thirty kilos it is a good yield," said Mesfin. Certain forests that are more open, with more light, might provide a couple hundred kilos of coffee per hectare. Even that, though, is cyclical: a (relatively) bounteous year is followed by a slack one. "It is like the teeth of a saw," said a coffee collector encountered in another part of Mankira's forest. "If this harvest is good, then next year's will decline."

Cultivated coffee exists because it is meant to exist, Mesfin had said in Kombo, south of Bonga. "Plantation coffee trees are bred, planted, and trained to produce. They are expected to do so."

Not so these gangly wild ancestors. A coffee tree is here because it won the space. More than one seed fell in the same place, and many other plants want the nutrients of the humus beneath it, the water, and those flickers of precious sunlight that pierce the overhead canopy. "It exists not just to exist but to survive," Mesfin said. Or because it *has* survived. This is one reason wild trees produce so little. Heavy bearing weakens a tree, and resources go into fending off diseases, pests, and beating competition— into simply surviving.

In the deep forest, Arabica trees are spindly, thin, and unusually tall as they stretch toward light filtering through a canopy of towering *warqa* (*Ficus vasta*, a type of wild fig tree), hundred-foot-tall *butoo* with yellowish leaves, and red stinkwood. Coffee trees have large leaves that are more supple than leathery in the shade, long gaps between the internodes, and few low branches. The more undisturbed the forest, the denser the canopy, the slower the trees grow, and the fewer cherries they produce—just enough to ensure the survival of the species.[3]

In Kombo, Mesfin pulled off a piece of moss and inhaled deeply. "The smell of the forest is the smell of dust. On the coffee tree there is a moisture which falls on the trunk, on the wood part, and that attracts dust, and in the dust mosses and ferns grow." The moss was fine and a touch brittle. "On that insects also feed and live. Some of the insects are the most important pollinators." He paused. "Listen." Under the wispy silvery-green covering was a slight shifting.

The unkempt coffee trees are just one among four hundred other species of plants growing in the dense understory of the coffee forest,[4] and an intricate piece of Kafa's rich floristic diversity.

Woldegiorgis pinched the end of a fresh coffee cherry and shot the beans into his mouth. They have a delicate sweetness, with subtle hints of hibiscus, cherry, and watermelon, even mango. He spat out the seeds, pinched another pair into his mouth, and set off deeper into the forest.

Threading quickly through the dense woodland, skirting potholes dug by shy, nocturnal creatures, he stopped to point out fresh buffalo tracks, and then, farther along, baboon scat filled with pale coffee beans. "Snakes are active and more aggressive in the dry season when they are hunting," Alemayu had warned. Green mamba—the most feared of the local creatures—lurked among the leafy foliage. (The electric-green skin of one spotted earlier was almost too vibrant to be real, and certainly too gorgeous not to be deadly.) A white-cheeked turaco, as stylized as a hand-painted ornament, scurried down a slender branch and then flashed its crimson wings as it darted off with a ripe fruit clamped in its orange beak. Deeper in the forest a solitary De Brazza's monkey announced itself with a booming call.

Woldegiorgis finally stopped on a thickly treed slope. He wore a soiled army-green polo shirt with a yellow checked collar and cuffs and a grubby baseball hat whose logo had long since peeled away. Throwing an arm around one tree's stout, forked trunk, he said, *"Bune inde,"* the "mother coffee tree." Small tree ferns sprouted from its aging bark, and beardlike tufts clung to its branches. "The oldest in Mankira."

Wild coffee trees can reach one hundred years old,[5] and eventually they just topple over. *Bune inde* was much older, Woldegiorgis insisted. He remembered it as the same size when his father showed it to him as a boy seven decades before. Its trunk wasn't thick, just five inches or so in diameter. In eastern Ethiopia, old cultivated Arabica trees growing on the sunny terraced hills around Harar are significantly stockier. This one had put its energy in growing upward through the middle strata. In the Gela coffee forest, they grow even taller, reaching fifty to sixty-five feet as they compete for light.

High, and seemingly out of reach, were a couple dozen still-yellow coffee cherries. "I will collect these myself," Woldegiorgis said somewhat improbably. Only he gathers the fruits from *bune inde*.

All around, coffee trees and saplings of all ages sprouted up. This was the hidden wealth of Kafa. But pulling away a piece of gauzy moss and inhaling, one smells not profit but survival.

Back with the four others, Woldegiorgis told them to pack up and return to the hamlet for lunch. Those venturing farther into the forest to reach their designated area carry food with them—boiled beans, some cabbage, and *kocho*, a staple flatbread made from the fermented starches of enset— and, snug in a wicker basket, a jebena of coffee corked with a corncob. Collectors who go into the deepest reaches of the forests travel with horses and mules and set up makeshift camps to stay for a month or longer, returning in late December or January once the harvest has been collected and the coffee dried.

Woldegiorgis had hired these four to pick for the day. Some laborers receive 10 percent of the cherries they gather. Woldegiorgis prefers to pay cash. The rate was one birr (five cents) per kilogram. Because they had to carry the coffee some distance back from the forest, he paid them an additional birr per kilo. A basket held five kilos, and each could fill it once, maybe twice, in a morning, earning up to a dollar for their work.

The oldest girl, wearing a crudely carved wooden Orthodox cross and two small knotted cloth charm bags around her neck, held open a jute sack for the others to dump their baskets. A second sack had already been filled. She and another girl each balanced one on their heads and followed Woldegiorgis back through the forest, crouching with their loads under lianas and low branches.

The troop of colobus monkeys hadn't moved far and were quietly plucking and chewing leaves. A cloak of spirituality clings to their patient, aloof demeanor, their stillness. "We call them monks," said Alemayu. "They have fasting days." People tolerate colobuses, unlike baboons or mischievous grivet monkeys, as they tend not to bother garden crops.

The forest eventually opened, and a trail that had taken form curled up into the hamlet. A stick with a white flower as big as a trumpet's bell had been driven into the ground in front of a tukul, a sign that home-brewed *tej* (mead) was for sale.

Woldegiorgis turned into the compound of his home, a sturdy rect-angular-shaped house with a corrugated roof. Years of smoke escaping under the eaves had blackened the top half of the mud walls. Coffee trees had been planted around the side and back. A rudimentary raised bed some four or five paces long and made with thin bamboo poles held drying coffee. The pods from the last few days had turned auburn and buff chestnut color, while the oldest ones, collected the previous week, were leathery and almost uniformly purplish black. He unknotted the gunny-sacks and poured the fresh cherries at the far end of the bed, raking them with his fingers into an even layer to dry in the sun. Depending on the weather, they'd be ready in one to two weeks.

Each year Woldegiorgis harvests about a thousand kilograms of coffee cherries* from the forest, he said, running a palm over the taunt smooth-ness of the fresh fruits, and another five hundred kilograms from the trees he tends on his plot and around his home. Half or so he sells to Mankira's cooperative straightaway. The remainder he keeps until the market prices go up, and to use at home.

As he spoke, leaden clouds appeared over the hill, and soon after, a handful of pregnant drops splattered down. Woldegiorgis hurriedly pulled a plastic tarp over the bed. Once the clouds had bundled past, he uncov-ered the cherries again.

While the mill in Bonga can peel away the dried fruit and parchment surrounding the beans, coffee kept to use at home must be painstakingly peeled by hand with the help of a stone mortar. Woldegiorgis's wife roasts the beans and brews coffee three or four times a day. (Preparing coffee is strictly a woman's job in Ethiopia.) She pours the coffee out into small, smooth-worn bamboo cups glossy as horn. The handleless chinaware ones are only for when guests come. Woldegiorgis likes to add a dollop of butter and a pinch of salt to his coffee, transforming the brew into a lusty concoc-tion. "If there is no butter, then honey," he added.

Sometimes, before he takes his first drink, he tips out a bit onto the

---

* It takes 6 kilograms of fresh coffee cherries to get a kilo of dried coffee with the husk, which gives about 800 grams of clean, green coffee. The beans lose 15 to 20 percent of their weight when roasted, leaving around 660 grams, or 1.5 pounds, of roasted coffee from 13 pounds of fresh cherries, a rough nine-to-one ratio of picked fruit to ready-to-grind beans.

smooth-worn earth floor of his home. Others in rural Kafa shake some coffee along the inside of the door, but Woldegiorgis does it around the central pillar. It is a libation in the purest sense, a small offering to Showe Kollo, the spirit of the land. Without *kollo*, there would be no coffee.

The previous week, before starting to collect the year's coffee harvest, Woldegiorgis and a dozen or so other men from the hamlet had walked to a secluded part of the forest carrying *kocho*, maize, and *tella*, a home-brewed beer made from teff.* They also had a live chicken. "Everything in the forest belongs to *kollo*," an anthropologist recorded in his field notebook back in the 1960s. "If you wish to take something from him then you must give something in return."[6]

Beside the buttressed trunk of a towering wild fig tree, they dug a shallow hole. The soil in Mankira is soft and loamy and easy to dig up. Kneeling, one of the men held the chicken, while Woldegiorgis unsheathed his knife and slit its throat, letting the blood seep into the ground at the base of the tree. He carved away a small piece from each part of the animal and placed them in the hole as an offering to Showe Kollo. He left, too, some *kocho*, maize, and *tella* at the base of the tree. Woldegiorgis then said a prayer and gave thanks for the harvest they were about to collect.

As a young boy ran back to the hamlet to announce that the sacrifice had taken place and the rest of the family could begin the celebration, the other men—only men attend these ceremonies—moved to a different part of the forest to roast the remainder of the chicken and eat it along with other foods they had brought with them. A few hours later, the group walked back out of the forest to join the festivities in the hamlet, which, fueled by *tej* and *tella*, continued until late.

In the morning Woldegiorgis returned to the sacrificial spot to see if the offering had been accepted. It had. The pieces placed at the base of the tree were gone. It would be a good harvest.

Saturday is the main market day in Bonga, and the sloped field in the center of town transforms as hundreds of traders, coming by bus, on foot, and

---

* The tiny-seeded cereal is indigenous to Ethiopia and mostly used as a flour to make injera, the large, fermented pancake type of flatbread with a spongy, crumpet texture that, literally, is the base on which many meals are served.

with mules from miles away, display their goods on plastic tarps. Women with colorful wraps and black head scarves sit behind small mounds of pinkish garlic, hunks of orange squash, and piles of yams and white potatoes still smeared in earth. There are dried wild cardamom strung on lengths of twine like necklaces, folded enset leaves that hold fresh butter and cheese, wild honey with bits of comb and wax, piles of used clothes, black jebena coffeepots, and, down at the bottom, livestock.

In the center are the coffee sellers. Squatting among the half dozen or so of them that had gathered on a late-October morning was a barefoot man wearing a sweater, bunting coat, and loose khaki pants. His gunnysack of dried coffee berries was only a third full. He was asking two and a half birr (twelve cents) for a generous scoop with a plastic water cup. Four scoops equaled a kilogram, making it about twenty-five cents per pound. The season had just begun, and this was some of the first new coffee of the harvest. Women crowded around him, taking out handfuls to inspect. The most interested bit a pod between their molars and peeled away the dried coating to look at the beans on the inside.

A woman with braided pigtails nearby was selling "clean" coffee. Measuring with a similar plastic cup, she sold heaped scoops of the beans for thirteen birr, about fifty birr a kilogram (one dollar a pound).

"From Mankira," said a guy standing beside her.

Pale, almost khaki green, and smelling of fresh peas, the beans ranged in size—wild coffee is more irregular than its cultivated cousins—with broken beans, grit, and small stones mixed in.

"Mankira," he repeated, shielding his eyes from the midmorning sun with a notebook.

"*Wof zerash,*" the woman said.

This is the wild side of that glorious morning cappuccino with a leaf doodled in its foamy surface: the untamed side of coffee, the unknown one. This is the original side.

CHAPTER 2

Island Ethiopia

A crown of an island in the Horn of Africa, Ethiopia rises up above some half dozen countries that border its lowland peripheries: Sudan and South Sudan on the west; Kenya, Somalia, Somaliland, and Djibouti along the south and the east; and, across the north, Eritrea. The high central plateau, ranging from four thousand to ten thousand feet above sea level and covering two thirds of the country, is split diagonally into two unequal parts by the Rift Valley. The crevice in the earth's crust averages thirty miles wide and runs like a narrow diaphragm, broadening into a flute shape in the northeast toward the Red Sea as the land flattens out into the Danakil Desert, among the lowest and hottest places on earth. Here, where the Rift widens, is the home of mankind. In 1974, archaeologists unearthed Lucy—or Denqenash as she is known in Ethiopia, "you are marvelous"—the 3.2-million-year-old skeleton of the oldest known hominid.

This is just one of the unique species to have developed in Ethiopia. Through a combination of geographic isolation and climate, it is an archipelago-like center of endemism with many unique species of animals and plants, from Prince Ruspoli's turaco[1] to staple crops such as teff and the drought-resistant enset, known as "false banana" because it looks like a banana tree but bears no edible fruit. And, of course, Arabica coffee.

Coffee comes from the *Coffea* genus of the large Rubiaceae family. Of the 124 known species of *Coffea*, only two are widely cultivated and considered commercially important: Arabica (*Coffea arabica*) and Robusta (*Coffea canephora*). Arabica accounts for the majority of coffee, and all of the fine coffee. It's milder, more balanced, and has higher acidity, a positive attribute responsible for many of the fruity flavors experienced in a bright, lively cup. More difficult to grow but better appreciated by professional cuppers (tasters) as well as Main Street consumers, it fetches higher prices on the global market.

Arabica's center of origin and diversity is the montane forests of Ethiopia.[2] The natural range is restricted to the cool, forested highlands, predominately in the southwest of the country on the north side of the Rift, with the core wild coffee forests falling within the historical region of Kafa. The Harenna Forest, in the southern Bale Mountains, on the other side of the Rift, has some wild Arabica, too. A small population also is just over the South Sudan border on the Boma Plateau.*

It rains all year round in Kafa, peaking in June and July, with yearly rainfall across the region averaging between 1,500 and 2,500 mm (about sixty to one hundred inches;[3] Seattle averages about thirty-six inches). The dominant greens, verdant lushness, and clouds that wedge into the valleys each morning dispel any preconceived notion of Ethiopia as simply an arid country of drought and famine. "When the Creator made the great Central African forest," wrote the German explorer Max Grühl a century ago, "He took a piece and cast it down among the mountains bordering on the northern shore of Lake Rudolf.† Hence it came about that Kafa is a forest land of dark beauty."[4]

Kafa is hilly, with few level stretches. According to local legend, the land had once been completely flat. "One day [the sky god] Yero came to the earth and lived with the people for a certain amount of time. The people hated him and tried to drive him away. The earth, on the other hand, loved him and did not want to leave him. Because of the hate of the people, Yero went back to the sky. The land began to follow him. He ordered it not to follow him anymore." Of course it did. "You can see which hills followed him the furthest. They are the highest."[5]

The low wetlands, with swamps and marshes—hippopotamuses, silvery-black African buffalo, and gangly yellow-billed storks that troll slowly for fish with their submerged bills partially open—quickly give way to savanna with shrubs and grasses, then to woodlands and the

---

* There might be another tiny population in the sixty-square-mile patch of montane forest on northern Kenya's Mount Marsabit. If it was originally wild remains disputed. Coffee's leading taxonomist, Aaron Davis at the Royal Botanic Gardens, Kew, is inclined to say that it was not.

† Renamed Lake Turkana in 1975.

cloud-covered montane forests, where the sun does not appear for days at a time. Above these are dense stands of bamboo. The tallest peaks reach 11,000 feet.

Coffee forests—Mankira, Boginda, Kombo, Gela, and Bonga (outside its namesake town) are among the best-known—thread through the middle strata. Arabica grows between 3,200 to 6,500 feet above sea level but thrives from 4,250 to about 6,000 feet on flat or gentle slopes.

Ethiopia's geography long protected its mile-high plateau from invaders and allowed it to develop in virtual isolation for more than two thousand years. It was, Homer said, "at the farthest limits of mankind," where "the Sungod sets" but also "where the Sungod rises."[6] Covering the southwest corner of the plateau was the Kingdom of Kafa, which ruled these forests for five centuries. Grühl called it the "African Tibet."[7] It was inaccessible, unknown, and mysterious, a heightened version of what defined Ethiopia well into the twentieth century.

Historically, the northern half of Ethiopia's plateau was a loose collection of kingdoms, principalities, and feudal states whose power shifted. They were ethnically and religiously diverse and often either at war with one another or paying tribute to remain at least somewhat autonomous. The most powerful ruler among them was the Negusa Nagast—King of Kings.

Little was known about Ethiopia at the time, even after the first Europeans made it into the emperor's court. A handful of Venetian, Genoese, and Portuguese adventurers gained access in the 1400s; they were treated well, given land and wives, and even official positions. Nicolò Brancaleon painted for the church and state, while his fellow Venetian Hieronimo Bicini served as secretary to the emperor, with whom he reportedly traded rooks and knights over the chessboard for hours at a time. But visitors were essentially barred from leaving. Secrets of the empire could not be taken out.[8] The mystique remained.

In the sixteenth century, the Basque knight-turned-mystic Ignatius of Loyola, founder of the Society of Jesus (the Jesuits), took interest in Portuguese reports of the Ethiopian emperor's refusal to convert from Orthodox Christianity, for twelve hundred years the main religion of northern Ethiopia, to Catholicism, and sent a six-man mission.[9] It required a number of years, but the Jesuits eventually succeeded in their proselytizing, at least at the highest level: Emperor Susenyos converted and even changed the state religion to Roman Catholicism in 1622. After a decade of internal upheaval over the decision, he abdicated in favor of his son, Fasilides, who reinstated Orthodox Christianity to its official capacity and expelled the Jesuits.

Ethiopia's flirtation with the West was over. Europe was rejected, and interaction with it simply ceased, marking the beginning of a long period of isolation. While European powers remained keen to establish themselves there, Ethiopia, nearly impenetrable and largely self-sufficient, remained aloof. It was, as Grühl put it in the 1920s, "a citadel."

Through the seventeenth and eighteenth centuries, only a couple of Westerners managed to pierce its seclusion. Charles-Jacques Poncet, a French physician and pharmacist living in Cairo, traveled by invitation to the emperor's court to treat his skin disease.[10] When Poncet crossed the Ethiopian frontier in June 1699, he was the first Frank (Christian) to reach Ethiopia since the Jesuits had been driven out.[11] The book of his journey describes a great many things of interest, including no less than the first description of the coffee plant in its country of origin. Christians in the north, though, did not "esteem it much,"[12] and Poncet didn't mention drinking coffee.

The first Westerner to record that was James Bruce. In 1769, the thirty-nine-year-old Scot arrived on a quest to find the source of the Nile and was served coffee not long after landing in Massawa. He called it "excellent."[13] Standing six foot four inches in his stockings and topped with a mop of red hair, Bruce was an unexpected, striking figure in Ethiopia. While he had a remarkably strong constitution and was both a gifted marksman and competent horseman, his survival was nothing short of miraculous.

To reach the rugged center of the country after an often-difficult journey across the sea—Bruce's ship wrecked off the coast of Libya and he lost his equipment—travelers had to first pass through the lowlands controlled by Muslim tribesmen who viewed Franks with disdain and distrust. Then came the climb. "The mountains of Abyssinia* have a singular aspect from this place," Bruce wrote, "as they appear in three ridges. The first is of no considerable height, but full of gullies and broken ground, thinly covered with shrubs; the second, higher and steeper, still more rugged and bare; the third is a row of sharp, uneven-edged mountains, which would be counted high in any country in Europe."†[14] It is a dramatic, broken land-

---

* See note on page xi for the use of the term Abyssinia.

† He was not exaggerating. Just shy of fifteen thousand feet, Ras Dashen in the Simien Mountains is nearly as high as the tallest peaks in France and Switzerland.

scape, craggy and eroded, with rows of jagged summits, steep escarpments, and sharp, barren massifs that hurl upward and then slope down into grassy hills. Dotting the fretted plateau are *ambas*, tabled mountains topped with churches, monasteries, and fortress prisons.

Inland, rivers and ravines interlace the plateau, making travel difficult in the dry season and all but impossible during the wet one. It was necessary to leave the west of the country with the approach of the rains, a Portuguese expedition in the 1540s reported, "before the rivers rose, which are heavily flooded in that part and quite stop travel on the roads; because the winters are very rainy and the land mountainous; the rivers collect much water from these mountains, and swell vastly."[15]

Bruce managed to reach the source of the Blue Nile on the southern end of Lake Tana, yet spent much of his energy trying to keep from being strangled in the web of the feuding court machinations. Bruce's toughest challenge was getting permission to leave. When the emperor granted it in late December 1771, Bruce hurriedly departed Ethiopia via the Sudan, becoming the first European to trace the Blue Nile to its confluence with the White Nile. The route, though, was significantly more dangerous than returning via Massawa, and he came precariously close to dying during the leg across the desert.

Upon returning to Britain, Bruce was first feted but then mocked. What he told of Ethiopia was simply too wondrous to be true. A favorite jeering point was his description of eating raw beef that had been cut away from a living animal. Among his most vocal detractors were three highly influential men of letters: Horace Walpole, James Boswell, and Samuel Johnson. Considered the authority on Ethiopia, Johnson ridiculed Bruce, going so far as to cast doubt upon the Scot's having even entered the country.[16] Among Bruce's claims was that coffee came from "Caffa" and grew "spontaneously everywhere in great abundance, from Caffa to the banks of the Nile."[17] This was ignored.

Bruce withdrew to his family's crumbing laird in Scotland and married. After his second wife passed away nearly a decade later, he began working on a five-volume travelogue,[18] published in 1790. It would be another fifty years after his death in 1794, as other travelers reported similar experiences, before the public began accepting that much of what Bruce had written about Ethiopia was generally true.[19]

By then, a trickle of missionaries and envoys were arriving in Ethiopia, and with them scientists and explorers. The hope was that proselytizing would help prize open area for trade.[20] Neither really came about.

The 1869 opening of the Suez Canal turned the Red Sea from a cul-de-sac to a highway that stretched twelve hundred miles south to Bab el-Mandeb (Gates of Tears), the wasp-waisted entrance between Africa and Arabia, and steeply increased European interest in the region. The Scramble for Africa soon pitched into high gear as the great imperial powers rushed to divvy up the continent. In the Horn, Italy controlled Eritrea; the British, French, and Italians carved up Somalia; the French established a colony that would become Djibouti; and the British held Sudan and Kenya. Jutting up in the center of the jigsaw was the Ethiopian plateau. Not only was it uncolonized by Europeans, but it had the only African leader actively taking part in the continental land grab. Among his chief targets was the Kingdom of Kafa.

In the last quarter of the nineteenth century, Ethiopia's ruler, Menelik II, began expanding outward from the Amharic heartland, attempting to knit together a disparate array of territories. He was not the Negusa Nagast, but rather the ambitious ruler of the central Shawa kingdom.

Not long after Menelik's father, the *negus* of Shawa, died in 1855, the newly crowned emperor of Ethiopia, Téwodros II, imprisoned the young heir in the sprawling hilltop fortress of Magdala. After nearly a decade of Menelik's incarceration, the emperor made a reconciliatory move by offering his own daughter's hand in marriage to the Shawan.[21] Menelik agreed, but left her a year later in an audacious escape. Back in Shawa, he killed Téwodros's loyal governor and declared himself king. The reign of two emperors and a quarter of a century would pass before Menelik himself would become the King of Kings.

He did not wait to begin annexing his neighbors, though by paying an annual tribute to Téwodros and not challenging him in the far north, Menelik had a free hand in his territorial ambitions elsewhere. In the mid-1870s, his forces moved west to conquer Gurage, Gojjam, and then areas south of the Blue Nile, and in the 1880s, he occupied a series of wealthy kingdoms along the Gibe River, between Kafa and present-day Addis Ababa.

Menelik's forces had superior weapons, but were also driven by an ideology of a greater Ethiopia. "Menelik certainly believed that his was a holy crusade," wrote his American biographer, "and his soldiers presumed, with considerable justification, that they would help their sovereign restore Ethiopia to its historic grandeur and size."[22] There was also motivation in the golden, ivory, and even human spoils, as prisoners became slaves. Menelik used the loot plus fresh tax revenue from the expanding empire to reward his generals, who raised and maintained their own armies; motivate the soldiers who fed themselves by pillage and plunder; and buy guns and ammunition to equip their swelling ranks.[23]

In 1884, Menelik's forces arrived in Jimma, Kafa's powerful Muslim neighbor and the largest of the Gibe states. "When you reach a city or land to fight against its inhabitants," advised the thirteenth-century *Fetha Nagast* (Law of the Kings), which Menelik was heeding in his expansion,[24] "offer them terms of peace. If they accept you and open their gates, the men who are there shall become subjects and give you tribute, but if they refuse the terms of peace and offer battle, go forward to assault and oppress them, since the Lord your God will make you master of them."[25]

Abba Jifar, who claimed to be the twenty-sixth in an unbroken line of rulers of Jimma,[26] took the advice of his mother and opened the gates. He agreed to pay a hefty annual tribute of 29,065 Austrian Maria Theresa silver thalers,* along with cattle, mules, and various household items.[27] While Menelik's government would appoint its own loyal men to key positions in newly acquired territories and nominally govern them from the central capital,[28] compliant rulers remained on the throne as vassals, had their territory left more or less intact, and were given near autonomy—as long as they continued to pay tribute. Abba Jifar kept paying and ruled until his death in 1932, after fifty-four years in power.

Sitting on a hilltop about five miles outside Jimma, Jifar's rambling, three-story wooden palace is derelict but surprisingly still standing after decades of rain, neglect, and political upheaval. Carved leaves and trees trellis along beams, hand-tooled dowels line stairwells, and stout wooden pillars whittled into Greek columns hold up sagging balconies. The intricate metalwork limning the eaves of the red tin roofs evoke the Swahili Coast.† Crowning the building is a watchtower with four windows, each looking in the direction of a powerful neighboring kingdom.

---

* First minted in 1741, the coins were carried by merchants to the eastern Mediterranean, the Arabian Peninsula (used to pay for coffee just a decade after being struck in Vienna), and elsewhere, including Ethiopia, where it was the unit of currency for two centuries.

† The style was perhaps not random. Among Jifar's effects in the Jimma Museum is a bed with a red velvet canopy, a gift from the sultan of Zanzibar. "Jifar was 210 centimeters

At the entrance of the compound, across a grassy expanse where thick-billed ravens—large, heavy birds with blunted black bills—dig for grubs, is a mosque. "He had six wives, fourteen children, and fifty-five slaves," the mosque's custodian, a gaunt man in a white skullcap and thin beard, recited as if by rote. Historians put the number of Jifar's personal slaves considerably higher, to as many as ten thousand.[29] He gave them as gifts and used them to work on coffee plantations and produce food for the court.[30] Inside the mosque, an open lattice of wood ribs ran across the high-peaked ceiling, and patterned red carpets covered the floor. A scrappy green plastic sheet had been strung up to divide the men's and women's sections. It was the first day of Ramadan, the Muslim month of sunrise-to-sunset fasting, and the mosque would be full that evening, the custodian said.

On a grassy knoll not far below the palace stands a newer mosque. A broad covered porch built for heavy rain encircles the square, cupola-topped portico, and a pair of white minarets trimmed in baby blue flank the squat building. Two young boys appeared and led the way along a barely discernible path, through scraggy trees and gravestones overgrown with weeds, to Jifar's tomb. It was ten feet long and shin high, with flaking plaster and a broken flowerpot sitting on one end. Set like a fin in the middle was a tombstone inscribed in Arabic. Surrounding Jifar in the form of a constellation were his wives. Spinning a slow circle with an arm outstretched, the oldest boy recited their names as he pointed toward the brush-covered grave of each.

Jifar had originally been buried in the other end of tomb, the boy explained. When it didn't rain for three months, the people said it was because the body had been placed in the wrong position. The tomb was opened, and Jifar's remains were shifted to the other end. "Soon after," the boy said, "it rained."

After annexing Jimma, Menelik's forces didn't continue across the Gojeb River into Kafa to conquer that kingdom next, but instead turned their attention east. The pastoral Oromo in Arsi had rebuffed an advance some years before with spears and bows and arrows,[31] but not this time. Menelik used Arsi as a stepping-stone for Harar and conquered the powerful city-state with rich grazing lands and control of the caravan routes to the coast.

[six feet ten and a half inches] tall," the museum attendant said. "It was only for sitting, not sleeping."

By 1887, befitting his expanding territory, Menelik relocated his capital farther south, building around a hot spring about eight thousand feet above sea level. His consort, Queen Taytu, named it Addis Ababa, "new flower." Almost immediately, it was a boomtown, sprawling over several hills.*

When Emperor Yohannes died in 1889, the Shawan leader at last proclaimed himself the King of Kings and took the name Menelik II. That year also marked the beginning of a devastating three-year-long famine that struck all but the southernmost part of the country, triggered in part by a rinderpest outbreak and followed by drought and cholera. Menelik ordered his generals south—and to send food back north if possible. Over the next few years, as Menelik's armies continued their slow domination of region, and to control territory closer to Kafa, they drew the large Ogaden region, Bale, and Sidamo into an expanding empire.

Meanwhile, rhetoric was escalating with Menelik's main European antagonist, Italy, which was establishing itself in neighboring Eritrea. Initially the relationship was decorous. With unusual openness for an Ethiopian ruler, Menelik welcomed an Italian Geographical Society mission.[32] The two countries grew closer, signing a treaty of amenity and commerce in 1883 and then another of alliance and friendship, even after Italy had seized Eritrea's key port of Massawa. But a third treaty in 1889, recognizing Italy's occupation of Eritrea, led to conflict. The problem stemmed from Italian subterfuge in producing different versions of the pact. The Italian-language one gave them power over Ethiopia's dealings with other European nations; the Amharic one made no such provision.

In 1895, with tensions mounting, Italy moved forces from Eritrea across the border into northern Ethiopia. Menelik summoned his governors and amassed an army of more than 100,000.[33] On March 1, 1896, an Italian contingent of 14,500 prepared a surprise attack at Adwa. The Ethiopians got word of it and struck first early that morning.

The Battle of Adwa was a rout. Within hours, the outmaneuvered Italian army lost nearly three fourths of its force, with four thousand Italian soldiers and two thousand Eritrean *askaris* killed, and numerous thousands more wounded or taken prisoner.[34] The surviving remnants fled in haste, abandoning weapons and vehicles.

With this unprecedented victory of an African army over that of a

---

* Within twenty-five years it had seventy thousand permanent residents, with another thirty thousand to fifty thousand temporary ones (Pankhurst, *Ethiopians*, 195). Today Addis Ababa is by far the country's largest city, with an estimated 3.5 million inhabitants.

modern European power, Menelik's standing soared. Italy signed a peace agreement recognizing Ethiopia's borders. The two other great powers in the Horn of Africa, France and Great Britain, hurriedly signed treaties as well, while the Ottoman pasha and Russian tsar sent missions.[35] For a continent almost entirely subjugated in colonialism, the triumph offered a flash of hope. For Ethiopians, it was the defining, founding event of a new nation, its first great national epic.[36]

Defeating the Italians and sustaining Ethiopian sovereignty turned Menelik into a hero, an emblem of African freedom that paradoxically granted him a freer hand in conquering other autonomous territories in the Horn.

The emperor ordered his first cousin Ras Wolde Giorgis* to lead an army southwest. Motivated and well armed with modern weapons, his forces were finally ready to conquer their last great territorial prize, Kafa.

---

* The title *ras* signified a commander of an army of the emperor who, in times of peace, acted as the governor of an annexed region. Wolde Giorgis and Woldegiorgis are popular names in Ethiopia today.

CHAPTER 3

The Kingdom of Kafa

Highway 5 runs southwest from Addis Ababa, through wide fields of teff, maize, and gaunt oxen tilling with wooden plows. The road drops down and along the scorching northern edge of the Rift Valley with acacia trees and onion-shaped birds' nests, the sky charged with raptors wheeling on updrafts, before climbing back up on the high plateau. The soil darkens and runs from chocolate browns to orangish crimson, and the landscape begins to breathe with soft greens. Kids hold out handfuls of small, intensely sweet bananas and mangoes to sell to passing cars and herd skittish goats down the road. Clouds gather ahead, and the first gardens with some coffee trees appear. Nearly across Jimma, another historically powerful kingdom and major coffee producer, the highway drops down again, and one reaches, some nine hours after leaving the capital, the Gojeb River, a muddy torrent that marks Kafa's eastern boundary. Along an upstream bend of riffles, people bathe in the shallows. By the bridge itself, when the water level is low, partially submerged hippos float in nearby pools. WAAMA DIGGOONA BUNEE DANE XAA'OOCH KAFA WAATOTE a listing billboard reads in Kafinoonoo, with Amharic and English equivalents below: WELCOME TO KAFFA* THE BIRTH PLACE OF COFFEE. It is an underwhelming announcement to a place where coffee, and coffee drinking, began.

Once over the Gojeb, the road climbs up through broad steps of cul-

---

* Like virtually all of the region's place names, *Kafa* has multiple spellings. I have left the original when quoting, but elsewhere use the most common version. See page xi for a note on spelling.

tivated hills and profuse shade trees that edge fields of teff, barley, and sorghum. After a dozen or so miles, a narrow pull-off appears beside the kilometer 441 marker post. A pair of young men picked up at the first village inside Kafa strode down the steep embankment to the beginning of a spiky seam of vegetation that ran across the undulating landscape and disappeared over the crest of a distant hill. It wasn't a hedge but a *hiriyo*, a trench now overgrown with trees and shrubs. As the first line of defense against invasion, Kafa's ancient kingdom had been ringed by them. Places particularly susceptible to enemy intrusions had two or three rows of deep ditches. Locals, one of the men said, knew the secret paths around them.

The two climbed down into the trench, which measured some twenty-five feet deep and thirty feet across. In the past, the ditches had sharpened bamboo spikes hidden by leaves to ensure that a leaping horse couldn't make it across alive, one of the men explained after he had climbed out.

Back up on the road, they crossed above a small quarry of hard orange rock that had recently been used for road-building materials and dropped down into another *hiriyo* running in the opposite direction. How far did this one go? One, wearing an Ethiopian national soccer jersey with its distinctive broad yellow and green stripes, put his hands on his head and made a sound meaning "Who knows?" The other pointed to the horizon and named a far-off village.

The defense ditches formed an inverted version of the Great Wall of China and had once helped seal the kingdom almost hermetically from the surrounding territories.

Independent, well organized, and a source of legendary wealth, the extensive Kingdom of Kafa had twelve provinces, each with a royal residence.[1] The most important was in the capital Andiracha, "a sort of African Lhasa."[2] The king forbid foreigners from entering and restricted traders to the commercial city of Bonga, about a dozen miles away.

"The king's palace was very nice, and very luxurious," said Tetera Mekonen Yemer, one of Andiracha's elders. Ninety years old and bedridden, he lay propped up on a handful of flattened pillows in the front room of his home just down the hill from where the palace had stood. A dozen jute gunnysacks of coffee sat stacked in the corner beside a small TV. His daughter sat on a low stool in front of the door and picked through a dish of dry red lentils. Beside her, on a coal brazier, a black jebena with coffee was reaching a slow boil. "The king had his own ministers, his own borders, his own government," Tetera said of Kafa's ruler at the end of the nineteenth century. "It was like a country at that time."

While stories tell of some five hundred years of kings, the end of the seventeenth century marked Kafa's consolidation into a strong, unified state,[3] with territorial expansion and economic growth well into the nineteenth century.[4] At its apogee around the turn of the eighteenth century,[5] the kingdom stretched from the grassy plains of the Sudan to the string of soda lakes that run along the Rift,[6] and as far south as Lake Turkana, the brackish opaque-emerald body of water that straddles the Ethiopia-Kenya border. The northeast boundary was the Gibe River and included the states of Jimma and Limu.[7] While the kingdom had shrunk from controlling thirty-eight kingdoms and chiefdoms that were paying it tribute in the early 1800s,[8] Kafa remained one of the most powerful and populous states in Ethiopia through the nineteenth century.

Unlike the Amharas of northern Ethiopia, who have for centuries had a body of literature written first in Ge'ez, the ancient Semitic language, and then Amharic, those living in Kafa had no way to indelibly record their stories in their own language until quite recently.[9] The name of the local language conveys its oral nature: Kafinoonoo literally translates to "Kafa mouth."

Tetera's daughter set down small, handleless cups filled to the brim with coffee. The tablecloth was a jute sack that had been cut open along its seam. Once it had cooled, Tetera picked up his cup, sloshing a bit into the saucer, and drank it quickly before continuing his story of a kingdom whose unbroken line of monarchs stretched back to A.D. 1390. His daughter, adding details to his comments, sat on the stool and sifted through the legumes for tiny stones as chickens fluttered in and out of the open door in front of her.

"Perhaps the absence of a script and written records blurs the past," V. S. Naipaul wrote of African cultures like that of Kafa with spoken rather than written histories; "perhaps the oral story gives them only myths."[10]

In Kafa, the stories—and myths—have survived, often told like this over coffee.

The Portuguese first mentioned Kafa, and it was known by name, or at least legend, in Europe centuries before travelers offered any firsthand

Vincenzo Coronelli's 1690 map showed Kafa—Regno di Cafate (bottom left)—for the first time.

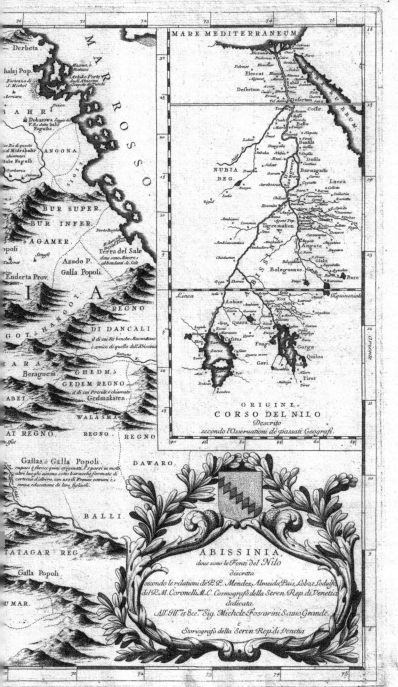

MARE MEDITERRANEUM

MAR ROSSO

NUBIA REG.

Derbeta

BAHR

ANGONA

BUR SUPER.
BUR INFER.

AGAMER.

Terra del Sale
che sono Miniere,
abbondanti di Sale

Azado P.
Galla Popoli.

Enderta Prov.

I A

REGNO

DI DANCALI
il di cui Rè benche Macometano
è amico di quello dell'Abissinia

GHEDM.
GEDEM REGNO
il di cui Preside è chiamato
Gedmakaten

WALASMA

REGNO   REGNO

Beraguem

Gallas, o Galla Popoli,
rapaci e feroci quai originati, e sparsi in molti
altri luoghi niuuno sotto baracche formate di
cortecie d'albero, con uso di Femine comuni e
senza educazione de loro figliuoli.

DAWARO.

BALLI.

TATAGAR REG.

Galla Popoli.

UMAR.

Coffir

Tigre nation

Angote

Beleguanze

Linea   Equinoziale

Gorga
Quiloa

ORIGINE,
CORSO DEL NILO
Descrito
secondo l'Osseruationi de' passati Geografi.

ABISSINIA,
doue sono le Fonti del Nilo
descritta
secondo le relationi de P.P. Mendez, Almeida, Pais, Lobo, e Lodulfo
del P.M. Coronelli M.C. Cosmografo della Seren. Rep. di Venetia
dedicata.
All'Ill.mo et Ecc.mo Sig. Michele Fossarini Sauio Grande,
e
Storiografo della Seren. Rep. di Venetia

accounts. They had come in search of the mythical Christian ruler Prester John, a certain ally and friend in the largely Muslim region. In the *Narrative of the Portuguese Embassy to Abyssinia During the Years 1520–1527*, the priest Francisco Álvarez referred to "Cafates," a race in the west bordering the Christian kingdoms of Shawa and Gojjam. They were "pagans and great warriors," Álvarez claimed, who "came to kill and plunder" his group "chiefly at night," and then "by day they took refuge in the mountains and thickets, and the mountains (as they say) consist more in ravines than in heights."[11] Another Portuguese report twenty years later repeated much of the same hearsay about these people who "have much land, and are rich with gold," but added a magical touch: "They say there is in the country an invisible wood that makes men invisible."[12] The Italian Franciscan friar and cartographer Vincenzo Coronelli included the "Regno di Cafate" on his 1690 map—the first to show Ethiopia being the source of the Blue Nile—as a narrow kingdom wedged between a Nile tributary and a mountain range. There was no hint that Kafa held coffee, and James Bruce's claim a century later that it did made no impact.

Some reliable details on Kafa, including its location and rivers, finally surfaced in the 1840s from a German Anglican missionary named J. L. Krapf,[13] even though he did not reach the kingdom himself. The first European to do that was the Dublin-born French Basque explorer Antoine d'Abbadie, in 1843. He had joined the caravan of a prince heading to fetch his twelfth wife in Kafa and spent eleven days in Bonga.[14] Yet not until 1890, nearly fifty years later, did d'Abbadie publish his account in *Géographie de l'Éthiopie*.

At the end of 1855, a Capuchin friar (and later Catholic cardinal) Guglielmo Massaia, promoting Catholicism in Ethiopia, sent a priest named Cesare da Castelfranco and an Ethiopian convert to establish a mission in Kafa. Castelfranco married a local woman and was swiftly excommunicated, yet stayed on. Massaia himself arrived in 1859 with more local converts,[15] and lived with Castelfranco until being expelled from the area two years later. Massaia lost his records and wrote of his time in Kafa from memory nearly three decades later.

In 1875, the Italian Geographical Society dispatched a scientific mission to the north of Ethiopia. Menelik gave them a large estate to use as a base to launch a series of expeditions.[16] Two explorers traveled to Jimma and Kafa. En route, they were held as prisoners. One died. The other, Antonio Cecchi, made his way to Kafa through "a mixture of bribery and force."[17]

Cecchi arrived in Kafa during the reign of Galli Sherocho, the penultimate king of Kafa, at a time when the kingdom was the richest in south-western Ethiopia.[18] The account Cecchi published upon his return is the first of the kingdom with real substance or veracity.

Being hard to reach and well defended was alone not enough for the Kingdom of Kafa to endure for more than five hundred years, a stagger-ing length given the upheavals, wars, and conquests that embroiled the Horn of Africa. Another key factor was its unusual political stability. While not completely static, the basic structure remained in place from at least the end of the sixteenth century.[19]

At the top was the king, the *tato*. "The king is the law," went a Kafa saying.[20] Adorned in a green robe and gold jewelry—a bracelet on the right wrist, a ring on the right pinkie, and earrings[21]—the king was revered and worshipped by his subjects, who sacrificed a young boy each year to ensure his health.[22]

Once crowned, the *tato* could not touch the ground, and a cloth was laid before him as he walked.[23] Nor was he allowed to eat with his own hands,[24] in order, some said, to reserve them for fighting the enemy.[25] Official feeders known as *made nao*, "slaves of the table,"[26] placed small morsels in his mouth. (When not performing his royal duties, the official feeder kept his arm covered in a cloth sack to keep it from being contami-nated or bewitched.)[27] The king couldn't drink by himself, either, and the royal cup bearer tipped ox horns of *tej*, beer, and coffee into his mouth. At mealtimes, a relay of drums sounded across the kingdom to warn the people to keep silent while he ate.[28]

For the majority of the population, the *tato* remained effectively invis-ible. Not daring to look him in the face,[29] subjects prostrated themselves with their arms stretched forward and said, "For you I eat the soil."[30] Royal roads that only he and his entourage could travel connected his dozen palaces,[31] and when he gave an audience, a curtain carefully obscured him.

Directly beneath the king were seven powerful councilors known as *mikireco*, and below them, a dozen provincial heads, who handled admin-istrative, judicial, political, military, and economic elements. Under these came numerous occupational castes, including weavers, tanners, and *satto*, wandering bards, who sang, danced, and told stories of wars, celebrations of personal triumphs, and past glories. A massive class of serfs followed, making up one third to one half of the population.

The lowest on the hierarchy, and one of the original inhabitants of

Kafa, were the Manjo, or hunter caste, who inhabited the dense forests. They served as trackers and trail finders, and border and royal-palace guards.[32] As skillful tree climbers, they hung many of the hives in the forest and then retrieved them some months later, climbing with smoking branches to calm the bees. Yet the Manjo tradition of eating wild animals made them an ostracized community. They were the only ones in the kingdom who hunted for their food[33]—few Kafecho even ate meat[34]— and their diet consisted largely of porcupines, monkeys and baboons, and wild pigs.[35] Other castes considered any item touched by a Manjo contaminated. Encountering a non-Manjo required a greeting that translated to "Let me die for you," or, if it was a noble, "I bury myself in the ground."[36] When the king passed, the Manjo prostrated themselves on the ground like others but didn't merely say they would eat soil for him, they literally did so.

Another factor in Kafa's longevity was economic power generated through key trade routes that began around Bonga and connected the interior with northern Ethiopia and the seaports along the Red Sea and the Gulf of Aden. Originating in medieval times, they reached their peak of prominence in the nineteenth century.[37]

From Bonga, the northern route passed through a string of key commercial towns as it headed to Gondar at the foothills of the Simien Mountains.[38] Founded by Emperor Fasilides in 1635, following his expulsion of the Jesuits, the strategically situated city served as imperial capital for 250 years. At Gondar the route forked. A western branch traveled inland to Matamma, along the Nile. The hot, lowland riverside frontier town on the Sudan border linked trade up the Nile to Egypt and the Mediterranean. Another branch from Gondar crossed the plateau northeast via Aksum and Adwa and then dropped down to the port of Massawa on the Red Sea.

The other main route from Bonga traveled east to the coast. Caravans passed through Jimma and Shawa and across the Rift Valley to Harar, the main political and commercial center in the east and key trading link with the Arabian Peninsula. From Harar, it was a perilous stretch across Somalia to the ports of Zeila and Berbera.

Woven baskets strapped to mules and camels held forest coffee, honey, pods of dried wild cardamom, and butter wrapped in enset leaves. They carried, too, gold mined across the Rift, ivory from the elephants that roamed to the south in herds of thousands, and leopard skins. Musk was another key item. The secretion from the perineal glands of civet cats was extremely valuable as a fixative for floral perfumes. About the size of a raccoon, with a coat of darker stripes and blotches, civet were trapped in Kafa's forests, kept in small bamboo cages, and fed a rich diet of meat, millet, milk, butter, and thin maize porridge. The cats had their anal pouches scraped of a secreted waxy pomade, which was packed in ox horns.[39]

Of all the trade items from Kafa, slaves were the most important. Slaving was endemic, and slaves considered plentiful, constituting, at times, between one half and two thirds of Kafa's population.[40] They were taken in raids from the tribes to the south of the kingdom, captured during wars, received as tribute, or bought on the market. People could be enslaved as punishment for debt, theft, the evil eye, or being found by a traditional priest of turning into a hyena at night.[41] Women could also be sentenced to slavery for adultery or even, according to Massaia, eating alone.[42] While some researchers estimate around half a million slaves were exported through ports along the Somali-Djibouti coast during the nineteenth century, Ethiopia's most eminent scholar put the number at 1.25 million in only the first half of the 1800s.[43] As part of the large Red Sea Islamic slave trade, most were bound for Arabian and Ottoman households rather than New World sugarcane, tobacco, or cotton plantations. Ethiopia was a source of eunuchs and, famous for their beauty, women for harems.

Caravans coming to Bonga brought beads and glass along with thin iron bars that could be smelted down for plowshares and agricultural tools. The prime imported good, though, was *amole*, salt cut into blocks. The salt was much sought after for people and for cattle and used, with the iron bars, as a form of money. Its value was not static but depended on how far it had come from the salt mines in the northeastern Danakil Depression and increased with each day along the caravan route. In the market of Andiracha in the 1870s, the Italian visitor Cecchi found coffee among "magnificent lion skins," "chunks of black tobacco," and silver ornaments. A *mulletto* (skin bag) that held ten to fifteen kilograms of dried, unhusked coffee pods was considered valuable and cost three or four salt bars.[44] (For fifteen or sixteen kilograms of honey he had to barter only a single bar.)[45] Trading with salt lasted well into the twentieth century. "Here above on the highland of Kaffa, money is an unknown concept," the Austrian explorer Friedrich Bieber reported after visiting Kafa in 1905. They were using only salt bars.[46]

During the second half of the nineteenth century, coffee rose as one of the southwest's most important commodities.[47] As synthetic fixers replaced musk in perfume ateliers, as ivory stocks fell, and when authorities managed to finally halt the slave trade in the 1930s, coffee became its main export.[48]

When the Kafa king Tato Galli passed away in 1890, after twenty-two years in power, news of his death was kept secret for seven days.[49] The councilors gathered at Andiracha to choose his successor. As he had neared death, all of the male members of his family had been put in chains until the council made its decision.[50] While succession was not necessarily hereditary—"kingship was cosmologically conceived and transcendentally sanctioned"[51]—Galli had followed his father, and the nobles chose one of his sons, Gaki, to follow him.

With the announcement of the king's death along with the name of his successor, public mourning began. Men shaved their heads and cut themselves on the crown with knives, while women, dressed in rags, scratched their shorn scalps with thorns until they bled. Mourners gathered at the royal palace in Andiracha, where all of the king's possessions had been spread out on display.[52] In the throne room, the body, washed, anointed with butter, and dressed in royal attire,[53] laid in a coffin made from a hollowed tree.

Three days later the burial procession set off for the royal graves, and until then the people did not eat.[54] Led by seven priests, who sacrificed oxen to purify the road that the body would take,[55] it took a day to reach Shosha, traveling up through the forests of coffee and into the dense thickets of bamboo. Among the mourners walked the newly tapped Gaki, dressed symbolically in the rags of a peasant.

On the twelfth day after Galli's death, attendants lowered the body into a twenty-foot-deep burial chamber. Along with an oxen sacrificed by each of the attending priests, fourteen more were slaughtered. Their hearts were placed on the supine king and his face sprinkled with their blood.[56] A slave was sacrificed and buried alongside the *tato* to join his master in the next world. Inside the tomb of the king were placed jars of mead and cups of coffee.[57]

"The Kaffa bury their dead in very deep graves at the bottom of which they make a cave," the Russian aristocrat, explorer, and military officer Alexander Bulatovich wrote at the very end of the 1800s. "They usually wrap up the corpse in palm branches, and, at the burial, lower coffee, money, and ivory together with it into the grave."[58]

"These were things that were important to Kafecho," said Mesfin Tekle. Coffee was considered special enough to be desired in the afterlife.

"Even nowadays," Tetera said in his Andiracha front room that smelled of smoke and old leather, "if you are rich and you die, your family puts in some things—your gold, your ivory . . ." Glancing at the dozen jute sacks in the corner, he added, "Your coffee."

For one year slaves and servants visited Galli's grave to mourn, bringing with them food and drink.[59] Once that time had passed, it was forbidden for anyone to come again. The grave was left to return to the wild. "Only the animals of the forest were permitted to be near it from then on," wrote Bieber.*[60]

After a short period of seclusion for Gaki following the burial of his father, the head bard placed the gold bracelet on Gaki's wrist and the ring on his pinkie, investing him with the royal insignia. People revered the office more than the person, and these symbols of kingship were key to his power.

Gaki Sherocho was in his twenties when he began his reign. Within a decade, five centuries of a sovereign Kafa would end. Cecchi had been one of the first outsiders to visit Kafa. He was also the last to see it in its independent splendor. Soon it would disappear like the tombs of Gaki's royal predecessors.

* It remains impossible to visit it today, even for Kafa's supreme traditional spiritual leader. "It is near the caves. There are guards—Manjo—they know where it is," said Mesfin. "It has been converted to nature, so you don't have the possibility of finding it among the bamboo groves."

CHAPTER 4

The Last King of Kafa

Menelik II had been making unfulfilled claims on Kafa for nearly two decades and even managed to extract a never-fulfilled promise of tribute in the form of slaves, musk, and coffee from Gaki Sherocho's father during his reign.[1] By 1896, though, Kafa was isolated, nearly surrounded by territories under Menelik's control, and ill equipped against the large and powerful coalition force that the emperor could now muster.

Gaki had prohibited the import of arms into Kafa after repelling an incursion by the Ethiopians a few years before, most likely to avoid an internal uprising,[2] and only three hundred or so outdated muskets were in the kingdom,[3] hardly enough to slow, much less stop, Menelik's troops. When the council of nobles gathered in Andiracha, Gaki proposed following the example of his neighbor Abba Jifar in Jimma and paying tribute to Menelik. The councilors, though, despite having few illusions as to the outcome,[4] voted to wage war instead, vowing to "fight with the help of our forests and animals in our territory."[5]

It would have to be a cunning defense. As Kafa had no standing army, every male from eight to eighty years old was called up[6] to mount a guerrilla resistance. Gaki ordered the destruction of the grain supplies[7] and forbade the planting or harvesting of any crops. He wanted to starve out the enemy, who would supply themselves exclusively from what they could find or pillage. "He hoped that the lack of provisions would force the Abyssinians to retreat, and that only the Kaffa, who were used to it, could nourish themselves," wrote the Russian military adviser Alexander

Bulatovich, who traveled with Menelik's forces in Kafa the following year. "To this end, word was spread among the people that a revelation had come to the high priest that by exactly this means the Kaffa would defeat the Abyssinians."[8]

During the June-to-September rainy season, when roads were muddy and rivers impassable, military campaigns were traditionally suspended.[9] The Ras waited patiently. Once the trails dried and the rivers receded, a thirty-one-thousand-strong army with twenty thousand modern rifles launched its attack on the medieval kingdom from four different directions, including Jimma with the help of Abba Jifar.[10] The warning drums begin to echo as Manjo guards beat the hollowed trunks from their posts every five or so miles along Kafa's defensive ditches.

As people of the forest, the Kafecho could draw on unique resources in their fighting arsenal to accompany a primitive assortment of knives, swords, bows and arrows, lances, and shields made from hippopotamus and buffalo hides. Soldiers kept pots of bees along riverbanks and in other cool spots where they would stay calm, then used them to disperse the unsuspecting enemy when fighting at short range. (The bees could, of course, also attack Kafa troops, but simply knowing about them minimized the risk.)[11] Less fierce but more effective at close range were red ants.[12] Collected by dropping pieces of food or bones and kept in sacks made from animal skins, the parcels of feisty ants were hurled at the enemy in hand-to-hand combat.

"They had their own traditional ways of fighting," said Tetera Mekonen Yemer in Andiracha. His grandfather had come from the north with Ras Wolde Giorgis's soldiers and had told stories about such unique tactics. "They were clever in their fighting," Tetera said with a light smile. Although the Kafecho had primitive weapons, he added, fingering his sparse gray beard, they were much feared as an enemy.

"Their spears are not the same simple shape as the Galla's,* but are very intricate and almost always poisoned," Bulatovich noted. "The Abyssinians consider war with them much more difficult than with the Galla. It is said that they poison the water and resort to all possible measures of war against

---

* Galla is an outdated and often derogatory term for the ethnic Oromo people. In the past it was often used to mean the non-Amhara people of the south and west, including Kafecho, and shorthand for those that had been conquered. Bulatovich is one of the few early Europeans to differentiate.

the enemy, in which the terrain which is rugged, mountainous and forested helps them greatly."[13]

Heightening their fierce renown was the custom of severing an enemy's private parts. "All these tribes of Galla gird Abyssinia round at all points from east to west, making inroads, and burning and murdering all that fall into their hands," wrote James Bruce. "The privities of the men they cut off, dry, and hang them up in their houses."[14]

In Kafa, they didn't hang them for decoration. To receive generous rewards for fighting—cattle, slaves, fiefs, black-leopard skins—the warriors had to present the enemy's genitalia.[15] They wore the trophies on their foreheads at victory celebrations, then buried them under the hearthstones.[16] During September festivities in Andiracha, the warriors, stripped to the waist, their foreheads blackened with charcoal, would go before the seated king, shout out their heroic deeds, and toss the severed dried pudenda of the enemy at his feet.[17]

"They cut more than that," Tetera said, raising a hand to the side of his face, indicating disfigurement, even mutilation. "You would be afraid if you see someone has no ear or something. Then the rest of the soldiers will not come."

But reputation, rusty muskets, poison-tipped spears, and skin sacks of red ants could hardly match a force that had just defeated an Italian army in a single morning.

Ras Wolde Giorgis led his troops across Kafa's eastern border, over the defense ditches, and made straight for Andiracha. They demolished the royal capital and established a military camp on the hill, from where the Ras directed a severe and remorseless campaign,[18] razing whole villages, killing men, and enslaving women and children.[19]

While the coalition managed to take quick control of Kafa, the campaign would not be complete until Gaki Sherocho had been taken prisoner, and capturing him proved surprisingly difficult.

The dry season passed without sign of Gaki, and the rains began again, tentatively at first with late, battering showers. Ras ordered his soldiers to plant peppers and cabbage.[20] As the rains steadied, the rivers rose, the trails became impassable, and nothing would dry. Mud and filth covered the camp. Dysentery broke out. "The troops of the Ras were totally worn out by hunger and disease," wrote Bulatovich, who stayed shortly after at the military camp. "There arose an intolerable stench from the quantity of corpses in Andrachi."*[21]

The Ras even began to consider abandoning his plans and returning to Addis Ababa.

Over the months, Gaki had been traveling with progressively fewer servants, sometimes dressed in rags and disguised as a peasant. With the Ras's snare tightening, the king made a dash for the region to Kafa's south, out of Menelik's control. "He decided to break through the guard posts, at night, dressed as a simple Kaffa, accompanied only by a single servant," soldiers told Bulatovich. "They noticed him and raised the alarm. [Gaki] ran into the nearby forest, which the Abyssinians quickly surrounded." But they couldn't locate him. "In the morning, they passed through it several times in a chain, but did not find the King."[22] It was as if he had vanished, perhaps using the magic wood that centuries before the Portuguese had claimed grew in Kafa's forests.

That night, September 11, 1897,[23] a solider looking in the brush for his missing mule accidentally stumbled upon Gaki, according to Bulatovich.[24] The king hurled a silver and then a copper spear at him but missed. He had been on the run for nine months.

When news of the capture reached the camp, the Ras announced that the fighting was over. Prisoners were released, and word spread that war with the Amharas had finished.

The Ras ordered Gaki dressed in his finest clothes and brought to him.[25] Upon meeting, both men bowed to the ground in respect. Gaki removed the gold bracelets from his arm and asked the Ras—the first to ever conquer Kafa—to accept them. "If you refuse to wear these bracelets, then I will despise you," he said.[26]

The Ras instructed the guards to shackle Gaki. "I am not a wild animal to be chained with an iron chain," he supposedly said, and offered one of his own made from gold.[27] The Ras would need permission from Menelik for that, but compromised in allowing a silver one instead. Soldiers looped it around Gaki's neck and hammered it closed. Attached to the other end of the chain was a servant, a traditional religious leader named Kameto.†

Before they could travel to Addis, the soldiers needed to recover Gaki's crown. It was a symbol of Kafa: the kingdom would remain strong as long

---

* Andiracha. See note on page xi on spelling.

† Friedrich Bieber identified him as a slave named Aruru. Grühl called Aruru a "guard."

as the crown remained in its land. When Menelik's armies invaded, Gaki had hidden the headdress along with the royal three-legged stool. Soldiers forced informants to reveal their hiding place,[28] in the caves among the bamboo thickets on Mount Butta.[29]

With a small contingent left behind to govern the newly conquered territory, and Gaki's wives living on an isolated farmstead a day's journey outside Bonga,[30]* Ras Wolde Giorgis set off for Addis Ababa with his prisoner. Gaki rode a mule and held an umbrella open above himself.

The caravan stopped at the Gojeb River. Gaki dismounted and slipped the gold ring from his pinkie. It was the end of the rainy season. The water would have been running high and swift, twisting the brush along the shore in its urgency toward the Omo River. The hippos that congregate at dusk in the pools when the water level is low would have been absent. The Kingdom of Kafa has ended, Gaki supposedly said, as he threw the ring into the murky water.

"He dropped it into the river that runs around Kafa," a government official in Bonga said recently with emotion, "so that a future generation may one day find it."

On November 6, 1897, fettered and carrying a rock on his shoulder in a symbolic show of submission, Gaki passed through the gates of Menelik's court in Addis Ababa.[†31] "Finally he reached the imperial presence, where he fell flat and placed a stone upon the back of his neck, and thus waited for Menelik to speak," wrote the head of the first U.S. diplomatic mission to Menelik's court. "The Emperor's wrath rose with the recollection of the wrongs which the Prince of Kaffa had done him, and his soldiers cried out injury after injury upon the unhappy King."[32]

According to Menelik's biographer, the famously forgiving (and certainly pragmatic) emperor would have allowed Gaki to be restored as head of Kafa in return for regular tribute payments. However, the crowd, includ-

---

* Bulatovich photographed the wives three months later. "On a spread out oxhide in the shade of banana trees, a young, rather beautiful woman sat, and behind her stood the chief guard of the captive harem—a large beardless eunuch. Two other wives were with her, as well as four concubines of the king and his bold beautiful twelve-year-old sister." Bulatovich, *Ethiopia Through Russian Eyes*, 253.

† Versions told in Kafa often depict a more defiant king. When Kameto knocked at the first palace gate, the guards would not open until Gaki bowed. He refused. Guards wound his neck chain around a heavy stone to force him down. Only then did the gate open.

ing soldiers who had fought in the Kafa campaign, keenly aware of the long opposition that caused the deaths of many of their comrades, bayed for his execution.[33] Ras Wolde Giorgis suggested a third alternative: imprisonment. The emperor agreed. The Ras also told Menelik that he wanted to rule Kafa himself. Menelik agreed to that, too.

There is a single photo of Gaki Sherocho taken after his capture. Wearing a dark robe, and with a light-colored shawl draped over his right arm, he stands behind a low wooden gate in what looks like the dock of a small-town courtroom. A thick chain encircles his neck like a noose and sags to his servant, whose face is tipped down and mostly covered by a wrap, at the edge of the image. Gaki appears unshaven. His hair has not been cut for some time and stands out in an unruly Afro. Looking directly at the camera—likely the first he had ever faced—he stands erect, even defiant.

The only known photograph of Gaki Sherocho
was taken after his imprisonment.

Gaki was imprisoned first in the old Shawan capital of Ankober, then in the northeastern province of Wollo, and finally in Addis Ababa, where he died in 1919, after more than two decades in prison.*

Gaki's body was not returned to Kafa to be buried among the imperial graves on Mount Shosha. He was interred north of Addis Ababa in the

---

* Gaki outlived Menelik II. The emperor, ailing with syphilis and partially paralyzed since 1907, suffered a string of debilitating strokes and lingered on until his death at the end of 1913. Fearing civil war, authorities kept his death a secret for nearly three years. Marcus, *History of Ethiopia*, 110; and Underhill, "Abyssinia Under Menelik and After," 49.

monastery of Debre Libanos, reached at that time through a cleft in a cliff.* Founded in the thirteenth century, it was the leading monastery in Shawa, Menelik's heartland, and center of the Orthodox Church in the Horn of Africa during the Middle Ages. Undoubtedly Gaki was put to rest without the heart of an oxen laid atop his own, nor coffee and *tej* placed in his tomb for the afterlife.

Bulatovich offers the closest account of the conquest of Kafa and its immediate aftereffects. A classically educated cavalry officer from the Cossack regiments, he had joined the Russian Red Cross's mission to treat Ethiopian soldiers wounded in their victory over the Italians at Adwa. Before heading home to Russia, he accompanied a military expedition to conquer a far-western region along the Baro River. Bulatovich returned to Ethiopia straightaway as part of a trade delegation. In Addis Ababa the Russian actively but unsuccessfully petitioned Menelik to allow him to help Ras Wolde Giorgis capture the elusive Kafa king, who was then still on the run, and managed to photograph the arrival of the Ras and his captive in the capital.

After delivering Gaki, Menelik's southern strongman headed back to Kafa to establish his rule over the territory. But almost immediately, Menelik sent the Ras farther south to claim the lands between Kafa and Lake Rudolf on the Kenya border for Ethiopia.[34] On his previous visit Bulatovich had impressed Menelik, perhaps with his legendary horsemanship. Concerned about clashing with the British, who claimed the adjacent territories, Menelik invited the Russian to join Ras Wolde Giorgis's army as an observer.

Bulatovich crossed the Gojeb River in early January 1898 and entered Kafa on his way to Andiracha, where he would meet up with the Ras. The Russian wrote rapturously of the landscape as he climbed through dense forests: "In nature some kind of joy of living was felt—a surplus of strength hidden within it. The charming beauty of the place carried one off to some place far away, to a magical world. It was as if in front of you stood the enchanted forest from Sleeping Beauty. All that was missing were the princess, her palace, and her subjects. But instead of the poetic circum-

---

* In Kafa today some are skeptical of the official version and claim that there is no proof of when or exactly where Gaki was buried.

stances of a fine story, before us appeared the dreadful signs of death and destruction."[35]

Only a few months had passed since Gaki's capture. The kingdom lay in ruins. "Amid the green grass, the white of human bones shone here and there. Settlements were nowhere to be seen—only thick weeds, growing on plots of recently cultivated earth, bear testimony of the people who once lived here," Bulatovich wrote. "The closer we came to the capital of Kaffa, the more noticeable became the signs of recent battles. Near [Andiracha] itself, clearings were completely strewn with human bones."[36]

With fields destroyed and gardens unplanted across Kafa, Bulatovich encountered "unending files of bearers—tall and strong Galla, carrying on their heads to Kaffa big skins of grain, or returning from Kaffa loaded with coffee and mead."[37] Wild coffee was one of the only products people could still find, and they bartered it for food. Coffee was a livelihood and cultural touchstone; now it was a salvation against starvation. "On the large area in front of the palace, a market assembles twice a week, to which the natives of the neighborhood throng. For bread from Jimma, they exchange coffee, which today constitutes the only wealth of the region."[38]

Camped in Kafa, Bulatovich found the situation dire. "Completely naked hungry Kaffa children wandered around our bivouac, picking up any garbage. It made you feel sorry to look at them. They had lost the appearance of humans and were terribly thin; more precisely, they were skeletons covered with skin. On their thin legs, which were almost devoid of meat, the joints at the knees were sharply delineated. The cheeks and eyes were sunken, and the stomachs were distended."[39]

Up to 60 percent of Kafa's one million people were killed or displaced in the war and its aftermath.[40] In the first quarter of the twentieth century, the population of Kafa fell to perhaps as low as 100,000,[41] just one tenth of what it had been. The two areas that showed the strongest resistance to Menelik—Arsi and Kafa—were effectively depopulated.[42]

Bulatovich was in the recently conquered Andiracha for nearly two weeks as a force of thirty-two thousand men assembled. Before the rains set in, they marched south to Lake Rudolf, making the Russian the first foreigner to cross Kafa. The journey was arduous and uncharted, but the soldiers met little resistance. Two months later they planted Menelik's green, red, and yellow flag and gave a five-thousand-gun salute,[43] marking the far southwest corner of the empire. Ras Wolde Giorgis and his army had just annexed eighteen thousand square miles,[44] an area the size of New Jersey, Connecticut, Delaware, and Rhode Island together.

Menelik's aggressive expansion was effectively over, with Ethiopia's modern, and current, size established. From the isolated, semi-independent Kingdom of Shawa, Menelik had extended his reach to all of the areas of East Africa not colonized by Europeans and created an immense empire encompassing some 435,000 square miles—as large in size as France, Spain, and Portugal combined—with Addis Ababa as its perfectly centered capital. It was landlocked, requiring access to the sea through Somalia, Djibouti, or Eritrea. But it was vast, with the core central highlands protected by a buffer zone of arid or tropical lowlands.

Bulatovich spent four months in the company of the Ras and the officers and soldiers who had recently fought in Kafa. *With the Armies of Menelik II*, published in Russian in 1900, and finally translated into English exactly one hundred years later, offers nearly the sole record of the conquest of Kafa.* Only a single report about the war appeared in the international press, a short piece in the Parisian daily *Le Temps*.[45]

The story of the loss of a great African kingdom and the world's first coffee culture has not so much been forgotten as simply not known. Menelik's forces destroyed what they could of it in a literal scorched-earth campaign.

"They burnt everything," said Tetera, sitting up in his bed. Fire was a weapon of war, and the soldiers wielded it with alacrity, burning down nearly every major town in Kafa. They destroyed not just the buildings, but evidence of the kingdom with it. "These detachments laid waste to the country," wrote Bulatovich, "setting fire to everything that could burn."[46] In the mid-1920s, Max Grühl reported that Bonga "no longer exists. Only a few huts peep out from the luxurious green covering the Castle Hill and

---

* Before leaving, Bulatovich received many gifts from the Ras, including the silver spear that Gaki had thrown at the Ras's solider. In Addis Ababa, Menelik awarded him a gold shield, a rare and outstanding decoration (Bulatovich, *Ethiopia Through Russian Eyes*, 380). Not long after returning to Russia, Bulatovich gave up his army commission, became a monk, and lived on Mount Athos, where he led a dogmatic movement within the Eastern Orthodox Church. But the soldier in him never fully disappeared. During World War I, he served as an army priest and is said to have led battle charges himself. He was excommunicated for heretical beliefs and killed in eastern Ukraine by bandits in 1919 (ibid., 417).

the neighbouring ravine cut by the Dincha. Not a trace remains of the magnificence of the Imperial days."[47]

The same happened to Andiracha and its royal palace. "The Abyssinians, having torn the city asunder, had to spend a long time trying to destroy this colossal building, until they finally succeeded in burning it down," Bulatovich wrote.[48] A few years later, Friedrich Bieber visited the site and found only a few palisades and a hut. Soon there was even less. "Of the Imperial palace nothing remains," reported Grühl. "A peasant was ploughing on the spot where the throne room (Harabi) had formerly stood. Thick brushwood covered the sites of the living-rooms and the women's quarters." Only a quarter of a century had passed since the kingdom had been conquered. "The palace is vanished and forgotten like all the rest of the glory of the Kafa Empire."[49]

In 1954, the Ethiopian ruler Haile Selassie visited Vienna. He went to the city's Museum of Ethnology to see the Friedrich Bieber exhibition, with objects the Austrian explorer had collected in Kafa. Peering into cabinets with swords, woven belts, and notebooks propped open to particularly interesting pages, the diminutive emperor, swaddled in a double-breasted woolen overcoat, asked if anyone knew what had happened to the royal crown. Bieber's son, Otto, accompanying the entourage, explained that it was in a Zurich bank vault. Not long after the crown had arrived at Menelik II's palace in Addis Ababa, a group of Kafecho managed to steal it. They headed back with it to Kafa, but soldiers apprehended them en route. Menelik understood its emblematic power and gave it one of his longtime close advisers, a Swiss engineer named Alfred Ilg, with instructions to send it to Switzerland.

Selassie cut short his visit to Vienna and went immediately to Zurich. He met with Ilg's widow and two sons and began negotiating for the crown's return.[50] Ten days later he flew back to Ethiopia on a Swissair DC-6 transport plane with it.

On display today at the Institute of Ethiopian Studies in Addis Ababa, the crown sits in a framed glass case the size of an antique telephone booth. Beside it is a three-legged stool whose stubby legs curve up like field hockey sticks. Gaki's old crown does not have the traditional corona shape or even that of a wreath. The curious piece is more like a two-toned metal joker's hat with a large phallic spout at the front. The nozzle morphs into a trio of similar phalli with bulbous, mushroom-shaped tips. White ostrich feathers rise from the top of the crown and in various clumps around the front and sides, and thin, foot-long silver chains dangle around the base like hair extensions.

The local Kafa government has asked Addis Ababa for its return for their new museum in Bonga. The museum is grand but unfinished, and nearly empty of its cultural heritage. Officially it is the National Coffee Museum. But for people in Kafa, their own culture irrevocably intertwines with coffee: to celebrate one is to celebrate the other.

The request for a talisman of memorabilia so heavily imbued with nationalist symbolism and sentiment is unlikely to be granted, especially given the current ethnic tensions in nearby Gambela and with the Oromo people, whose protests caused the Ethiopian government to enact a draconian state of emergency in 2016.

CHAPTER 5

Origins

At the center of Bonga is a small empty roundabout whose central island held the city's symbol, a giant jebena coffeepot. It was removed a few years ago during road construction and now sits junked in a weedy lot. A few hundred yards up from the traffic circle is the town's new symbol, the National Coffee Museum, with its distinctive burgundy roof topped by a giant cutout of a coffee bean. In front is another giant coffee bean that looks like a giant war shield. Around the platform are the names Kafa and Mankira printed a dozen times.

The cornerstone of the building had been laid in 2007, and the Ethiopian prime minister inaugurated it in 2015, but it remained unfinished and still closed to the public in late 2016, although access was possible on certain occasions. On a July day, wires stood out of the vast walls awaiting light fixtures. A stairwell curled around a thick column at the center of the oversize building. A couple feet of stagnant water flooded the basement level. The rooms were locked and mostly empty. A worker opened the three that held information on Kafa (a chart of the political structure of the old kingdom, a hand-drawn map of the four-pronged attack on Kafa in 1897) and a paltry collection of coffee curios: rusted, Italian-era espresso machines, heavy scales used at the cooperative for weighing burlap bags of beans, and, in dusty glass cases, ox-horn cups and clay jebenas. A couple of stout wooden mortars with rodlike pestles leaned against the corner.

Lending the white walls some color was a selection of paintings of Kaldi, the Ethiopian goatherd who discovered coffee.

Kaldi's story is familiar. One day, according to the standard version retold in books and on coffee companies' websites around the world, he fell asleep and his herd of goats wandered off. He blew his *washint* (bamboo flute), but they didn't respond. After searching for a while, he finally found them—not placidly grazing but acting excited and dancing on their hind legs. Kaldi noticed that they were eating red berries growing on the branches. He chewed some himself, felt their stimulating effects, and began dancing alongside his goats. Filling his pockets with the strange fruits, he returned home. When he showed his wife, she made him take them to the local monastery. The abbot was less than enthusiastic about Kaldi's discovery and tossed them into a fire. Enticing aromas soon filled the room, drawing in some of the abbey's monks, who raked the toasted beans from the embers, crushed them, and prepared a hot drink. After imbibing, the monks found themselves unusually alert during their lengthy nighttime prayers. Word—and the drink—gradually spread, initially among monks and then the rest of the people.

This old tale was included in the first printed treatise devoted solely to coffee in Europe. Written in Latin by Antoine Faustus Nairon, a Syrian Christian professor of languages at the College of Rome, it was published in 1671. The story spread widely, although almost immediately it had its critics. The French orientalist Antoine Galland—official antiquarian of King Louis XIV and the original translator from Arabic of *One Thousand and One Nights* and the sixteenth-century manuscript by Abd al-Qadir al-Jaziri describing coffee's origins—criticized Nairon for accepting or even inventing the story of the goatherd. "[Galland] says they are unworthy of belief as facts of history," wrote coffee's supreme authority, William Ukers, in 1922, "although he is careful to add that there is *some* truth in the story of the discovery of coffee by the Abyssinian goats and the abbot who prescribed the use of the berries for his monks."[1]

But the story also holds certain similarities to versions of coffee's discovery that those living around the wild coffee forests themselves tell.

"At a stretch of a hundred to two hundred kilometres, everywhere the eye randomly looks, the undergrowth of the jungle consists of the wild coffee shrubs," wrote Friedrich Bieber at the beginning of the twentieth century.[2] In Ethiopia as part of an Austrian trade commission, he was the first foreigner since Alexander Bulatovich to see the region. Menelik had granted Bieber's specific request to visit Kafa once he had finished his trade business in the capital and helped outfit a caravan that included fifty men, seven riding horses, and twenty mules carrying luggage.

With a lifelong obsession for Africa and Ethiopia in particular, Bieber had become fluent in Amharic on a previous trip to the country and added Kafinoonoo to his linguistic repertoire. In Kafa, conquered just a half dozen years before, he asked a continual stream of questions about the land, its people, and their history and wrote everything down in his notebooks, earning him, according to his grandson, Klaus, the nickname Abu Kitaba (Father of the Book). Bieber spent a month in Kafa and collected five hundred objects and enough information to write the most substantial work ever produced on the region, an unrivaled thousand-page monograph that captured details of the culture before they had completely vanished. "We have our oral tradition," said a civil servant in Kafa's Department of Education, "but we also have Bieber."

Traveling through the countryside one day, Bieber stopped for a midday rest near a rural farmstead, where he found an elderly Kafecho preparing coffee. Bieber set the peaked white pith helmet he wore on the ground by his feet, "slurped the exquisite coffee with joy," and listened as the man told him the story of its discovery. Bieber recorded in his diary, according to his son, Otto:

> A long time ago goats and sheep from a herd nibbled on the coffee beans lying on the jungle ground and instead of lying asleep during the night, they kicked and jumped around. So, they have been told, the shepherds would have become aware of the strange effect of the small bean. And then as they themselves ate the beans, they quickly gained strength and endurance and also needed no sleep during night. And later, as the Kafecho told it, they burnt the beans of the coffee shrub over an open fire in small containers.[3]

The resemblance between this and the early European version is certainly of interest, especially considering the isolation of Kafa at the time. Only a few other Europeans had ever reached Kafa before him. Bieber, moreover, heard it not from a well-traveled merchant in Bonga but at a random farmstead.

The differences, though, are even more compelling. While some might appear trivial—there are goats *and* sheep; they eat berries from the ground, not the tree—other elements are weightier and correspond with the half dozen versions of the tale recently heard in coffee forests around rural Kafa.

However, in local versions monks never appear in them, and for good reason. Orthodox Christianity probably didn't reach Kafa until the six-teenth century—the earliest churches date to the 1520s—by which time coffeehouses in Mecca, Damascus, and Cairo were already serving the drink. The coffee in the tales had no immediate religious use.

More significant, the classic version conflates the discovery of the coffee fruit with making a beverage from its roasted and ground beans and gives monks credit for an immediate eureka moment. Brewing coffee would come later. The drink as we know it evolved gradually. Coffee began as *food*.

"The king of the area around Mankira had a goatherd named Kali Adu—Adu being his father's name," began Tamirat Haile, a man in his twenties wearing a track suit tucked into low rubber boots, in a Mankira Forest hamlet. He spoke in Kafinoonoo, and the dozen or so men that had gath-ered around a raised bamboo bed covered with drying wild coffee listened closely. "One day when he took out the king's flock, they were acting dif-ferent, with a very different character. All night they continued to act excited. In the morning, the king said to Kali Adu, 'Follow the goats to see what they have eaten. Then bring some back.' The goatherd did so, gathering the leaves and red berries that they ate. The king looked them over and ate some of the berries."

"Fresh?"

"Yes," Tamirat said. "But then later the king roasted them."

"He didn't just toss them into the fire? And then smelled . . ."

"No. It was not accidental." Tamirat shook his head. "Other things we gather we roast and they taste better. Things from the forest. Or things from the garden, like maize."

A couple of the men nodded in agreement.

"After the king had roasted the coffee, smelled it, and ate some coffee beans," Tamirat continued, "the king announced the news to his followers."

"The king didn't *drink* it?"

"Pounding the beans to make a drink came with the next king."

In local versions of coffee's origins, tales like Tamarit's learned from village elders, people first ate it. Early bands of gatherers no doubt appreci-ated the berries: the brilliant crimson-red coffee cherries, enticing on the trees, are slightly sweet, somewhat refreshing, and have a mild stimulat-ing effect from the caffeine.

While it is impossible to say precisely how early people in Kafa began using coffee beans, in 2004 and 2005 an American-French archaeological project found among primitive flints and tools a pair of coffee beans in a rock shelter just south of Bonga, not far from Mankira. According to the carbon dating, they are at least eighteen hundred years old.[4]

Those living around the coffee forests of Kafa not only chew the cherries when ripe but also cook them. In the nineteenth century Antonio Cecchi wrote of the fruits being salted and fried in butter, a dish that people still prepare on special occasions during the harvesting season.

Woldegiorgis Shawo has a different version of coffee's founding, one that he had heard as a boy. On a damp March morning some months later, the forest still wet, he cut plate-size leaves with his panga and layered them along a low dirt bank to sit on and tell his story. It was something of an origin story, too, as it also explained that the Manjo clan became outcasts not from hunting and eating monkeys, per the standard account, but from their leader's greedy desire to taste coffee.

"Before," Woldegiorgis said in a low, laconic voice, "nature was dense, and people stayed in their houses. They got food from the forest but they didn't know coffee. One day, the goatherd of a *gepetato** found the flock full of energy. He tasted some of the berries that they were eating. He liked their flavor and began bringing them home for his wife to cook." Woldegiorgis took off his baseball cap and set it beside his panga. The morning clouds that stubbornly clung to the forests were finally burning off. "Kafa had a king called Matto, with three wives and three houses. As a present to the king, the wife of the *gepetato* taught one of them to prepare coffee fruits. The Manjo had their own king. He heard about the coffee and wanted to taste it. Manjo had ninety-nine wives and ninety-nine houses, and he told Matto, 'I will give you forty wives and forty houses for your one wife that makes you coffee.' Matto refused. But Manjo was desperate to taste the coffee. He hired some people to kill the king and kidnap the wife that knew how to make coffee."

Woldegiorgis stood up. The half dozen oxen he was grazing had wandered off. He listened for a moment and caught from deeper inside the forest the faint tinkle of bells they wore around their neck. "The people of

* A powerful traditional spiritual leader.

Kafa didn't like the Manjo after that," he said, drawing the story to a quick end, "and still today avoid them."

The fullest, most nuanced local version of coffee's discovery comes from Kafa historian Bekele Woldemariam. While a folktale, it illustrates the gradual progression of coffee from a food to a drink.

Nothing in the woodlands is wasted; everything has a use. Those who live around the forest learn to take advantage of all that it offers. People usually begin with the most accessible. For coffee trees, that is their leaves. These—rather than beans—were the first used from the tree to brew a drink.

It was some time in the second century A.D., Woldemariam's story begins:

> a shepherd of goats and later his family noticed the special smell of coffee from the breath of goats. The shepherd was called Kalli or Kalliti.* Kalli followed the route of the goats and noticed the type of plant leaves which the goats anxiously ate. Kalliti then picked some of the leaves, took them home and told the story of how he had discovered them. The family of Kalliti curiously and eagerly put the leaves later to be known as coffee in the boiled water. When they tasted the water they found it to have a pleasant and unique taste. The discovery of this taste soon spread throughout Kaffa. The leaves of the coffee were ground and boiled for drinking purposes for an uncertain period of time; i.e., before the beans of the coffee were discovered.[5]

While berries are only ripe for a short period, leaves can be found year-round. They are easy to gather, require none of the labor of drying and peeling the coffee fruits to get to the beans, and need only to be steeped in hot water to make a drink. A tisane from coffee leaves has long been prepared in Kafa not only by poor people foraging along the forest fringes,

---

* According to Woldemariam, "Kalliti (or when shortened to Kalli) is the local name of a Kaffa man or Kaffecho. It literally means 'brave,' 'fast,' 'alert'" (Woldemariam, *History of the Kingdom of Kaffa*, 56). The spelling is a transliteration that might be more accurately rendered as Kali Di'i.

but even the ancient kings, who drank a brew of "yellow coffee leaves ground and mixed with honey."[6]

Yellow—or, more precisely, bronze—is the key trait when gathering the leaves in the forest, as locals stress that these are the most flavorful. They are left to dry for a few days before being pan-toasted until brittle. (Some go about it in an easier fashion, simply gathering dry leaves and crumbling them into hot water.) The brewed flavor of the infusion is similar to a light pu-erh tea, earthy with a natural sweetness. (The infusion is also high in antioxidants.)

Kuti is especially prevalent in eastern Ethiopia around Harar and Dire Dawa as an accompaniment to khat, the mildly narcotic leaf chewed fresh in the afternoons. "But not only with khat," insisted Mignot Solomon, on a balmy late morning in Dire Dawa, as she tossed a handful of leaves onto a hot, wide steel disk. With a metal hook she stirred the leaves until toasty brown, then placed them into a teapot of boiling water along with a pinch of salt. After a couple of minutes, she strained the liquid into teacups and added a large sugar cube to each. The infusion glowed the bronzy tone of a fine black tea. The luminous brew was mild and lacked astringency, without tannins coating the gums.

Children in Harar also sip the simple infusion. "Kids here start drinking coffee at twelve or thirteen," said a Harari in a coffee bar. "But *kuti* at any age."

Kafa also has a more complex leaf infusion called *chamo* (literally "bitter"), which includes wild garlic, foraged forest ginger, the aromatic herb rue, and even chilies. One version, popular to the south of Kafa, simmers toasted and ground leaves with chilies, wild cardamom, and a dollop of seasoned clarified butter, making a savory concoction that explodes on the palate and blows out the senses. "For flavor," said Mesfin Tekle on drinking *chamo*, "but also medicinal. It's strong but good for the throat." Parents give it to kids as young as two years old in Kafa, he said, the same age they start giving them coffee.

"It is not surprising that in Ethiopia," wrote anthropologist Rita Pankhurst, "where there is so much popular knowledge about the properties of the country's extensive flora"—according to the United Nation's Food and Agriculture Organization (FAO), more than 85 percent of the population uses herbal remedies or products from wild animals as their primary source of health care[7]—"the wild coffee plant should also, at some unknown period, have yielded its secret."[8]

That secret included, finally, its beans, and using them to brew coffee.

"Many years later the elderly people of Kaffa noticed the red and green beans of coffee," wrote Woldemariam, continuing his story. "They also noticed that birds were eating these coffee beans. So they picked the beans and put them in an earthenware pan. The aroma from the roasted beans gave off a stronger, and a more attractive sensitive smell than the former leaves."

At first people ate the beans toasted—a habit not lost today among Kafa residents, who eat handfuls of them like nuts—but then they began pounding the beans and simmering them in water to prepare a drink. "They also discovered that roasted, ground, and boiled coffee [beans] had a more stimulating power and more flavor than the ground and boiled leaves."[9]

While Arabs or Sufis generally get credit for first brewing coffee, preparing the decoction was most likely begun by those living here among wild coffee trees. The progression would have been natural, more gradual than wholly accidental. In London, Aaron Davis, head of coffee at the Royal Botanic Gardens, Kew, said, "Roasting coffee, or cooking with it, at some point you are going to produce a liquor, aren't you?"

How the Kafecho first brewed it is unknown. Without a written language, they were unable to record their methods themselves. But scouring the works of the first Europeans to reach the region yields some intriguing clues on early—and unique—methods of preparing coffee at its source.

In the mid-1920s, the German explorer Max Grühl drank "superb Kafa coffee made with butter, honey and spices."[10] Grühl asked his guide Chinito how the women made the coffee, then quoted him at length on the precise process:

> They take the beans and roast them well over the fire. Before each meal they roast the beans afresh until they are a fine brown colour and then they grind them into a very fine powder. The powder is in a modo (a wooden mortar about twenty inches long with a wooden pestle over three feet in length), mixed with a little butter and honey, and made into tiny balls. The balls are placed in the coffee-pot and well boiled. The woman who

makes the coffee, at this stage adds a few grains of ofio (spice of some kind—paradise or African pepper—the pods strung together on a thread). The coffee is then ready for drinking. Coffee has always been made in this way in Kafa. In very early times the Mancho [Manjo]—the predecessors of the Kafitsho in Kafa—prepared it in the same manner. The coffee is often made to-day without butter and honey, in the Habesho [Ethiopian] manner. But that is not Kafa coffee.

Learning the authentic version thrilled Grühl. "I suppose Chinito had given me the oldest recipe in the world for making coffee!"[11]

Or at least one version of it. Two decades earlier, Bieber had witnessed an even more rudimentary method from the "old Kaficho" on the rural farmstead who told him the story of the goatherd. Bieber watched the coffee beans being "finely pulverized between two rough stones, then mixed with wild, dense honey, made into small balls, and thrown into boiling water."[12] This, Bieber wrote, was "the original way."

To have butter meant having cattle, and not everyone in Kafa did so. Even for those with cows, it took time to collect the milk and churn. Wild forest honey, though, was plentiful. It has a light woodiness to its sweetness and overtones of ripe fruits, and Kafecho slather it on soft bread for breakfast or ferment it into their beloved, headache-inducing *tej*.

Honey was also traditionally used in a way to carry roasted and ground coffee by those going into the forest or taking a journey. Unlike the typical runny variety from Western supermarkets, Kafa's forest honey is dense and opaque and can be shaped into a sticky ball with coarse coffee grounds and carried in a pouch. A pinch of the mixture could be dropped into hot water for a cup of essentially ready-to-brew instant coffee or simply eaten on its own.

Pastoralists with herds of cattle often used butter instead of honey for carrying coffee, which early European travelers in Ethiopia found highly surprising. "It is not a matter of small curiosity to know what is their food, that is so easy of carriage as to enable them to traverse immense deserts, that they may, without warning, fall upon the towns and villages in the cultivated country of Abyssinia," the eighteenth-century Nile explorer James Bruce wrote.

This is nothing but coffee roasted, till it can be pulverised, and then mixed with butter to a consistency that will suffer it to be rolled up in balls, and put in a leather bag. A ball of this composition, between the circumference of a shilling and half-a-crown, about the size of a billiard-ball, keeps them, they say, in strength and spirits during a whole day's fatigue, better than a loaf of bread, or a meal of meat.[13]

These were essentially early energy bars.

The early travelers to Kafa came across people drinking coffee so frequently that each made note of the zealous habit. When Alexander Bulatovich crossed Kafa in 1898, he found locals sipping it "several times a day, up until and after eating. They boil coffee in earthenware vessels and pour it out into little cups made of ox horn."[14] Along with the "original way," Bieber saw that women prepared it fresh and hot before each meal, "roasting coffee beans on the baking bowl, crushing these roasted beans to powder in the mortar, and then boiling up the powder in the coffee-boiling jug on the hearth with water."[15] The coffee was served from the pot and drunk from small horn cups, and those who liked it spiced, he noted, added some grains of paradise or a pinch of cloves.

Horn cups can still be found in Kafa, although many have replaced them with small, handleless ceramic ones made in China. Some people—Woldegiorgis in Mankira among them—continue to prefer cups made from bamboo.

"I cannot have more than three cups of coffee," Mesfin said, laughing. "But the rural people can have eight or nine cups in one day"—two or three times at home, and the remainder with friends in their homes. Every invitation includes coffee. ("If coffee is not part of an invitation," Woldemariam counsels, "it is said that the invitation is incomplete.")[16] But even that is not needed. If you smell coffee being prepared, there is nothing strange about simply walking inside for a cup, Mesfin said. There will always be extra coffee and plenty of cups on the low table. "You don't need to feel ashamed or embarrassed. You go into the house and they will serve you coffee."

From traditional sacrifices to the forest spirits and socializing to a family's economy, coffee is always present. "For those in Kafa it is part of their life," Mesfin explained. "Most of the time when they are shopping, when they're buying clothes or whatever, they think in coffee terms."

Coffee, the American anthropologist Amnon Orent noted after living in a rural hamlet in Kafa for eighteen months in the 1960s, is a measure of, and a means to, prosperity. "Wealth in Kafa today means the amount of coffee one can gather on his lands. This coffee is generally sold in Bonga for cash. Cash in turn is used to buy additional cattle, which raises an individual's status in the community. The cattle can then be used to arrange better marriages for one's children. These better marriages open up [beneficial] ties with higher clans."[17]

Coffee has long been central to Kafa's culture, and it retains unparalleled importance on numerous levels today. "People," Mesfin said, "consider coffee is their identity."

CHAPTER 6

Gift for King and Country

Coffee, in Kafa and in most of the numerous languages in Ethiopia, is a variation of *bun*.[1] "*Buno* means 'coffee' in Kafinoonoo," explained an articulate young manager in the Department of Education in Bonga. "But the word also means 'red fire.'" He was referring to an ember, a rather poetic reference to the color of a ripe coffee cherry. In his office at the end of an unlit corridor, large cupboards with their doors ajar held sloping stacks of dusty, donated chemistry, mathematics, and geography textbooks, many of them decades old. "There is also a village named Buna near Mankira," he said, "the original coffee forest." That seemed more telling as the source of the word. He thought for a minute and added that it also meant "warning."

These are coincidences, according to Mesfin Tekle, and have little to do with coffee's name. "The root of the word is a gift for the king." *Buno* derives from *bono*, a formal way to refer to the king, and *kaafo*, meaning a cover or wrapping for a gift. "*Bono kaafo, bono kaafo,*" he repeated in quick succession, "becomes *buno*." He formed the word slowly, pulling it out into two long syllables—*boo-noo*—with a soft ending, the *o* nearly as open as an *a*.

It was a quiet March weekend afternoon in Coffeeland's restaurant-bar. The two dozen white Land Cruisers that crowd the parking lot each day hadn't yet arrived. Behind him, a woman on a low stool roasted coffee on a flat metal disk over embers, rhythmically stirring as they darkened, and sweetly pungent smoke wafted about the room. She brought Mesfin a handful of warm beans. He popped one into his mouth and crunched down on it like a corn nut.

"It is related to a gift," he continued. "There is a gift that is owed to the king." He used the word euphemistically; it was a tribute. Different items were acceptable to give. "One was coffee. One was civet musk. And ivory. And honey. So these were the gifts to give to the king. In the early times, coffee was a valuable means which everybody can access, and because of that, his gift was coffee." In the 1850s, the Capuchin priest Guglielmo Massaia found that people in Kafa were obliged to supply coffee beans to the ruler.[2]

The cover for the gift was made from an enset leaf. Held over fire, the stiff, banana-like leaves become flexible, and skilled hands shaped them into containers. They are still used, and in Bonga's weekly Saturday market, certain goods—cheese, butter, salt, *kocho*, coffee—are sold wrapped in them.

Mesfin crunched another coffee bean. "When [Kafecho] people go on a journey, they take coffee with them. People want to not only drink coffee, but to *smell* it. Because of that, they take coffee beans with them and put them in a container." From the saucer on the table he picked up another bean. It was a deep shade of brown, nearly black. *"Bono kaafo, bono kaafo,"* he said again quickly, *"buno."* He crunched the bean. "That is the legend."

With news of its discovery, coffee "spread from village to village and from province to province of the Kaffa Highlands," wrote Bekele Woldemariam. "In the traditional way, the people of Kaffa who had coffee plants at their disposal sent a parcel of berries or coffee beans to their friends and families in the distant areas."[3] Nearly all could get some, either from nearby forests or trees planted around their homes. At the end of the 1870s, Antonio Cecchi, a member of the Italian Geographical Society, found few huts in Kafa not surrounded by coffee trees. He reported two ways of cultivation, transplanted from the forest—simply going into the woods and pulling up saplings, or raised from seeds.[4] This remains virtually unchanged today, and in rural Kafa it is rare not to have at least a few coffee trees growing beside the house and a simple raised bed for drying the beans.

Merchants traveling in caravans throughout the Ethiopian highlands took coffee farther. "There were houses along the ancient trade routes," Mesfin explained, permanent settlements that acted as places to stop, rest, and resupply. Traveling with servants, merchants were gone for months, even years, at a time. "They took seeds and seedlings, planting them, little by little, on the way," he said. These are the tales that have been passed down. Mesfin is a keen collector of such stories, but he is also a trained scientist. "This is the most probable," he added as a caveat.

Along the paths that radiated out from Kafa, coffee also spread in less intentional ways. "The Arabica coffee plant exhibits weedy tendencies as indicated by the rapid spread of the plant along trails, under isolated trees in abandoned fields, and in clearings in the forest area near village sites," reads a 1960s Food and Agriculture Organization report on Ethiopian coffee. "Humans, mules, monkeys and other animals are factors in the dissemination of coffee seeds."[5] Hornbills and other large birds and certain primates might have been an especially effective if haphazard means of spreading Arabica, but merchant caravans contributed to the accidental scattering as well.

The main trade routes can be traced directly over Ethiopia's key coffee-producing areas: north from Kafa through Limu, Illubabor, and Wollega on the way to Gondar; and east through Jimma, across the Rift to Sidamo, Arsi, and Harar. Bonga was the starting point for both routes.

The dried coffee berries were carried in rudimentary containers made from woven palms and strapped to mules or camels. They were imperfect and unsealed, and beans trickled through gaps in the weave along the journey as the animals bumped into things (or each other), scraped their loads against trees, and were loaded and unloaded by handlers. Some of the beans would germinate and grow along the path. On these tracks, locals also took seedlings or seeds from trees and planted them in their own gardens.

Slaves traveled along these same routes, and one idea—anecdotal, intriguing, not improbable—is that they helped spread coffee as they chewed fresh cherries and spit out the seeds on their journey. These caravans departed once the rains had stopped, the rivers had receded, and the mud had dried. This was also harvest time, and they would find ripe cherries on the trees. The slaves traveled on the forced marches in shackles or wooden halters, barefoot, usually naked, and with scant food.[6] Coffee fruits have little pulp, but they are somewhat refreshing in the mouth and offer a bit of caffeine stimulation.

Halting for the night in the 1850s along one of the main routes from the Somali port of Zeila inland to Harar, an area with a long history of coffee cultivation, the explorer and linguist Richard Burton encountered people chewing coffee fruits. It must have been somewhat common, for his comment about it is offhand and alludes only to an associated superstition: "Those who chew coffee berries are careful not to place an even number in their mouths."[7]

Once Menelik had a hold over a united country, road connections improved, movement increased, and the spread of coffee quickened. Menelik rewarded victorious generals—many of whom were relatives—with annexed areas to govern. These were unpaid positions, and the new governors received fiefdoms "to eat."[8] In Kafa, Ras Wolde Giorgis confiscated land from the Kafa nobility and redistributed it largely among outsiders. In lieu of a salary, settlers from the north, mostly soldiers, received rights over land or labor.[9] Departing governors stripped the fiefdom of what they could. When Ras Wolde Giorgis was transferred in 1910, his soldiers rounded up as many slaves and as much livestock as possible to take with them.[10] In 1926, Max Grühl came across a column of hundreds of naked captives that took hours to pass him on the muddy trail: "Men and women practically naked chained to one another, leading naked children by the hand or carrying them like bundles on their backs, dragged themselves through the filth and were driven like cattle by their heartless captors."[11] Seized by an outgoing governor, they were likely heading to Jimma to be sold.[12]

From Kafa, there was not only rife plunder in slaves, ivory, and musk, but also coffee.[13] Elders in Yirgalem, Sidamo, say that when Haile Selassie's son-in-law Ras Desta Damtew left Kafa in 1932 after serving as governor for four years, his soldiers carried coffee seedlings to his new posting in their region. Today it is one of Ethiopia's preeminent coffee-growing areas.

In most of the world, the single way to farm coffee is on plantations, in orderly and often large fields of well-tended rows. In Ethiopia, the first modern plantations were established to the southwest of Kafa just a half century ago. Bebeka, Tepi, and Limu are the largest in the area, with a scattered handful of smaller ones. Yet despite modernization, particularly over the last decade, the system still remains uncommon in Ethiopia and accounts for less than 5 percent of the country's exportable production.

The most common method of cultivation is "garden coffee." Grown on small patches in a family compound or on nearby small plots, and generally intercropped with various fruit trees, enset, maize, and, in the east, khat, this style accounts for at least half of Ethiopia's coffee. The country's three best-known producing areas—Sidamo, Yirgacheffe, and Harar—rely completely on garden coffee.

One unique way of farming in Ethiopia is called semiforest. Along the edges of wild coffee forests, farmers remove some of the canopy to allow more light, slash back lianas, shrubs, and undergrowth a couple of times a year, and even slightly trim the coffee trees themselves, stimulating growth and substantially increasing yields.

Too much openness, though, can kill trees accustomed to growing under heavy shade. The spindly, slow-growing wild Arabica luxuriates in the newfound light and nutrients and bears more fruit. However, without the upper canopy, they often suffer from overproducing; the trees require more nutrients than they can take from the soil, and the roots begin to die. With a significant amount of cover removed, they also lose some of their resistance and become more prone to diseases. "Nature is always the winner," Mesfin said with a droll grin.

The fourth way is wild forest coffee. This only amounts to a fraction of Ethiopia's total production, up to 5 percent. Quality is mixed, and yields are extremely low. With little manipulation, the trees follow a natural biennial up-and-down crop cycle.

In Kafa, people consider forest and semiforest the same and refer to both as *wof zerash*. The only difference is some slight tending and more open growing conditions in the latter. The trees themselves are wild and have been naturally sown.

Apart from a few companies that have begun marketing it in Europe,* wild coffee is nearly impossible to find outside the region—at least unblended. Homes around the coffee forests use foraged beans, which also get traded in Kafa's local markets. Some of it ends up being mixed in with other beans from around Kafa, Limu, and Jimma with similar flavor profiles and auctioned on the Ethiopian Commodity Exchange as Jimma Grade 5.

The coffee beans need to be dried after picking, and there are two main methods to do this. The first is sun dried or "natural": the fresh cherries are spread out on beds to allow the beans to dry inside the fruit before being milled and cleaned.

---

* A collaborative project launched in 2014 between Union Hand-Roasted Coffee in East London, Aaron Davis at the Royal Botanic Gardens, Kew, and local partners in Ethiopia has worked to improve the quality of wild beans from Yayu Coffee Forest Reserve and bring them to a market abroad.

This indigenous method of drying brings out wild-berry flavors and tropical aromas in the coffee and gives the body density and a creaminess in the mouth. The final cup, though, has less uniformity. It is nearly impossible to control that only perfectly ripe red cherries have been picked. Farmers sell natural coffees to mills and cooperatives only once they have already been dried, at which point the pods all look the same. A green cherry and an overripe one have a near-identical bluish-purple color when dry, even if their eventual flavors in the cup are wildly dissimilar.

The second style of drying is "washed." It's modern, large scale, and requires expensive equipment. A machine removes the outer peel of the fruits just after picking. The beans move to a large cement tank of water, where the sugars and alcohols of the dense, sticky mucilage break down through soaking and then rinsing in a washing channel. Workers spread out the beans on long raised beds in the sun to dry. Still wet and greenish yellow in color, they give off a slightly fermented, pickled aroma. As they dry over the next few days, the outer parchment turns the color of bleached bones (and will later be removed when milled). The beans feel like small shells when raked through the fingers.

Immediately removing the fruit after picking yields a cleaner, brighter, and more mild final cup of brewed coffee. Fruity flavors turn gentler, rounder, and more delicately complex. The fermentation that happens when soaking away the mucilage improves acidity—leaving not the tangy, sour acidity of a lemon but that of a green apple. A crisp sensation is left in the mouth, and the coffee feels lively rather than flat.

The first washing station in Ethiopia opened in 1972. In 1975, washed coffee accounted for just 5 percent of Ethiopian exports.[14] The method is more expensive. It requires substantial water and creates more waste, including the mucilage-rich water from soaking. The resulting coffees are more consistent and fetch more on the international market than sun-dried. The Ethiopian government and aid agencies such as USAID and TechnoServe, as well as Menno Simons's import company, Trabocca, have helped finance and set up washing stations. While today washed coffee has grown to 20 to 30 percent of Ethiopia's production,[15] it makes up the majority of its exports.

In Harar, coffee is exclusively sun dried, and in Kafa it remains the main method. Only seven of the forty-three cooperatives that form the Kafa Forest Coffee Farmers' Cooperative Union have washing stations.

In the mid-nineteenth century, merchants divided Ethiopian coffee into two categories: Abyssinia—largely wild beans from the southwest—

and Harar. It continued to be mainly exported under those two names in the 1920s.[16] The crop expanded, and during the twentieth century coffee took on an unrivaled importance in the country's economic life. During the first decade of the twenty-first century, the country's production more than doubled. In 2014 coffee exports brought Ethiopia $880 million.[17] Somewhere around 95 percent of the production is done by smallholders with less than two hectares.

Ethiopia is the largest coffee producer in Africa, and the fifth largest in the world. Its 2016–17 crop was around 6.5 million sixty-kilogram bags, or 390,500 metric tons (860,905,134 pounds) of green coffee. It produces purely Arabica coffee. Usually referred to as Ethiopian heirloom, the variety is a wily mix from wild, old-growth trees, taken, over time, from the forests and raised in gardens, and seeds selected from the best-producing trees and passed around. This gives Ethiopian coffees the broadest spectrum of flavors found in any producing country. In the cup, it tends to be smooth with intense aromatics and flavors, carrying a berry fruitiness with some citrus notes and chocolaty tones. "Ethiopian coffees are irreplaceable in their flavor profiles," said Menno Simons, the most important importer of specialty coffee from Ethiopia.

Coffee accounts for about a third of the country's foreign exchange and is one of the few sources of hard currency, necessary to buy refined petroleum products and equip the military, the third largest in Africa. The government requires that export-grade coffee be exported; only low-quality coffee beans can be sold on the domestic market, meaning that Ethiopians are forced to buy rejects, broken beans, or ones damaged by moisture or insects. Yet demand is so great that prices are often higher than for export-quality coffee. If the laws were liberalized, the export market would largely collapse.

While certain Central and South American countries might be synonymous with coffee, Ethiopia is the only country that consumes over half of its own production. That's almost five hundred million pounds of coffee for a population of nearly one hundred million, a particularly impressive quantity as nearly half the population is under fourteen years of age. (By contrast, Kenya consumes just 3 percent of its production, while Colombia exports over 86 percent of its coffee.)

Coffee, though, was not immediately popular everywhere in the country even after it had spread across Ethiopia's plateau. In the north, Orthodox Christians initially saw it as the drink of Muslims, who controlled trade and also grew it in the east. "The Abyssinian Christians, probably to distinguish themselves from Moslems, object to coffee as well as to tobacco," noted Richard Burton on his travels to eastern Ethiopia and Somalia in the 1850s.[18] Prejudice against drinking coffee died away in the second half of that century, and coffee became not just the national drink but a staple.

Interwoven in the country's distinctive fabric, coffee is an incomparable strand in Ethiopian life. "It is so much part of the culture," wrote the social anthropologist Alula Pankhurst, "that it is a symbol of sociability, a metaphor for social relations and a vehicle for spiritual blessings."[19] It is everywhere, seemingly all the time.

The common phrase for getting together, to talk, is *buna tetu*, which literally translates to "drinking coffee." This captures both aspects of its significance: a meeting rarely lacks coffee, and coffee rarely lacks company. Drinking *buna* in Ethiopia is a communal rather than solitary activity and is rarely done alone. Or quickly.

At the core of Ethiopian life is the traditional coffee ceremony, which many consider the most important part of their culture. The ritual binds the diverse population from eighty different ethnic groups, a cohesive to a disparate country cobbled together not much more than a century ago.

On a small knoll edging a brooding patch of forest, Lemlem Dubale spread out long grasses and ferns and then arranged two dozen pink and bell-shaped yellow blossoms around the spot that she had cut just inside the forest. In a semicircle facing it, she arranged chairs. Wearing an ankle-length short-sleeve dress of coarse white cotton striped with red, her hair pulled back in a short bun, she lit the charcoal in a brazier and patiently fanned until it was glowing. She pinched an ember with tongs and placed it in a second, smaller brazier with chunks of chalky incense, sending up puffs of fragrant white smoke. The coffee ceremony was beginning.

This was in Sidamo, on the south side of the Rift, but it could have been nearly anywhere in Ethiopia, so prescribed is the ritual, so familiar are its steps. Appreciation and pleasure come in the exquisite execution of each anticipated step.

On an ornate wooden serving tray sat tiny cups with slight tulip lips. Lemlem had more than a dozen of them even though she only expected half that number for coffee. Others might smell it being prepared, she said in a low voice, and come to join the ceremony. "All would be welcome."

She shook some green coffee beans from a tin onto a wide, slightly concave metal disk. After carefully picking them over for broken beans and small stones, she washed the beans with a touch of water. Setting the griddle down on the brazier, she began to slowly roast the coffee, moving the beans around with a bent strip of metal. Sitting on a fallen tree stump, she stirred steadily as the beans darkened to chocolaty brown and began to smoke, the aromas blending with the freshly cut grass, charcoal, and incense.

After almost fifteen minutes, once the beans were shiny and nearly black, she took the griddle off the brazier and fluttered a hand through the aromatic smoke. Alerted by the aromas, a handful of people had begun to gather and take a seat. Lemlem made a slow pass among the plastic chairs, allowing each person to take in the evocative aroma of the just-roasted beans. Showing appreciation is key, and impressed *aah*s came from the small group.

While the roasted beans cooled for a few minutes, she filled the jebena with water and nestled it into the hot embers.

The most important among the requisite tools of the coffee ceremony is this bulbous, long-necked pot. Made from clay and darkened black to a high polish, the jebena had a short, pointed spout. "Coffee comes from the forest," said Jacques Dubois, author of a book for UNESCO on traditional Ethiopian crafts, in his Addis Ababa pottery studio. "The spirit in the forest sometimes manages to get in with the coffee. And inside the jebena." The front spout, he said, offering one theory for the shape, allows the spirit to slip away peacefully during the ceremony.*

Lemlem placed a fresh ember on the incense burner. From a small wooden box she took a generous pinch of crumbled incense. ("Special blend?" "Yeah," she said, leaving her mouth slightly agape and letting the soft *h* fade to whispered exhale.) She sprinkled it over the top. Aromatic smoke billowed up. The smell was reminiscent of an Orthodox church, and with the association of sacred rituals, voices became hushed.

---

* In Mankira, the traditional jebena is less bulbous, with a long, narrow unflared neck, and no front spout. They call it *Kafeo jebena*, a woman in Mankira explained, "the original style." Ingredients go into the top opening and brewed coffee is poured out the same. Butter is a common ingredient. It floats on the surface and comes out only if there is just the single opening, she said, not if there is a front spout.

Scooping the beans into a cylindrical mortar made from a hollowed tree stump as thick as a thigh, she began to pound using a blunt, rodlike piston, keeping a hand cupped around the top of the mortar to stop any grounds from being flung out. The crushed beans released a strong, fruity aroma. In parts of Ethiopia, wild cardamom or a clove sometimes gets pounded with the beans, or, near the Sudan border, a curl of cinnamon bark. In Kafa the addition, if any, is fresh wild ginger. Lemlem tipped the grounds down into the slim neck of the jebena.

While the coffee brewed, she passed around wooden bowls of popcorn and puffed barley.

A man named Alemayhu from a nearby compound took a handful of kernels from the bowl. "In your country, you drink for the taste," he said when asked about the savory accompaniments. He meant that the actual experience largely focused on that singular sense. "But here it is for all five senses," a complete sensual experience. He touched a finger on his hand and said, "First: seeing. The setting. The grass. The way the flowers are arranged. The woman preparing coffee who is smiling, happy." Touching a second finger, he said, "Smell." Of these there were many: the just-roasted coffee, the incense, the cut greens and flowers, the fresh grounds. He indicated his ear. "Grinding the coffee in front of you by hand, the sound. That is the third." There was also the crack of the roasting beans, the pebbly tinkle during stirring, and the riverlike hush of pouring coffee. Then there is touch. "Drinking," he said, "we use a handleless cup. It fits nice in the hand and warms the fingers."

He took another handful of popcorn from the bowl. From inside the forest a hyena called. Its deep bellow started low and finished on a sharp, quick upward pitch: *WHHHHooop!*

A guard from the compound passed through and at the edge of the woods dumped out a bucket of food scraps. He cupped his hands around his mouth and shouted, *"Amba! Amba!"* ("Come! Come!")

"And taste?"

"Yes. And taste." Alemayhu laughed. "To satisfy these five senses with coffee takes time," he said, finally getting at the answer. "Half hour, one hour. More. So we are giving a coffee 'breakfast.' That's why you need something to eat. Popcorn. Injera. *Kocho.* It's a special meal, not lunch or dinner, but a coffee ceremony meal."

A murmur of bubbling came from the jebena. Alemayhu put a finger back to an ear, indicating another of the pleasing sounds. Lemlem lifted the pot off the embers and set it on the ground. The bubbling stopped, and the grounds began to settle. As the jebena doesn't have a filter, letting the grounds settle and using a method of pouring that does not disturb them are paramount for a good cup of coffee.

It was dusk, and the light was quickly fading. A pair of spotted hyenas lumbered silently out of the forest and approached the scraps. When a couple of vultures fluttered heavily down, one of the hyenas charged to flush the birds off.

Lemlem wiped each of the cups with a clean cloth and arranged them on the tray so that their lips touched. She poured out the coffee in a graceful, continuous stream from high above. Alemayhu touched his ear again and raised his eyebrows, indicating the cascading sound.

Lemlem carried around the wooden tray, offering coffee to the dozen people who had quietly gathered. The warm cups nestled snugly in palms.

It had taken an hour to prepare. Anticipation had built. In a moment the cup was empty. The coffee had a familiar thickness to it, a smoothness, and an evenness that wild coffee from Kafa often lacks. These beans had come from trees growing among avocado, banana, and enset in a walled garden attached to a compound.

Lemlem collected the empty cups. But the ceremony was not over. Like tea in the Sahara, coffee traditionally comes in three rounds, each diminishing a touch in strength. Lemlem added water to the jebena and set it back on the embers. Bowls of popcorn and barley came around again, and also *kocho*, with its spongy, almost rubbery texture. Prepared using the pulped starch of enset that has been buried and fermented in pits for months, it is unfamiliar, even unpalatable at first. ("This bread is inedible to anyone not accustomed to it," wrote the Capuchin friar Guglielmo Massaia after encountering it in the mid-nineteenth century.)[20]

Those sitting in a semicircle facing Lemlem watched her delicate and precise movements. Conversation had slowed. The leisurely, almost meditative pace of preparing the coffee seemed to contrast, or perhaps counter, the energizing effects from the caffeine. *WHHHHooop!* a hyena yipped.

Lemlem poured out the second serving, then added water for a third. The last one—called *baraka*—bestows a blessing on the guest, and to leave before it is served is considered rude. Or worse. In Kafa, people say *bune marako gačheto* when someone has had an accident. "It means that you didn't respect the coffee spirit," Mesfin explained at the Coffeeland in Bonga while crunching on just-roasted coffee beans. "The ceremony needs to be finished before you leave. You cannot just drink and go." If you do, he said, "You'll break the coffee spirit."

When a gurgling came up through the neck of the jebena, Lemlem took the pot from the coals and set it on the ground for a moment. It was nearly dark. The sky had turned an inky purple. *WHHHHooop! WHHH-Hooop!* came from the forest. The shadowy figure of a hyena slunk along its edge as Lemlem poured out the final round.

PART TWO

Out of the Forest

CHAPTER 7

Coffea aethiopica

T he horse-drawn carriage jolted along the Herenweg, the road running from Haarlem, outside Amsterdam, to Leiden, some twenty miles south, past grand summer estates built by those wealthy enough to escape the pungent sewer smells of Amsterdam in the heat. About halfway, near the famed Dutch bulb fields, the carriage turned into the short drive of Hartekamp. The name means "deer park," and while *herten* no longer roam wild on the grounds today, a weather vane of a leaping stag atop the pale-yellow main house recalls its more bucolic origins. Once the coach halted, the young Swedish botanist Carl Linnaeus alighted.

Linnaeus had been developing a system of classifying plants according to their sexual organs, innovative work that would transform the son of a Lutheran vicar and avid gardener into the father of taxonomy and one of the greatest natural historians. But on that mid-August 1735 day, he was largely unknown. He had come to the Netherlands two months before to take a medical degree, awarded in mere days after he presented an already-written thesis.[1]

Hartekamp's owner, George Clifford III, welcomed his guest. Part of a wealthy Anglo-Dutch banking family, the widowed fifty-year-old was a director of the Dutch East India Company, the powerful trading company. Clifford's real passion, though, was the natural world, and he had spent many guilders indulging it. The house and the conservatory had been built before his family had purchased the estate. Clifford bought the adjoining land, expanded the gardens, and had four heated greenhouses erected[2]— one for plants from southern Europe, another Asia, a third Africa, and a fourth the New World. These complemented a research library and world-class herbarium with thousands of dried specimens.

Linnaeus was "dumbstruck" and "captivated" by Hartekamp's renowned treasures. "I was enthralled by your menageries, crowded with tigers, apes and monkeys, wild dogs, antelope, wild goats, peccaries [jave-linas] and warthogs, and by the myriad flocks of birds whose calls and songs echo through your garden, among them parrots, pheasants, peacocks and doves," Linnaeus wrote of his visit that summer day. "I was astonished when I entered your hothouses, crammed with such profusion, such variety of plants as to enchant a son of the cold north, uncomprehending of the strange, new world into which you had brought him."[3]

Linnaeus's botanical knowledge and ability to classify plants new to him impressed his host, and Clifford asked him to organize and care for Hartekamp's collection, and to prepare a record of its contents.[4] This last item particularly interested the Swede: "I had no greater desire than to see an account of such a garden made public, and no greater fear than that I might not be able to extend a helping hand."[5]

Within a week he had accepted the position of *hortulanus* (superintendent of the garden) and resident physician. Clifford was something of a hypochondriac, and Linnaeus would act as his personal doctor as well. Along with room, board, and salary, Linnaeus received a generous budget to buy books for Hartekamp's library, specimens for the collection, and even travel expenses to visit England. He lived, though, "like a monk"[6] and focused his attention on work, including cataloging Clifford's collection. He prepared the manuscript of *Hortus Cliffortianus* in just nine months.

With the support of his patron, Linnaeus published a limited edition of the large, folio-size work in 1737. Written in Latin and heavily illustrated, it detailed some 1,251 living plants growing in the greenhouses, gardens, and nearby woods of Hartekamp, and the 2,536 dried ones preserved in the herbarium. Among the latter was coffee.

In preparing the coffee entry, Linnaeus consulted the work done two decades before on the plant by Antoine de Jussieu at the Jardin du Roi* in Paris.[7] Jussieu had made the first study in Europe of the coffee plant and offered its original taxonomic description, identifying it as a member of the laurel family.

---

* Renamed Jardin des Plantes after the French Revolution overthrew the Bourbon monarchy.

Linnaeus's dried sample was a direct descendant of the one that Jussieu had studied.[8] Fixed to the sheet with slim strips of strapping tape, the foot-long branch appeared to be standing upright in an ornate vase. In eighteenth-century Holland, decorative vases, medallions, elaborate labels, and pennants helped identify the owner of the collection. Kept unbound, herbarium sheets could be lent and duplicates exchanged.

In *Hortus Cliffortianus*, Linnaeus included the Frenchman's account— *Jasminum arabicum, lauri folio, cujus femen apud nos Caffé dicitur*[9] ("Arab jasmine, with laurel leaves, the beans of which we can call coffee")—but rejected the conclusion that it was a laurel. Instead, he created a new genus, *Coffea*.

Linnaeus left Hartekamp not long after publishing *Hortus Cliffortianus* and, back in Sweden, continued to perfect his taxonomical system to make a clearer, simpler way to identify plants, then animals, and eventually all manner of living things. To each he gave a binomial name. The genus was the first part of Linnaeus's scientific classification. The second part, the specific name, was the species epithet, an adjective that indicated the origin or gave a characteristic.

The first clues to what he might name coffee had appeared in Jan Wanderlaar's allegorical frontispiece of *Hortus Cliffortianus*. The crowned goddess Mother Earth (Europe) holds the heavy keys to the garden of Hartekamp (the botanical kingdom), whose gates open just behind her.* A map of the estate unfurls on the floor among garden tools, a compass, a Celsius thermometer (which Linnaeus helped invent), and a pair of cherubs. Sitting atop a lion and a lioness, she accepts horticultural tributes: an American Indian proffers hernandia from the New World, an African woman aloe, and an Arabian woman a heavy flowerpot with a coffee tree.

Inside the book's page-long coffee entry, Linnaeus was less coy: *Crescit in sola Arabia felici*—"It grows only in Felix Arabia [Yemen]."[10]

The Linnean Society of London keeps the dried specimen sheet from Linnaeus's personal herbarium in its secure vault beneath Burlington House on Piccadilly. In a subterranean, wood-paneled room lined with Linnaeus's library, a librarian carefully unwrapped the *Coffea* sheet. Unlike the

---

* Bursting into the elaborate scene is the young god Apollo, wearing little more than a laurel wreath. He pins the slain, fork-tongued dragon of ignorance and falsehood underfoot, while his left hand holds a lit torch bringing light and his right pushes away the shroud of darkness. The face of Apollo is none other than that of Linnaeus himself.

Jan Wanderlaar's allegorical frontispiece of Linnaeus's *Hortus Cliffortianus*.

ornate sample from the Clifford herbarium,* it was plain and unadorned. Two of the leaves had come off, leaving fossil-like veined imprints on the sheet. On the left side, and somewhat smeared, read "Caffe." At the bottom, written in a lighter ink and in Linnaeus's own hand according the librarian, was "arabica."

In 1753, Linnaeus published his botanical magnum opus, *Species Plantarum,* which included all known plants, some fifty-nine hundred of them. He gave coffee its official binominal. To *Coffea* he added the epithet *arabica.* "From Arabia."

The Horn of Africa juts far out into the Red Sea, nearly pinching it off at the Gulf of Aden. A mere twenty miles across at its narrowest point, and only some two hundred at its widest, the slender slip of sea has been a key commercial trade route since antiquity, a well-traveled strip connecting Egypt and the empires of the Mediterranean with India, the Indian Ocean, and the East. Along the eastern side of the sea is the Arabian Peninsula, homeland of Islam and the Arabs, and one of the oldest inhabited regions in the world.

Tucked just inside the Red Sea's southern entrance on the Arabian side is the port of Mocha. "The edge of town is like the concavity of a half moon, and is flanked by two mouldering castles," wrote an English traveler who visited in 1795. It had stucco buildings of mud or coral, white fortifications, and towers crowned with battlements. "The coast is low, sandy, and deficient of verdure; it seems to have been, formerly, part of the sea, but inland mountains rise, at a great distance, among fertile valleys. The opposite coast of Abyssinia, which is dimly visible in clear weather, appears more mountainous."[11]

Established in the thirteenth century, Mocha came to prominence after the Ottomans took control of it in the mid-1500s as they gradually conquered Yemen (and the nearby Islamic holy cities of Mecca and Medina). Mocha grew quickly from fishing village to prosperous port. A Dutch East India Company cloth merchant named Pieter Van den Broecke, calling at Mocha in 1616, reported more than thirty ships from as far away as India and Persia in port,[12] as well as the arrival of a caravan numbering one thousand camels.[13]

---

* In 1791, Clifford's widow sold his herbarium to Joseph Banks, the director of the Royal Botanic Gardens, Kew. London's Natural History Museum now holds the collection.

Ottoman rule of Mocha was soon truncated by the al-Qasimi dynasty, which ousted the Turks from Yemen in 1635.[14] Under the al-Qasimi, Mocha flourished as a key Red Sea port and important destination on the global trade network, an entrepôt of spices from the Indies, Indian cotton textiles, New World silver, and Chinese silks.[15] But coffee was its key commodity.

Yemen was the first to commercialize coffee on a large scale, and Mocha held for nearly two centuries—into Linnaeus's lifetime—a virtual global monopoly on its trade. As coffee drinking spread across the Middle East and Europe, the Arabian Peninsula was synonymous with the product, and the port the sole source of beans.[16] Mocha became so closely associated with it that coffee sold in its markets took the port's name.*

Loaded onto Arab and Turkish ships, sacks of coffee traveled up the Red Sea to Jeddah and then Suez, where camels carried them to the warehouses of spice and coffee merchants in Cairo and Alexandria.[17] From there, traders shipped the beans around the Mediterranean.

As demand grew in Europe, trading companies wanted to cut out intermediaries, and merchants began visiting Mocha. The British East India Company established itself first in Yemen, followed by its Dutch counterpart in 1696.[18] The Dutch received permission to open a "factory"— a trading establishment headed by a commercial agent known as a factor— and to send six hundred bales of coffee annually free of duty.[19] French and English factories followed.

By 1720 Mocha's coffee trade had peaked,[20] and it lost its monopoly. Demand shrank, and competition increased sharply from coffee grown in European colonies. The port's decline was steady.[21]

The Ottomans regained control of Mocha in the mid-1800s, but the port had already suffered a competitive blow when the British conquered Aden in 1839—the first acquisition of Queen Victoria's empire—and made its fine natural harbor their main regional port. Other Europeans did likewise. "All of the Mokha [coffee] comes from here," wrote a French trader in Aden in 1885, "because Mokha [the port] has been deserted."[22]

Mocha remained under Ottoman control until World War I. But its wells dried, the port sanded up, and the town slowly wilted as the popula-

---

* There is some confusion today, as in many parts of the world *mocha* has come to mean coffee with chocolate added to it. This perhaps comes from the natural chocolaty notes in coffee from Mocha.

tion shrank and the magnificent merchant houses crumbled, leaving few traces of its past importance.

Until the mid-sixteenth century, the global coffee market was still quite limited, and Ethiopia was perhaps able to fulfill Mocha's requirements for beans.[23] While cultivation had begun on a formal but limited scale in Yemen earlier, significant coffee farming started once the Ottomans brought Yemen under their control around 1550. With surging demand from coffee's growing popularity in the Middle East and the Eastern Mediterranean, the Turks financed construction of terraces, irrigation networks, and planting on the slopes running between Ta'iz and the port of Mocha, and along the western escarpment that runs parallel up the coastline. Farmers cultivated coffee in the moist bottoms of wadis (ravines that fill with the seasonal rains) and on hillside terraces, some wedged so tightly into the narrow valleys that their stone faces rose up twenty feet.

Within half a century, Yemen usurped Ethiopia as the main source of coffee.[24] It was an improbable achievement. Just over 2 percent of Yemeni land is arable and suitable for farming.[25] Even if conditions were somewhat better at the time, water was scarce, conditions harsh, and most of the coffee needed to be irrigated. On a royal Danish expedition to Yemen in 1762–63, Carsten Niebuhr and Peter Forsskål trekked into the hills to see the coffee terraces. They noted the careful, snug cultivation in beds placed stepwise above each other. Some were watered by rain, others used a sophisticated system of gravity-fed irrigation: The upper levels had large cisterns or wells that channeled springwater downward through terraces so densely planted that the sun rarely struck the ground.[26] The Yemenis excelled in cultivating not just coffee but a wide variety of fruits and vegetables on their dry terraces by having complete mastery of the scant water resources available.

Yemeni coffee farmers had a reputation for taking care of their fields, selectively harvesting the coffee, and meticulously tending the fruits as they dried naturally. They loaded the dried pods into straw baskets and brought them to storehouses, from where camels transported the coffee to the port of Mocha to be sorted and sold.

In the high, hilltop citadels on the road down from Ta'iz, tower houses still rise up among the terraced fields. Fanlights with alabaster and colored glass arch gracefully over windows outlined in chalk, freshly

An engraving from the royal Danish expedition to Yemen (1762–1763) shows the steep slopes of coffee. In order to clearly illustrate the agricultural system, only a few trees are shown.

washed carpets hang out over the sills, and, on the flat roofs, spreads of drying red cherries turn plummy purple in the cool sun.

When he attached the *arabica* suffix in 1753, Linnaeus unintentionally hijacked Ethiopia's proprietorship of coffee. A decade later he published *Potus Coffea*, an eighteen-page pamphlet made of rag scrap with words running to the edges, adding that the plant grew spontaneously in "Arabia felici & Aethiopia."[27] It was too late. He had named it *Coffea arabica*, not *Coffea aethiopica*, and Arabia would continue to be regarded in the public mind as the original source of coffee.

From the earliest works on the subject, beginning with Abd al-Qadir al-Jaziri's treatise *The Best Defense for the Legitimacy of Coffee*[28] and Dawud al-Antaki's *The Nature of the Drink Kauhi, or Coffe, and the Berry of Which it is Made, Described by an Arabian Phisitian*,[29] Arabia was recognized as coffee's origin.

By the time Linnaeus was classifying coffee, only a small number of references had pointed across the Red Sea to Ethiopia. Charles-Jacques Poncet had recorded it growing in Ethiopia, and the English botanist Richard Bradley reiterated in *A Short Historical Account of Coffee* (1715) Poncet's observation that it was "a Native of that country; it was transplanted from thence to Arabia Felix."[30]

A decade or so after Linnaeus's misnaming, members of the Danish expedition to Yemen wrote that, according to Arabs they met, the coffee tree was originally brought from Ethiopia.[31] At the end of the eighteenth century, James Bruce, writing with extraordinary prescience, pinpointed "Caffa" as its specific source a century and a half before anyone else.[32] At the time, Bruce's observations were widely distrusted, and his point ignored.

While gradually more reports indicated Ethiopia as Arabica's native home, the belief that it originated in Arabia stubbornly endured well into the second half of the twentieth century, even among researchers. Following two years in Ethiopia and Yemen on a United Nations–sponsored coffee project in the mid-1950s, Pierre Sylvain wrote that the former could "be considered as the native home, and probably the excusive native home of *Coffea arabica* L."[33] But without irrefutable scientific proof, he still needed to couch his assertion in qualifiers. In 1958, A. E. Haarer published his referential *Modern Coffee Production*, where he argued that Yemen wasn't the native home of coffee not by offering proof *for* Ethiopia but by laying out a case *against* Yemen. Rainfall was far from sufficient "to provide the ecological conditions necessary for an 'Arabian' coffee and forest community." Wild coffees are always found under forest cover, which Yemen simply did not have. Or even had: there are no historical references to Arabian forests. The soil types were wrong, there didn't appear to be as many forms of Arabica in Yemen as in Ethiopia,[34] and no authentic records existed of Arabica growing wild in its namesake region.[35] In 1961, Frederick Wellman could be only slightly more forthright in his comprehensive work *Coffee: Botany, Cultivation, and Utilization*: "The place of its origin is well recognized as the highland of Ethiopia and its extension into the southeastern corner of the Anglo-Egyptian Sudan, not far from Kenya."[36]

How, and precisely when, coffee arrived in Arabia has been, Wellman noted, "lost in the haze of tradition and fable."[37] Even with the most advanced DNA techniques, it remains one of coffee's mysteries.

Coffee is strangely absent from early literature. There are no known mentions of it by the ancient Egyptians, who explored down the Red Sea coast and up the Nile, or the ancient Greeks, who also sailed the Red Sea. Nor do the Hebrew Scriptures have any clear references to coffee, or the Bible, or even the Koran, which was definitively compiled in the mid-seventh century A.D. The Persian-Iraqi physician and philosopher Rhazes (c. 865–925) wrote of a medicinal black infusion called *bunchum*—from the fruit called *bun*, the name in Ethiopia and Arabia for the coffee berry.[38] This is often considered the earliest reference, followed by a similar one by the Persian-born scientist and thinker Avicenna (Ibn Sina) around A.D. 1000. However, scholars have long asserted that *bunchum* actually referred to a root.[39] There are essentially no persuasive comments regarding coffee in historical documents, or depictions on pottery shards, until the fifteenth century, and not with any frequency until the sixteenth. (That both Rhazes and Avicenna were referring to coffee remains highly suspect, since no other reference would be made to it for this gap of five hundred years.)

So when did coffee arrive on the Arabian Peninsula? The range offered by the most esteemed experts is remarkably broad, between fifteen hundred and three hundred years ago.[40] Wellman placed the first movements of coffee in A.D. 575, when the Aksumite Kingdom was the most powerful state between the Eastern Roman Empire and Persia,[41] and its control stretched from northern Ethiopia to southern Arabia,[42] and then again about 890.[43] An Ethiopian Coffee Board publication claimed, "We know for certain that sometime before the 9th century A.D., Arab traders took coffee and planted it in Arabia."[44]

The sixth century seems far too early—it is implausible to not have verifiable references to coffee from such a highly sophisticated culture for eight or nine hundred years—and just three centuries ago far too late,[45] as coffee had long been growing in the hills around Ta'iz by then. It was probably the fourteenth century,[46] and certainly no later than 1400.[47] By the 1500s, as demand surged, cultivation was in full swing in Yemen.

In Ethiopia, pictorial versions of coffee's journey to Arabia hang on countless walls, from the National Coffee Museum in Bonga to hotel lobbies in Jimma, Addis Ababa, and Harar. The opening panels show Kaldi and his goats discovering coffee, followed by a woman preparing the drink. Muslim merchants sip the coffee and then buy bags of beans. At the seashore, the traders board a small boat that takes them to Arabia.

"This Kaffa bean tree was brought by Muslim merchants to Arabia," Friedrich Bieber wrote in 1920. "These merchants had so far been supplied with its beans via Massawa from Kaffa at the time of the reign of King Madi Gado or Wodi Gafo, who reigned from about 1530 to 1565."[48] That coincides with the period that Yemen was expanding planting and terracing under newfound Ottoman rule. "Wrongfully, Arabia is regarded as the home of the coffee tree," the Austrian explorer wrote in his journal. "Arab traders brought the coffee tree—Kaffatree or coffee tree—there to Yemen, and then from there it started its triumphal march over the whole world. Kaffa is the original home of coffee."[49]

In some illustrations the merchants appear sneaky, carrying bulging sacks of money and offering furtive glances. It's not clear if they are being devious or are simply afraid. "A story runs that at the risk of his life an Arab succeeded in smuggling coffee-seedlings out of Kafa and in bringing them safely to Arabia," the German explorer Max Grühl wrote. "Thus the way was paved for the establishment of the coffee-plantations in the highlands of Yemen."[50]

"It wasn't stolen," said Mesfin Tekle on a wet day in Bonga, shaking his head. "Trade, that was the way. The link [between Kafa and Yemen] is Tengola," he said, referring to the ancient mosque and trading center established by Muslim merchants.

Located halfway between Bonga and Andiracha, Tengola sits some fifteen minutes off the road down a slender, ambling path. On a November afternoon, sunbirds and flycatchers darted from the trees along the overgrown creekbed paralleling the trail. Enset with swordlike leaves veined in beetroot crimson surrounded a handful of small farmsteads on the hillside. The mosque's compound was a grassy expanse with a dozen or so mud homes girdled by a living fence of closely planted shrubs and spiny candlestick euphorbia trees cropped at chest height. The mosque itself, a low rectangular building with a rusted red corrugated roof and no minaret, sat along the back.

The first to bring Islam to Kafa was Abidir Selam, said the mosque's imam, Sheki Kedir Sedik, as he unlatched a pair of heavy padlocks on the wooden door. Abidir Selam came from Hejaz, the Red Sea coastal strip in Yemen and Saudi Arabia, and established a mosque on this spot, some seven hundred years ago, he explained. That original building, a traditional mud hut, had long fallen to the elements and had been rebuilt many times. The current one had an interlacing wattle of sticks smeared with mud that contained crushed white stones and a generous amount of teff that swirled through the crumbling walls like unbraided rope. Along the covered portico that ran the length of the building, a soft layer of hay had been spread.

Kedir pushed open the double doors and flicked a switch. A trio of bare lightbulbs dangling from the ceiling gave off an orange, low-wattage glow. The handful of patterned carpets didn't cover the entire earthen floor, and hay had been scattered across the remainder of it. Some fifty or sixty people gather for Friday prayers, but hundreds come during the important festivals, camping on the grassy field for a few days.

"The grove of Abidir Selam," Kedir said, gesturing toward a small patch of woods just beyond the mosque. The heavy gold ring he wore was loose and slid around his finger. "His house was there."

Kedir had been appointed imam of Tengola mosque forty years ago following religious training in neighboring Oromia. He was the eighth generation in his family to be imam, he said proudly. Though the afternoon was warm, he wore an oversize gray suit and knitted white skullcap embroidered with dull golden thread. His forehead was damp with perspiration.

Kedir knew the history from his father and grandfather, past imams of Tengola. Kedir's oral history dating Islam's arrival in Kafa to the 1300s is a few centuries earlier than historians generally put it. Arab traders, though, likely predated Abidir Selam and those who initially brought the faith. Islam in Kafa is *nagade gibino*, "religion of traders,"[51] and the name for a Muslim remains *negado*, literally "trader." Mesfin said, "First came trade, then friendship and gifts, and finally religion."

Between Tengola and Andiracha is the important ancient market grounds of Tiffa. While an hour off the road and no more than a tiny hamlet today, when Antonio Cecchi visited in 1878, the market still gathered four days a week and was the largest in the region. Muslims traded at Tiffa for coffee, honey, and musk from the nearby forests, and gold and ivory from the south, Kedir said. "They left with these and came back with salt." (He didn't mention slaves, but traders also bartered for them with salt.)

It would certainly have been possible to carry coffee seeds from Kafa to the Arabian Peninsula and have them arrive in viable condition some months later. Optimal germination happens by sowing fresh seeds, and a journey to Yemen would require ones that had been prepared in a way so farmers in Arabia could plant them.

In Kafa today, farmers such as Woldegiorgis Shawo continue to follow traditional methods of preserving some of the best seeds each year by peeling away the outer skin of the freshly picked fruit by hand, dusting with ash or charcoal, which acts as an antifungal, and storing in a cool part of the house. According to Jean-Pierre Labouisse, a global expert in preserving coffee resources with deep experience in Ethiopia, coffee beans that aren't fully dried and are stored at room temperature in a humid place can be kept viable for up to two years, which is plenty of time for the journey to Yemen and any wait for the correct moment to sow.

At Tengola, when asked about how coffee spread from the wild forests of Kafa, Kedir shouted impatiently, "Oromo!"—referring to Ethiopia's largest ethnic group. "The Oromo came and took coffee. They traded east, among the Muslims. Probably Harar." Kedir waved his hand vaguely eastward but also dismissively. "I only know what my grandfather told me." It came from the stories he had heard growing up. He shrugged, his bony shoulders marooned within his jacket, and crossed the overgrown field back to his home.

His grandfather was likely more correct than Kedir realized.

In the 1990s, using newly available DNA technology, studies began to indicate that Yemen's coffee might not be as closely related to the wild Arabica of Kafa and surrounding forests as to stock from further east, perhaps around Harar. "A clear separation was observed between the Ethiopian germplasm collected in the southwest highlands of Ethiopia (Illubabor and Kaffa provinces), and the cultivated material spread world-wide from Yemen," wrote Philippe Lashermes, coffee's leading geneticist, in 1995. "This result supports the hypothesis that the arabica plants transferred to Yemen for cultivation by the Arabs originated from the south eastern part of the evergreen mountainous region of Ethiopia (Sidamo and Harar provinces)."[52]

Looking out over his laboratory at the Institut de Recherche pour le Développement (IRD) in Montpellier, France, the low hum of expensive and delicate machines piercing the glass walls of the conference room, Lashermes rejected those findings. The work was done two decades ago, he said, using an outdated technique. The paper had been presented at a colloquium in Kyoto, he noted, and not peer reviewed. The study didn't have a broad enough range of samples, and a close reading suggested that it didn't fully lead to the conclusion. He shrugged. He didn't know if Harar was a transit point and didn't want to speculate.

His colleague Benoît Bertrand, though, had just completed a diversity study on Ethiopian and Yemeni coffee using the latest DNA technology and was putting the final touches on a paper. The study had sequenced the genotypes of 798 coffee samples, one hundred from Yemen. On a large, wall-mounted dry-erase board in his office, Bertrand, another of the industry's leading geneticists as well as one of its foremost coffee breeders, wrote:

"wild" Ethiopian
Yemen
modern

"All the modern varieties are coming from Yemen," he said, connecting the bottom two with a line. "And Yemen passed from Ethiopia." He made a short line between the top ones. "There was not coffee in Yemen before Ethiopia."

He vigorously cleaned the board and drew the rough outlines of the Horn of Africa and the Arabian Peninsula. "Somewhere between Ethiopia and Yemen was the first domestication of coffee." He traced the bulging curve of the Horn that swept in close to Arabia across the Red Sea. "But, if coffee came directly from Ethiopia to Yemen, or if Harar was the first center of domestication, we cannot say."

He moved to his computer and touched the mouse, waking the screen to the paper. "We can see that it started in Ethiopia," he said, scrolling down to a diagram mapping out three distinct clusters of coffee types— modern varieties, Yemeni coffees, wild Ethiopian ones—based on genetic markers.

From the data, though, it was impossible to know if there was a step in Harar. "It is not possible for the moment, no." Gaps remain in understanding coffee's complex heritage.

While "one bag of beans would have been enough" to start the entire Yemen industry, as Lashermes pointed out, it was almost certainly through disparate introductions.

The coffee from the southwest region in Ethiopia would have needed to adapt to the dry and sunny conditions in Yemen. Bertrand stood in front of the uneven hourglass outline of the Horn of Africa and Arabia. "This is forest." He pointed to the Ethiopian side. "There was an adaptation to the dry and sunny conditions of the population of Yemen." He tapped on the

Arabia part of the map. "But you lost lots of types of coffee. Only some were able to adapt to Yemen's conditions."

This seems why pinpointing the year of the original attempt is not precise. "The first one? I don't know," Labouisse said. He shrugged, as if to say that the exact date of initial introduction isn't important, as there were many of them over the years. That Yemen sustains far more genetic coffee variety than anywhere else outside Ethiopia indicates that Yemen's terraces of coffee were established not only with wild plants from the southwestern forests, but likely from elsewhere in Ethiopia, including around the legendary trading enclave of Harar. Of all the seeds carried to Yemen, those from the dry east of Ethiopia would have had the easiest time adapting.

CHAPTER 8

City of Saints

I n 1842, the British Royal Geographical Society published "Extract
Report on the Probable Geographical Position of Harrar." It included
extensive details on the annual *kafilas* (caravans) that left the city for
the thirty- to forty-day journey to the ports on the Somali coast, minutely
describing when they departed, where they halted, and what the camels
carried. It listed the number of weapons held in the city, the gates of the
protective wall by name, and the crops grown in the surrounding hills.
"Coffee is the most important article produced; at least 2000 bales* are
yearly exported to the sea-coast, to the ports of Berbera and Zeila, and
thence to Arabia and India; finally to European markets."[1]

But, as the "probable" in the title indicates, 175 years ago the august
geographical society still lacked one vital piece of information: Harar's
precise location. No Englishman, nor non-Muslim for that matter, had ever
entered the city.

For centuries Harar was the main trading post and transit point on
caravan routes from western and southern Ethiopia to the ancient seaports,
and for the annual Islamic hajj to Mecca. The independent emirate had
a highly organized fiscal system, elaborate trade network, a unique language, and even its own currency—wispy gold, silver, and bronze coins
so light to be barely detectable on the palm of the hand. Harar's noisy
markets were legendary for their ivory, musk, slaves, and coffee.

Local tradition places the founding of Harar in the thirteenth century

---

* An ancient measurement used for Mocha coffee. According to the *Oxford English
Dictionary*, one bale equaled 2 to 2.5 hundredweight (224 to 280 pounds).

when Sheikh Abadir Umar Ar-Rida arrived from Arabia with forty-three others and selected the site to found a new city.[2] But Harar existed before that. When UNESCO inscribed it to their World Heritage List in 2006, three of the city's mosques were dated back to the tenth century.[3] That fits better with the account of a local lord unifying a number of villages into Harar around that time. A banner hanging in one of the city's museums lists the seventy-two successive emirs who ruled Harar from A.D. 969 to 1887.

If Sheikh Abadir was Harar's spiritual father, then Emir Nur ibn al-Mujahid was its military one. While fighting an Ethiopian army in the mid-sixteenth century, Nur slew the country's emperor. Rather than attempting to conquer further Christian territory, Nur withdrew to Harar (with his enemy's severed head on a pike) to solidify rule over the city and the region around it. His greatest legacy was wrapping Harar in stout walls known as the *jugol*. Standing between thirteen and sixteen feet high and pierced by five gates, the hearty construction ran two miles in circumference.* During the reign of the emirs, guards locked the gates at dusk and took the keys to the ruler. No one could leave until dawn.

Oval in shape and built on a slight incline, Harar's medina-like knot of quiet, colorful alleys unspool through its compact 120 acres (less than a fifth of a square mile). The population inside the *jugol* peaked at around fifty thousand—an inconceivable number in such a small space—but has fallen to a crowded but manageable twelve thousand with the city's expansion beyond its ancient walls. Small iridescent birds bolt from eaves as the numerous minarets sound their calls to prayer, and spotted hyenas gather at the gates at dusk to be fed scraps. At night, they wander with their distinctive bearlike gait through the empty alleys looking for refuse that has been left out for them.

Packed tight against one of the gates is a spice market, where vendors sell Harar's famous coffee. In the mid-nineteenth century, there were four categories of coffee products on offer here[4]—*bun*, or ordinary beans; beans of highest quality, called *hamaratos*; dried husk of the fruit (*kottu*); and the leaves (*kashar*)—and this remains the case. An elderly woman squatted near the whitewashed city wall with a bag of fresh coffee leaves, a day or two old, vibrant green and only just beginning to wilt. Nearby, another

---

* Hararis sometimes refer to its length as measuring 6,666 cubits, a symbolic number often said to be the total sum of the Koranic verses. A sixth gate was cut through in 1933. The walls remain intact.

sold coffee husks, six birr (about twenty-five cents) for a pound or so measured out with an empty quart tin of Sheno vegetable butter.

The coffee beans themselves are among the cluster of jute gunnysacks with rolled cuffs containing sesame seeds and legumes, chilies dried on the flat rooftops, and gemlike chunks of incense. A trader took a fistful of beans the color of split peas and thrust his hand forward. "Best quality," he said as he opened it. He held the beans for a moment to be appreciated before spreading his fingers and letting them cascade back into the sack.

Harar is Madinat al-Awilya, the City of Saints, the spiritual heart of Ethiopia's Muslim community and the fourth-holiest city in Islam. Eighty-two mosques and some 102 shrines[5] stand within the *jugol.* The city was not only off-limits to infidels, but death awaited any foolish enough to try.

The first Frank to enter Harar and break its "guardian spell"[6] was Richard Burton in 1855. The British explorer, prodigious linguist, and future translator of the *Kama Sutra, Arabian Nights,* and *Perfumed Garden* had recently become famous as the first non-Muslim to visit Islam's holiest city, Mecca. His employer, the East India Company, was keen for him to next explore Somalia and Harar.

The perils of actually reaching the city were high. The five-week journey from the coast with a small entourage became progressively more perilous. Of the ten chapters of his subsequent bestselling two-volume travelogue, Burton devoted just a single one to the ten days he spent in Harar disguised as an Arab merchant. He certainly didn't try to hide. Upon arriving at the city's gates, Burton immediately asked for an audience with the young emir and gifted him a pair of pistols.

Burton's comments on the city's coffee are scant: "The coffee of Harar is too well known in the markets of Europe to require description."[7] He noted that the industry was so valuable that the emir forbade "the Harash, or coffee cultivators, to travel lest the art of tending the tree be lost."[8]

Afraid of not being allowed to depart, Burton began making excuses to leave almost straightaway. When the emir granted the request, Burton left before dawn the next day. "A weight of care and anxiety fell from me like a cloak of lead," he wrote, on passing safely through the city's gates and threading his way through the hills back to the coast. "The dew hung in large diamonds from the coffee trees, the spur-fowl crew blithely in the bushes by the way-side:—briefly, never did the face of Nature appear to me so truly lovely." His small retinue did not linger. "With arms cocked, a precaution against the possibility of Galla spears in ambuscade, we crossed the river, entered the yawning chasm and ascended the steep path."[9]

While Burton may have cracked the spell, Harar remained for the next decades largely off-limits and unvisited by Europeans. Twenty-five years would pass before one would reside in Harar. He was a young French coffee trader named Arthur Rimbaud.

In the center of the old city, among stocky shrines capped with turquoise domes, cobbled lanes shaded by overhanging wooden balconies, and women selling peanuts and sticks of sugarcane, is the Rimbaud House—a fine wooden mansion with an ornate façade and a third-floor gallery that offers long views across the flat city roofs and surrounding hills. Rimbaud never lived in it, though. It was built by an Indian merchant after the poet's time in the city. Both Rimbaud and Harar are so nurtured by myth that such a detail hardly seems to matter.

In 1871, at sixteen Rimbaud wrote one of the most influential verses in modern French poetry, the hundred-line "The Drunken Boat." He sent it to Paul Verlaine and soon after joined the married poet extraordinaire in a binge of absinthe and sex. The two fled Paris for London and then Brussels, where their tumultuous, thirteen-month-long escapade culminated in the jealous Verlaine shooting Rimbaud in the wrist. (Verlaine spent two years in prison for his act.) At eighteen Rimbaud penned his masterpiece, "A Season in Hell." In three dazzling years he had reinvented European poetry. But he was done with literature. He turned his back on it, burned his papers, and lit out on the road: Germany, Indonesia, the eastern Mediterranean. There is no proof that he wrote another line of verse after his twenty-first birthday.

By 1878, Rimbaud was zigzagging down the Red Sea looking for work in Jeddah, Suakin (northeastern Sudan), Massawa, Hodeida (Yemen), and in Aden, where a coffee seller named Alfred Bardey hired him. Rimbaud's first job was as a foreman, receiving the bales of coffee brought down from the highlands by camel. Coffee arrived in the warehouse dried but generally unhusked, and he oversaw a team of Indian women who removed the peel with grinders and then cleaned the beans. These were sorted, weighed, packed in giant gunnysacks that held over 150 pounds of coffee,[10] and shipped to Marseille.

Some of the coffee arriving in Aden came from Harar, sent via the port of Berbera. Bardey saw the commercial opportunity of having a presence in Ethiopia and, that winter of 1880, dispatched Rimbaud to Harar to open a company outpost. He crossed the Red Sea and traveled twenty days on horseback through the Somali desert to reach his new home.[11] He was twenty-six years old.

Egypt had ended Harar's many centuries of independence a few years before Rimbaud's arrival. The emir was gone, and Egyptians occupied the city. Today, on the north side of the main square, Feres Megala ("horse market"), behind waiting blue Lada taxis, is a simple café called Almadu with a couple of rooms above it. Once it was the offices of Bardey's company, exporters of coffee, ivory, skins, and musk. Here Rimbaud spent the next few years buying coffee and other goods from around Harar and organizing their transport to the coast and on to Aden. The coffee was packed into goatskin bags and loaded onto camels for the journey.

There are just eight known photographs of Rimbaud. One is a self-portrait taken "in a coffee plantation" in 1883. Visits like this must have been common, as that year he bought more than three million francs' worth of coffee[12]—an enormous sum; his monthly salary was three hundred francs plus expenses. Even if he himself was not getting rich, trading was brisk, and Bardey extended Rimbaud's contract for another three years. But then in early 1884 Rimbaud had to hurriedly close down the office and liquidate the stocks because regional fighting was severally hurting business.[13]

Back in Aden he continued working as a coffee trader, though business was down. "The main product is a coffee called Mokha," he wrote

Poet turned coffee trader Arthur Rimbaud on
a Harar coffee plantation.

in a letter. "There are a raft of other things, dried leathers, ivory, feathers, rubber, incense, etc., etc., etc., and imports are also varied. All we do here is coffee, and I am in charge of purchasing and expeditions." He was buying two hundred thousand francs of coffee a month.[14] "But Mokhas are dead in France; it falls in value day by day, and profits barely cover shipping charges."[15] He struggled in "the horrible pit that is Aden."[16] He was earning nothing but his meager salary. Getting ahead seemed impossible.

He gave up coffee and turned to running guns. He organized a venture to provide Menelik II with a load of arms. The leader was still actively expanding his empire. "His only interest is to gather enough guns to allow him to send his troops to commandeer Gallas," Rimbaud wrote.[17] The weapons would help arm Menelik's armies in defeat of the Italians and their conquest of independent territories, including Kafa.

After spending months in stifling Tadjoura in Djibouti—so hot, he wrote, that the air confused the senses[18]—painstakingly assembling a caravan to haul 1,755 rifles and 450,000 rounds of military ammunition and 300,000 hunting cartridges, Rimbaud set off with one hundred camels and an equal number of Ethiopians, Somalis, and Danakil (Afar) tribesmen. The caravan crossed the Afar Depression and along Lake Assal, a bleak and searing landscape five hundred feet below sea level, and followed the ancient salt trail—dry sand, scalding gravel, mummified camel carcasses—across the Rift Valley before climbing to the central plateau to the Shawan capital of Ankober, some eight thousand feet in elevation. Rimbaud had figured fifty to sixty days.[19] It took significantly more, perhaps as long as four months. He arrived, at last, on February 9, 1887.[20]

The intrepid, epic journey quickly turned farcical. Menelik had moved his capital to Entoto, another 110 miles southwest. The caravan carried on. When it finally reached Entoto, Menelik was away on a campaign to conquer Harar from the Egyptians. Rimbaud could only wait for his return. "[Menelik] arrived in Entotto heralded by musicians found in Harar blowing Egyptian trumpets as though their lives depended on it," Rimbaud wrote, "and followed by his troops and his spoils among which were two Krupp cannons, each carried by eighty men."[21]

Along with the cannons, troops had recovered a massive stash of weapons left by the Egyptians, sinking the market value of the rifles and ammunition that Rimbaud had brought. Dealing through Menelik's Swiss adviser, Alfred Ilg, Rimbaud reluctantly accepted about one fifth of what he had anticipated.[22] Feeling conned, he railed in letters about the emperor.[23]

Menelik paid Rimbaud not in cash but in signed bonds redeemable by Menelik's cousin Ras Makonnen,* the new governor of Harar. After three years away, Rimbaud returned to the enclave. "Once in the city," Rimbaud wrote in a long letter published in Cairo's main newspaper, "the Abyssinians reduced it to a horrible cesspit, demolishing houses, ravaging plantations, terrorizing the population as only the blacks know how."[24] While the soldiers destroyed a large number of coffee trees, they also improved roads, leading to a significant increase in coffee production.[25] Buyers such as Rimbaud gained easier access to the harvest, and farmers were better able to get their beans to the market in Harar.

Rimbaud left for Aden and, after a short rest in Cairo, returned in May 1888 to Harar. Working for a different French import-export merchant based in Aden, Rimbaud again organized caravans to the coast "carrying products from these lands: gold, musk, ivory, coffee, etc., etc."[26] The company claimed that for them Rimbaud was exclusively concerned with buying coffee and sending it down by camel to the coast. The other items were for his own dealings with various brokers.[27] He was also dispatching caravans to the Ethiopian heartland of Shawa with writing paper, bundles of wool and flannel, pearls and buttons, cooking pots, and other goods that had come from Aden.

Rimbaud had by then become a figure of respect.[28] He set up house with a mistress and a servant named Djami,[29] became close to Ras Makonnen, and had a circle of European friends scattered around the country (Ilg among them). Business, though, was poor. Still he stayed on: "And what would I do in France?"[30]

Yet his letters to his mother and sister are full of complaints—about the weather, the food, the mail, those around him. "I am bored all the time; I've never met anyone as bored as I am. And if that weren't bad enough there's the matter of living without one's family, without intellectual pursuits, lost in the midst of all these Negroes whose lives one is trying to improve and who, themselves, are trying to take advantage of you and make it impossible for you to sell your wares without delays," he wrote.[31]

The bristle and bitterness of such letters is in stark contrast to his beautiful teenage missives full of flair and flourish. Toward the end of February 1891, he asked his mother to send him a rubber stocking for the varicose

---

* His first son, Tafari Makonnen, become the future Ethiopian emperor Haile Selassie.

veins in one leg. It turned out to be a tumor on his right knee. The pain got so severe that he was soon unable to move. The next letter home, sent from Aden two months later, described his emergency evacuation from Harar. A group of sixteen bearers carried him two hundred miles to Zeila on a stretcher, ten days of "horrible suffering."[32] He crossed the Red Sea and, on May tenth, sailed for France, his first time in the country in a dozen years. Days after arriving, doctors amputated the cancerous leg high above the knee.

Despite such bitter complaints of Harar when he lived there, the city remained firmly on his mind. Within a week of the operation he wrote to Ras Makonnen that he would be returning in a few months. Even with his worsening health, Rimbaud did strike out again for the city before the end of the year. He made it only as far as Marseille, where he died. He was thirty-seven.

Coffee still grows around Harar, just not close to the city itself, nor near any of the main villages or even hamlets. All of the accessible farmland has been converted to fields of khat, which needs to be sold extremely fresh. The nearest small coffee farms to Harar are about three hours away. The main coffee areas take five or six hours to reach, rural places too danger-ous for outsiders to venture into without good connections and a local escort, and certainly only during daylight hours, as there are ragtag rem-nants of the Oromo Liberation Army, a rebel group that has been fighting the government for self-rule since the 1970s. ("They hide out on the farms," according to one international Ethiopian observer. "The farmers don't say anything because they will be killed if they do.")

The road west from Harar runs for a stretch along Lake Haramaya, where greater flamingos, sacred ibis, and storks wade among the shoreline reeds, and on barren trees rising from the water, motionless cormorants balance with their wings half-extended in the breeze. Just beyond the important khat market of Aweday is a rugged, pitted dirt road that descends from the ridge through dry hills planted with maize, sorghum, and khat, a dusty landscape given occasional pats of tropical green from groves of mangoes and guava. Toward one hamlet, women with colorful, diapha-nous wraps loosely draped over their heads walked toward the weekly market carrying baskets of produce, eggs, and live chickens held suspended by their feet. Nearby, women and children clustered around a well waiting to fill old yellow cooking-oil containers with water. Above a switchback, where a creek watered a group of stout shade trees, hundreds of humped charcoal cattle stood in a field. An hour farther along was the home of a farmer named Abdela Mume.

"They belonged to my father and his fathers," said Abdela in Oromo, walking the ten minutes to his coffee fields. He wore a ribbed tank top and an open, oversize men's dress shirt that flapped in the breeze, a patterned green sarong tied around the waist, and shiny red plastic sandals. The amount of land he had with coffee he didn't know in hectares. "Only in trees," he snapped. "Two hundred and fifty trees."

Once he was among coffee, his hands instinctively pressed fruits to check their ripeness. It was November and nearly all were still green. "The oldest trees were planted by my grandfather's father," the fifty-five-year-old Abdela said, making them 150 to 200 years old. Other trees in the area might be two centuries old, he thought, but he wasn't sure. A bit farther to the west in Jerjertou—where coffee grows, Burton noted, "in perfection"—farmers claim that the coffee fields go back eight or nine generations, some 250 to 300 years.

But there is certainly an even older history of cultivation around Harar, at least to the first part of the sixteenth century,[33] when Harar was being wrapped in thick walls and terraces for coffee were being built on Yemeni hillsides. The Arab chronicler al-Umari, writing about the powerful Harar-born military leader Ahmad Gragn ("the Left-Handed," 1507–43), mentions a placating gesture by nobles in the Dawaro region—not far southwest of Abdela's farm—of offering "three handsome mules, some sugar, some *qat*, and some coffee-beans."[34]

Walking to another section of his farm, Abdela pulled off a branch of khat that grew among the coffee, plucked off some tender leaves, and shoved them into his mouth. "When there is a good rain, we can collect ten quintals,"* he said. "If there is a shortage of rain, then five quintals." He dries the picked fruits on raised beds near his home and sells them to a buyer. (More isolated farmers bring their coffee by mule to the road.) The pods then head to a mill in Dire Dawa in flat-nose Isuzu trucks that blaze down the rural roads with such terrorizing speed that they are locally known as al-Qaeda.

While researchers do not know when or by what route coffee came to Harar,[35] Abdela was less uncertain. "From Kafa? No!" the grizzled farmer

---

* In Ethiopia, a quintal equals one hundred kilograms. Latin American coffee farmers also speak in quintals, but mean one hundred pounds, or forty-six kilograms.

shouted through a mouthful of khat. "Arabia!" He was adamant and leaned close to emphasize his point. Other farmers around Harar say much the same. Popular perception is that trees planted on these hills originally came from Yemeni seeds.

Even if genetic testing one day proves that coffee here came originally from the wild forests on the other side of the Rift Valley, or even from the Bale Mountains' Harenna Forest, Abdela wasn't alone in his thinking, or even necessarily wrong.

In 1958, Pierre Sylvain argued that coffee was probably introduced to Harar by Arabs in the fifteenth century. "Certainly, after visiting Yemen and Harar, one is struck by the similarities in the method of cultivation," the French researcher and UN coffee expert observed, "and there does not seem to be any doubt that this method was brought across the Red Sea as it is not used in other parts of Ethiopia."[36] The "method" included growing in open sun, without shade trees, and terracing, key to Yemeni coffee and found in Ethiopia only in the eastern highlands. There is particularly careful tending on the orchards, and similar uses of water. Abdela irrigates the trees individually by hand, while a square-shaped berm of earth formed around each keeps precious water from running off and allows it to soak into the soil. After one of the infrequent rains, Abdela places stones around the bases of the coffee trees to keep the roots moist. These ways, he said, he learned from his father and grandfather. They also taught him to sow by placing two seedlings in a single hole. Elsewhere in Ethiopia this is done with a single bean.[37]

The agricultural practices of Abdela and his neighbors are similar to those of Yemeni farmers, said Amin Al Hakimi, professor of plant breeding at Sana'a University in Yemen and the country's preeminent coffee specialist. While the landscape and growing conditions are comparable, only part of the cultivation techniques can be explained away by climate, geography, and poor, rocky soil.

Historical links between Harar and Arabia are lengthy and deep, beginning with those settling in Harar from Arabia, and continuing with the shared Muslim faith and yearly hajj that passed up the coast of Yemen to Mecca and back each year. Harar was a key link and way station between Ethiopia and the Arabian Peninsula.

With such close ties and frequent traffic between the regions, coffee seeds most likely traveled both ways. Aaron Davis at Kew Gardens speculated that the seeds may have initially gone from Harar to Yemen, but then flowed back, with improvements. Over time, there was a two-way sharing of information, improving of cultivation, and exchanging of seeds. Al Hakimi believes it went the other way, but only at first. "Seeds, techniques, peoples," he said, "flowed not in a single direction but back and forth."

When Menelik II conquered Harar in 1887, he gained control of the eastern caravan routes to the coast. Yet almost immediately he severed the city's strategic importance by building a rail line to connect Addis Ababa with Djibouti on the coast. The route bypassed Harar for Dire Dawa, a new city about thirty miles away down on the lowlands, and converted the ancient enclave into a tangent rather than transit point. Dire Dawa became the headquarters for the region's coffee industry.

Dire Dawa is Ethiopia's most international city. While the recent arrival of loud, fume-spewing Bajajs—Indian-made, three-wheeled diesel tuktuks—has broken the tranquillity of the once peaceful grid of roads, the city still feels midcentury and lethargic, with low buildings tucked under a shady canopy of jacaranda, acacia, and flamboyant trees in the searing heat. In the old Greek neighborhood, across from the long fence of the railway yard servicing the Addis Ababa to Djibouti line, is MOPLACO, a coffee-exporting company founded by an Ethiopian-born Greek named Yanni Georgalis and now run by his daughter, Heleanna.

In the cupping room, the head taster, Mignot Solomon, pressed the back of a forefinger to one of the dozen cups arranged on the marble table to check if it had cooled enough to taste. It had. Leaning over the cup, Mignot deeply inhaled a sample from eastern Harar before dipping her spoon into the liquid. Her pencil-thin eyebrows arched up as she took a couple of sharp, noisy slurps. "Brown chocolate," she said of the flavor. "And wine." As the cup cooled, blueberry notes began to stand out. She shook a small plastic tray of coffee beans from a different part of the region, slightly smaller beans that sounded like dry beach pebbles. She trailed her fingers through the dish to check for defects.

The similarities between Harar and Yemeni coffee in the cup are striking. Both are only natural, dry-processed (rather than washed) coffees and yield comparable flavors. "Harar is cleaner, more fruity than Yemeni coffee, much better in substance. By that I mean the overall quality of the coffee, the character, the mouthfeel, and the body," Heleanna said in MOPLACO's Addis Ababa warehouse. "I find good Yemeni less fruity, more chocolaty, though. Harar has very distinct winey notes—if it is a good Harar."

This last qualifier was key. Fine coffees from Harar have a specific and much-sought-after flavor profile—a classic mocha flavor, carrying hints of chocolates and blueberries—and a mild, gentle acidity and creaminess in the mouth, unique attributes eked out of the dry, stony hills. With Saudi Arabia continuing to hold it in the highest esteem, Harari coffee now commands such high prices that importers need to guard against the blending in of lesser beans smuggled from neighboring Arsi. (In both Harar and Yemen, yields are dropping due in part to farmers turning to khat, which they can harvest a few times a year.)

"To me," said Dutch coffee importer Menno Simons, "a good Harar is like honey sweet, with some raisiny flavors and chocolate in it. But not so spicy. Yemeni coffees are more spicy, in my opinion, and of course carry a sweetness."

Such differences are nuanced, subtle, and generally picked out only by experts. Most people simply taste the similarities.

With the surge in demand of coffee from Mocha during the sixteenth century as the popularity of the drink exploded, developing an industry in Yemen was a way to avoid the dangerous and costly, weeks-long journey to bring coffee from Ethiopia, made particularly perilous by roaming bands of marauding tribes, including the deeply feared Afar warriors.* It was easier to have coffee growing in the hills behind Mocha.

Yet for centuries coffee continued to be sent from Harar, even if eventual buyers didn't realize it. The Royal Geographical Society's 1842 report noted that Harar coffee was, at its final market, "sold as Mocha coffee."[38] The German missionary J. L. Krapf reported the same not long after, as did Rimbaud and, later, the American envoy Robert Skinner. "Arabian coffee retains to this day such prestige that the Harrar coffee, which is said to be the original Moka, and quite as good, if not better, is industriously mixed at Aden with the Moka of Arabia," Skinner wrote after his 1903–04 mission to Menelik's court, "or, as is frequently the case, is sold as Moka without any mixing at all."[39]

Today Yemeni Mocha is still often blended by unscrupulous traders, but no longer with coffee from Harar, which has become far too expen-

---

* This remained true for centuries. "When I visited Harar," Richard Burton wrote in the 1850s, "the price per parcel of twenty-seven pounds [of coffee] was a quarter of a dollar, and the hire of a camel carrying twelve parcels to Berberah was five dollars: the profit did not repay labour and risk." Burton, *First Footsteps in East Africa*, 2:26.

sive and relatively scarce. (In 2016, the area produced only around 7 percent of Ethiopia's total coffee.) Traveling in Gondar in 1855, Krapf noted that while both Kafa and Harar coffee were being exported and sold as Mocha, "the best quality of all" coffee in Ethiopia came from Kafa.[40] It was, at the time, presumably the most expensive in Gondar's weekly market. That is no longer the case. Harar—perhaps the "original Moka"—fetches the highest price on the Addis Ababa coffee exchange, and the majority of the dwindling, coveted production goes directly to Saudi Arabia.

CHAPTER 9

Out of Arabia

Historians have long associated Sufis, members of a mystical branch of Islam, with inspiring widespread use of coffee outside Ethiopia and the drink's international spread. They used coffee to concentrate and stay awake during their lengthy prayer sessions, then carried coffee beans with them to gatherings with other Sufis and to Sufi orders around the Middle East, Persia, and Egypt. Sufis were not part of a reclusive sect. They went to work and shopped in the market, prayed at the local mosque, and swapped stories in the public baths.[1] It didn't take long, then, for coffee to pass into the wider community. Once it did, coffee's conquering was swift, its appeal overwhelming.

With Islamic law prohibiting alcohol, small cups of the drink became popular. Coffeehouses opened in Mecca and Medina by the end of the fifteenth century, then in Cairo, Damascus, Baghdad, and Istanbul, where a Syrian opened the first *kahvehane* in 1555.[2] As restaurants didn't really exist, and bars and gambling establishments were far from respectable, coffeehouses made ideal places to meet friends and socialize. The open seating broke down social barriers, while the coffee itself stimulated conversation. "It brings to the drinker a sprightliness of spirit and a sense of mental well-being," wrote an early Arab commentator on coffee.[3]

Coffeehouses sprouted up in neighborhoods across the region's cities. Istanbul had more than six hundred within a decade or two.[4] Not all found the clientele of the highest standing, though. "All these people are quite base, of low costume and very little industry, such that, for the most part, they spend their time sunk in idleness," wrote the Venetian traveler Gianfrancesco Morosini in 1585. "They continually sit about, and for entertainment they are in the habit of drinking, in public, in shops and in the streets—a black liquid, boiling [as hot] as they can stand it, which is extracted from a seed they call Caveè . . ., and is said to have the property of keeping a man awake."[5]

As coffeehouses became a key part of social life in the Middle East, authorities took notice, especially when attendance at prayers dropped. Some Islamic clerics viewed the drink as an intoxicant and argued that it should be forbidden. The very source of the word for coffee in much of the world reflects this early illicit association. While *Kafa* is a logical source for the words *coffee, café, kaffee,* and other variants, etymologists generally trace its origins to the Arabic *qahwa,* meaning "wine."* The early Sufi mystics used coffee to keep focused on their prayers but also in their quest for "spiritual intoxication" as they chanted God's name.[6] There was even a word for the brew's blissful effects, *marqaha,* which can be translated as "coffee euphoria."[7]

Certainly it was not purely spiritual, even in the holiest of cities, Mecca. "The inhabitants of *Mecca* found this Drink so agreeable to their Taste, that, without troubling themselves about the Intention of the Devout and Learned, who may be said to have been the first Institutors of it," wrote the French traveler Jean de la Roque in the early 1700s after a trip to the Middle East and Yemen, "they made its Use so common, that it was sold publickly in Coffee-Houses, where they flock'd together, under that Pretence to pass away the Time more agreeably; there they play Chess, and at *Mancalah* [a shell game]; even for Money. There they sing, play on Instruments and dance; Things which the more rigid *Mohometans* cannot endure; which did not fail to bring Trouble in the End."[8] In 1511, Mecca's governor, Khair Beg, banned the drink. Among those unhappy with the decree was his superior, the sultan of Cairo, who intervened, reversing the ruling. "His Successour," wrote de la Roque, "after having receiv'd Orders to call him to an Account for his Conduct, put him to a tormenting Death the Year After."[9]

Over the next two centuries pious mobs wrecked the occasional coffeehouse and a few conservative rulers placed bans on opening them.

---

* "One may also consider the happy coincidence of the word *qahwa* with the place name Kaffa," wrote scholar Ralph Hattox. "It is possible that the berry or beverage was first called after Kaffa, and that subsequent to its introduction in Arabia those who knew of it there could not resist the poetical urge to apply to it a near-homophone that had been a term for wine." Hattox, *Coffee and Coffeehouses,* 19.

But such opposition did little to hinder the speed of their proliferation. Coffee became the iconic drink of the Ottoman Empire, whose historical reach can be defined by countries that prepare tiny, robust cups with fine grounds that need to settle before they can be sipped. The great sultan Süleyman I even appointed a *kahvecibaşi* (head coffeemaker) at Topkapı Palace.[10]

Many Christians considered coffee a Muslim drink and even the work of the devil. When it made its way to the Vatican around 1600, advisers to Pope Clement VIII wanted him to ban it. "Why, this Satan's drink is so delicious that it would be a pity to let the infidels have exclusive use of it," he allegedly said after tasting. "We shall fool Satan by baptizing it, and making it a truly Christian beverage."[11]

Coffee's popularity in Europe was equally immediate and intense, and any opposition as ineffective as it had been in the Middle East. "The passion of Europeans for this foreign luxury has been so lively, that neither the heaviest taxes, nor the most severe prohibitions and penalties have been able to stop it," the Frenchman Guillaume Thomas Raynal wrote at the end of the eighteenth century. "Having battled in vain against an inclination which chafed against hindrance, all governments have been forced to give way to the torrent."[12]

The drink was virtually unknown in Europe until 1615, when a shipment arrived in Venice. In 1650, a Lebanese Jew served it in Oxford.[13] It was served a year later at a London "cophe house" called the Sultan's Head, although a mustached Greek from Ottoman Smyrna named Pasqua Rosée generally gets credit for opening in 1652 the capital's first coffeehouse. By 1675 England had three thousand such establishments.

As in the Middle East, they became places to meet and debate ideas. The strong, caffeinated drink was an antithesis to ale and its stupefying effects: coffee was a catalyst for clear thoughts and clever talk. While certainly not all, or even most, of their chatter was high-minded, notable English coffeehouse habitués formed an illustrious bunch of poets, politicians, and rabble-rousers, great wits whose judgments made—and broke—reputations: John Dryden, Alexander Pope, Samuel Pepys, John Milton, James Boswell, Samuel Johnson, Oliver Goldsmith, Edward Gibbon, and Adam Smith.

Coffee was exotic, an oriental extravagance. Suleiman Aga, the Ottoman ambassador to King Louis XIV, brought coffee with him to Paris in 1669.[14] Wearing Turkish dress, his servants offered society figures small cups of the bitter brew on napkins embroidered with flecks of gold.

When an Armenian named Pascal opened the first café in the French capital in the 1680s, he fashioned it on an Ottoman coffeehouse. A few years later one of Pascal's waiters, the Sicilian Francesco Procopio dei Coltelli, founded the still-running Café Le Procope, an elegant place that welcomed ladies. While the café was decorated with refined, aristocratic French taste—large wall mirrors, crystal chandeliers, tapestries, marble tables—the Procope's waiters wore exotic, oriental garb.[15] La Fontaine, Voltaire, Rousseau, Beaumarchais, Victor Hugo, Benjamin Franklin, and Thomas Jefferson drank at Le Procope, as did France's most notorious coffee addict, Honoré de Balzac, with a reputed fifty-cup-a-day habit. A Balzac quote about drinking coffee on an empty stomach hangs in Addis Ababa's most famous coffeehouse, Caffè Tomoca: "Le café caresse la gorge et met alors tout en mouvement: les idées se précipitent tels les bataillons d'une grande armée sur le champ de bataille . . ."* According to the French bishop and diplomat Charles-Maurice de Talleyrand, the perfect cup was "black as the devil, hot as hell, pure as an angel, sweet as love."

Before long, coffeehouses were opening in the American colonies. The King's Arms was the first in New York City (in 1696, at what would today be Broadway between Trinity Church and Cedar Street), while Bostonians headed to the Red Lion, King's Head, and Indian Queen. William Penn gets credit for introducing such establishments to Delaware and Pennsylvania, the colony he founded as a sanctuary for Quakers. After the American Revolution, the drink traveled westward.[16]

As coffee flourished across the globe, Mocha successfully held a monopoly as a source of beans. Jealously guarding its market, authorities forbade foreigners from visiting coffee farms and reportedly only allowed beans to be exported once they had been boiled and their ability to germinate destroyed.[17] This was likely just rumor. Boiling all the beans would realistically be difficult and would probably spoil the coffee.† Later edicts merely banned the taking of plants.

Coffee became, simply, too popular not to eventually spread. In 1670, the Sufi Muslim Indian pilgrim Baba Budan,[18] stopping in Mocha on his

---

* A more precise translation than the abridged one printed on a yellow plastic sign dangling from an electric bug zapper in the café goes: "Coffee caresses the throat and sets everything in motion: ideas rush forth like the battalions of a great army on the battlefield."

† The French physician Charles-Jacques Poncet, traveling in Ethiopia in the 1600s, alluded to the Ethiopians doing the same: "'Tis a Mistake that they put Coffee into boiling Water, to prevent the Growth of it as some have affirm'd." Poncet, *Voyage*, 119.

way home from performing the hajj to Mecca, allegedly hid seven seeds in his waistband and carried them to Mysore, in the south of his country. But the Dutch would become the source for the rapid spread of coffee planting.

By 1720 Mocha's domination of the global coffee market had peaked. Within a few years, supplies from a newcomer forty-five hundred miles away overtook Mocha on the Amsterdam exchange.[19] One of the world's first great global commodities was quickly proliferating. By 1750, coffee was growing on five continents.[20]

During the seventeenth century, Dutch merchants were buying large quantities from Ottoman outposts in the eastern Mediterranean and later Mocha. Holding near-exclusive control of the market, merchants in Arabia fixed the prices. Grasping the commercial potential of growing and transporting coffee itself, the Dutch East India Company (Verenigde Oostindische Compagnie, or VOC) sought to establish its own plantations.[21] Coffee was an ideal product: it had a good value and growing market, and the dried pods could be stored in the hold of a ship and carried back to Europe without significant deterioration.

Chartered in 1602, the VOC controlled the trade of the East Indies—roughly modern-day Indonesia—with Batavia (Jakarta) on the island of Java as the heart of their Asian network. Before attempting to plant coffee on land under their control, the Dutch methodically sought to learn as much as they could about the plant. Merchant captains gathered information on trips to Mocha, Alexandria, and Venice, and, when possible, carried men trained in botany.[22]

In 1696, a VOC ship took stock from South India's Malabar Coast,[23] descendants of the seeds that Baba Budan had carried from Mocha,[24] and planted them in western Java. These, though, were lost in an earthquake and subsequent flooding.[25] The Dutch tried again in 1700.[26] They obtained more stock from Malabar and successfully transplanted them to the highlands outside Batavia.[27]

Beans propagated in Java arrived in Amsterdam in 1706 and impressed the coffee buyers. In 1711, the first lot of dried coffee beans were sold to a VOC merchant in Java.[28] Later that year, a shipment of 894 pounds of Java coffee went up for public auction in Amsterdam.[29]

Coffee grew well in Java's volcanic-rich soil, and production shot up in a rush of land clearing and planting. In 1717, 2,000 pounds of dried coffee were shipped to Amsterdam. By 1720, the amount had risen to 116,587 pounds, and just four years later, as more trees were bearing and traders packed an increasing quantity into East Indiamen ships among pepper, cloves, silk, and indigo, one million pounds of Java coffee arrived on the Amsterdam market.[30] By 1726, Java was supplying four million pounds of coffee a year. It had not only overtaken Mocha as the largest supplier, but prices were one third that of Arabian coffee.[*31] Over the next decade, four million pounds of coffee shipped annually to Amsterdam, an amount upped to six million in 1736.[32]

In the sample shipment of coffee beans that arrived in Amsterdam in 1706, Joan van Hoorn, the governor-general of the VOC, included a plant for Amsterdam's Hortus Botanicus. Founded as a medicinal garden in 1638, it was one of the world's first botanic gardens—and best. Exotica from the VOC as well as the Dutch West India Company, which operated from West Africa to the Americas and the Pacific Ocean, deeply enriched its collections.[33]

Planted inside a newly invented glass greenhouse,[34] the tree grew well, and Hortus gardeners successfully germinated seeds and planted out seedlings. "In the Physick Garden of Amsterdam are two Coffee Trees, about 17 Foot high each," wrote the English botanist and illustrator Richard Bradley less than a decade later, "which have been for some time in a bearing State, and have at most Seasons Fruit upon them."[35]

Coffee was a gift worthy of a king not only in Kafa but also in Europe. In 1712, Amsterdam's mayor, Nicolaas Witsen, sent a fine sapling as a royal present to the Sun King, Louis XIV, of France. It died. The following year[36] the Dutch sent a heartier specimen to the long-reigning bon vivant at his royal residence, Château de Marly.[37] The magistrates, reported an eighteenth-century tract on coffee, "presented to him an elegant plant of this rare tree, carefully and judiciously packed up to go by water, defended from the weather by a curious machine covered with glass. The plant was about five feet high, and an inch in diameter in the stem, and was in full foliage, with both green and ripe fruit."[38] The day after its arrival, the king

---

* "The Coffee of Yemen still keeps the preference," justified Carsten Niebuhr, who journeyed to Arabia in the 1760s, "probably because the Europeans do not cultivate theirs in the same manner, and upon such high mountains where there is so regular a temperature of air as in Yemen." Ellis, *Historical Account of Coffee*, 22.

sent it to the Jardin du Roi in Paris, placed it under the care of the young Antoine de Jussieu, and ordered France's first greenhouse built for it.[39]

The French successfully propagated from what is now known as the Noble Tree. Louis XIV himself had several trees in the gardens of Versailles that produced five or so pounds of ripe coffee fruits a year. Enjoying not just the drink but also the ritual of preparing it, he would roast the beans and make coffee himself for guests.[40]

In 1723 (or 1720, the date is disputed), a French naval officer named Gabriel Mathieu de Clieu obtained a sapling from the Parisian *jardin* through the intercession of a well-connected lady, boarded a Caribbean-bound ship in the port of Nantes,[41] and carried the plant to the island of Martinique. The source of the dramatic tale of the troubled voyage is the naval officer himself. It has been retold many times by others, always with a hearty dose of *galanterie* and *bravade*:

> He lost all but one plant, for the ship entered the doldrums and lay by for weeks on glassy seas with sails slack and the heat almost unbearable. Drinking water ran low and all were put on scant rations. A crazed passenger saw de Clieu giving half his daily drink to the tree and attempted to destroy it. A branch was torn off but the owner fought him away, and the ship's crew helped to keep the tree from the demented man. The ship finally came to Martinique with the gaunt chevalier and his living coffee seedling.[42]

Once in Antillean soil, the plant flourished. The first harvest was in 1726, the same year that imports of Java coffee in Amsterdam reached four million pounds. Plantings quickly spread, coffee estates multiplied, and in fifty years—by de Clieu's death in 1774—just under nineteen million coffee trees were growing on the island.[43] Martinique was already producing more coffee than Java.

The Noble Tree would become the parent for nearly all of the coffee in the Americas and West Indies,[44] as the European powers got stock from its rapidly scattering progenies and planted them out in the far reaches of their colonial territories. The official name of this variety is *Coffea arabica* var. *arabica*, better known as Typica.

Intrigue, theft, chance, and sex color the tales of Typica's spread, as its arrival in Brazil reveals. In 1727, a border dispute between French Guiana and Dutch Guiana (Surinam) drew in an administrator from neighboring Brazil, Lieutenant Colonel Francisco de Melo Palheta. The squabbling colonies both cultivated coffee, and the Brazilian was keen to bring some seeds back to his own country. He successfully negotiated a resolution and even bedded the young wife of the French governor, but was unable to get any coffee stock. At his departure, the woman presented her lover with a bouquet of flowers. Hidden beneath the blooms were prohibited coffee berries. These went into the ground in the northeastern state of Pará,[45] kick-starting an industry that is today, by a significant margin, the world's largest producer of Arabica coffee.

While Typica was making its way around the Atlantic, a second variety of Arabica from Yemen was also spreading global roots.

In 1708, two French ships picked up coffee seeds and sixty young plants at Mocha and took them to Île Bourbon (now known as Réunion), a small volcanic Indian Ocean island east of Madagascar. They failed to grow. The French tried again in 1715, and only two plants survived. But a third try in 1718 was successful, and by 1721 trees were fruiting nicely.[46] Within a century, Île Bourbon was producing about six million pounds of coffee a year.[47]

This variety of *Coffea arabica* took the name Bourbon—pronounced "bour-BONE"—after the island.* Compared to Typica, the bush is more compact and upright, less conical, and with more branches, broader leaves, rounder coffee cherries, and a 20 to 30 percent higher yield. Bourbon offers a sweeter and generally overall better cup, with bright acidity, lighter body, and good balance. But the variety tends to be more delicate, even temperamental in the field, and more susceptible to heavy winds or rains knocking down the fruits.

Typica and Bourbon were the first widely cultivated coffee varieties (or varietals). Developed either through natural section, selection of seeds by farmers from trees that perform well, or selective breeding that attempts to capture specific characteristics, a variety has distinctive traits, from the shape of the bean to flavors, body, and acidity. Such traits, though, can vary from place to place depending on environmental conditions such as elevation or rainfall. (Today around two dozen main varieties of Arabica are

---

* Bourbon is the surname of Louis XIV and the branch of the royal family that long ruled France. The name of the variety can also be seen as a nod to his hand in establishing both coffee drinking in France as well as the crop on French colonial soil.

being cultivated.* Their names frequently reflect where they were first grown.)

Paris merchants were initially not impressed with the new product from Île Bourbon, insisting that it "cannot call Itself coffee, as it only roughly resembles it, and is good for nothing."[48] "Up to now," another Frenchman commented in the 1730s, "the Coffee from that island which has reached Europe has smelt unripe, with a complex taste of mildew which it is impossible to remove."[49] Opinions changed as methods of processing and transporting improved.

As with Typica, Bourbon spread widely through the efforts of merchants, governors, and, following the tradition of medieval monks in Europe, planter priests. In East Africa, French Roman Catholic priests led the propagation. The fathers grew it around their settlements to provide themselves with coffee, but also as another source of income, as they were chronically short of funding from Europe.

Holy Ghost fathers brought coffee from Île Bourbon to mainland Africa in the second half of the nineteenth century. They mistakenly believed that coffee favored a warm climate and had only limited success in swampy, lowland areas, such as at their Bagamoyo Mission north of Dar es Salaam.[50] The plant found more suitable conditions on the slopes of Kilimanjaro in what was then German East Africa.

For the order, coffee farming carried considerable symbolism: they were planting seeds of faith and growing a community. One of their missions was to educate, and by 1905 the brothers had more than five thousand pupils attending a string of schools around Kilimanjaro. At the outset of the First World War, the 150 mission schools in the region had more than sixteen thousand pupils.[51] In what might be historically unique, the curriculum for local children included the planting and care of coffee.[52] While the order helped lay the foundations of a growing industry, its achievement with coffee in Tanzania would be eclipsed by its success across the border in Kenya.

In August 1899, the French Catholic bishop of the Zanzibar diocese and two other Holy Ghost brothers boarded the train at Voi, in the southern

---

* *Cultivar* and *variety* tend to be used interchangeably but do have a technical difference. A cultivar—from *cultivated variety*—is a variety produced using horticultural or agricultural techniques.

lowlands of British East Africa, for the slow journey upland on the Uganda Railway's "iron snake." In the special luggage van that the railway had put at their disposal, among holy books, candles, and mosquito nets, the men had packed a hundred coffee seedlings from the Bura Mission in the Taita Hills. As dusk fell three days later, the trio alighted their first-class carriage at Mile 325, only reached by the under-construction line a few months earlier. At almost six thousand feet in elevation, the spot would become Nairobi, but then it was a cool, treeless plateau with a few shacks.

Before long, the order purchased a tract of land from a local chief named Kinyanjui and established a mission, St. Austin's. The precious coffee seedlings went into the ground as they began planning the parish church. "There was here a fine big grey church with a bell-tower on it; it was laid out on a broad courtyard, above terraces and stairs, in the midst of their coffee-plantation, which was the oldest in the Colony and very skillfully run," wrote Karen Blixen, better known by her pen name, Isak Dinesen, in her 1937 book *Out of Africa*.[53]

Within a year, St. Austin's coffee farm was flourishing, with additional fields of trees added as the Bura Mission sent more seedlings up the line. When the first harvest was ready, a group of priests gathered to taste the coffee, eagerly wondering if it had preserved its qualities in the new surroundings. As they passed around the cup, each pronounced it the best he had ever tasted. The men were not alone in their judgment. St. Austin's won first prize for coffee at the Agricultural and Horticultural Society's Nairobi Show trade fair in 1905. Tins labeled "French Mission Coffee" appeared on Nairobi grocery shelves the following year and were soon being exported to France.[54] By 1910 the mission's fields had fifteen thousand coffee trees. They imported machinery and soon installed a new hydraulic wheel, pulper, and decorticator to process their picked coffee. Ex-president Teddy Roosevelt, interrupting a hunting safari, was among the many official, aristocratic, and curious visitors who came to see the operations.[55]

Rather than trying to create a monopoly on coffee, the mission was generous with its seeds and seedlings. A 1904 issue of the St. Austin's *Mission Journal* reported shipping thirty-five hundred *"petits arbres"* to Lady Delamere,[56] of the region's most prominent colonial farming family. When the market price of coffee rose in 1909, many other settlers decided to plant and obtained stock from the fathers.[57] At the outbreak of the First World

War, the mission had fifty-two thousand coffee trees and yet could still barely keep up with the demand.*[58]

After the war ended, priorities shifted at St. Austin's. It concentrated resources on education and upgrading schools and gradually sold off tracts of its land to help fund other Holy Ghost missions in East Africa. The fathers had started and supported the coffee industry through its infancy, and by 1920, when the protectorate officially became a British colony named Kenya, it passed out of their hands and into those dedicated to farming.†

Among the early generation of coffee farmers was Blixen, who sailed for Africa in 1914. The morning after landing in Mombasa, the twenty-eight-year-old Dane married her cousin Baron Bror von Blixen-Finecke, with Prince Wilhelm of Sweden as witness. The original plan was to have cattle, but Bror, swept up by coffee, had changed his mind. Six hundred of the farm's forty-five hundred acres[59] were being cleared and planted with coffee seedlings when she arrived.

The farm was just ten miles from the French mission. "The French Fathers were my best friends," she wrote, and though not Catholic, Blixen would attend Sunday mass—"partly in order to speak French again, and partly because it was a lovely ride to the Mission"[60]—and the Christmas services. They called on her, too. "The French Fathers sometimes rode on their motor-bicycles to the farm and lunched there; they quoted the fables of Lafontaine to me and gave me good advice on my coffee-plantation."[61]

On borrowed money the farm expanded to six thousand acres, one of largest in the region. The couple divorced in 1921, and throughout the twenties, Blixen managed the farm alone, struggling through drought and plagues of locus, continuously poor harvests,[62] and a fire that destroyed

---

* The coffee in British East Africa wasn't exclusively Bourbon. The missions also made some early introductions of Typica, which were not necessarily kept distinct. As well, German settlers brought a Typica strain from Java locally called Menado, and around 1902, the Scottish mission in Kikuyu, about a dozen miles west of St. Austin's, planted stock from Nyasaland (Malawi) that had come from Jamaica's Blue Mountains (which had originated in Martinique). Soon after they also began to experiment with a Typica variety called Kent's, developed in South India. Kieran, "Origins of Commercial Arabica Coffee Production in East Africa," 66.

† The fathers were certainly more successful at education and coffee than proselytizing. A principal superior complained in 1953 that in the five decades they had baptized a mere three thousand in the Kikuyu area. Gogan, *Holy Ghost Missions*, 27.

the coffee mill. "Coffee-growing is a long job," she later wrote. "It does not all come out as you imagine, when, yourself young and hopeful, in the streaming rain, you carry the boxes of your shining young coffee-plants from the nurseries."[63] Coffee prices plummeted. Debts mounted. The farm was in the wrong place for coffee: the elevation was a little too high,[64] the soil too acidic, there was not enough rain.

There was solace from those on her farm, in the landscape, and, most of all, in her relationship with Denys Finch Hatton, who took her flying in his bright yellow Gypsy Moth biplane named *Nzige* (Swahili for "locust"):[65] "I owe [him] what was, I think, the greatest, the most transporting pleasure of my life on the farm: I flew with him over Africa."[66]

In the end, the farm failed and was put up for auction.[67] Blixen stayed on for the final harvest in 1931. As she was packing up the house to return to Europe, Finch Hatton died in the crash of his plane near Voi, where the three Holy Ghost priests had boarded the train with their coffee seedlings just three decades before. Broke, broken, and ill, she sailed to Denmark, where she remade herself as a writer, telling, most poignantly, most nostalgically, of her years in East Africa growing coffee, beginning with that famous line: "I had a farm in Africa at the foot of the Ngong Hills."[68]

Today Arabica is cultivated in around forty countries stretching in an equatorial band roughly between the Tropic of Cancer and the Tropic of Capricorn. In the break room of Equator Coffees & Teas' head office and roasting facility, Ted Stachura, head of coffee for the Bay Area roaster, stood beside a wall map of the world and traced his finger along the peripheries. Brazil was at the southern limit, Hawaii at the northern one, he said, the tip of his index finger covering most of the archipelago. In Equator's warehouse, burlap bags of coffee beans sat stacked in long rows on pallets waiting to be roasted. In 2016, Equator bought one million pounds of green Arabica beans that came from nearly every major producing country in the world.

In 2016, 93.5 million sixty-kilogram bags of Arabica was produced around the globe, over 12 billion pounds. It's a staggering amount, fifteen times the weight of the Empire State Building or six times that of the Golden Gate Bridge. Eighty-five percent of that was grown in Latin America. Yet most of that came from just two varieties—Typica and Bourbon—that genetic testing proves originated in Ethiopia, went to Yemen, and passed through Dutch or French hands. Such a limited genetic base is causing serious repercussions today.

CHAPTER 10

Beyond Waves

T he Blue Bottle barista ground a digitally weighed amount of beans from Colombia's Huila El Playón region and sprinkled them into the cone filter. She moistened the grounds with a swan-necked Japanese kettle, allowing a slight bloom scattered with iridescent bubbles to form before slowly tipping a thin stream of hot water over top, circling her tattooed wrist to pour in a unhurried counterclockwise motion. A few minutes later she set the cup with its tiny blue-bottle logo down on the counter. The coffee, a wooden panel hanging on the wall informed, had notes of "butterscotch, blood orange, bay leaf," an intriguing, if seemingly unpalatable, combination.

Gorgeous light flooded the 110-year-old W. C. Morse building in Oakland, California. Once an auto showroom, it features windows reaching to the twenty-foot ceilings. Designed with the sumptuous minimalism and sleek aesthetics of a Jony Ive's Apple product, the café had only a few high pub tables and a single oversize one made of fumed ebony oak[1] and topped by a silver bowl of cow parsnip. Seated around the table were a dozen people quietly absorbed in their mobile devices while sipping high-priced cups of coffee on a late-summer afternoon. Apart from the light patter of music playing from symphony-hall-caliber speakers, the café was as hushed as an art gallery.

Coffee in the United States is big business. According to the National Coffee Association, in 2015 consumers spent $74.2 billion on coffee (and another $6 billion on brewers, sweeteners, and flavorings). The total economic impact of the coffee industry in the United States that year was $225.2 billion. Americans drink an estimated four hundred million cups a day. Consumption has risen 43 percent in the past decade and a half.[2] "The demand just keeps going up," said Tim Schilling, director of World Coffee Research (WCR). "But the demand is not for the crap. The demand is for the better-tasting, the higher-quality coffee." He was referring to specialty coffee. Twenty-five years ago it accounted for 1 percent of the industry. Today it's between 20 and 30 percent, according to Schilling.

Originally specialty coffee referred more generally to special microclimates that produced beans with unique flavor profiles. According to the Specialty Coffee Association of America (SCAA),* the term came to mean high-quality coffee made from green beans that are free of defects, roasted to their highest flavor potential, that brew a cup that has a distinctive character and scores 80 or above on its standardized 100-point tasting scale. Below 80 is considered commodity or commercial level.

While the W. C. Morse Blue Bottle might be among the ultimate specialty coffee cafés on the West Coast, thousands of places in the United States serve high-scoring single-origin coffees roasted in micro lots and brewed using a range of methods.

But American coffee drinking didn't reach such connoisseurship in a single bound. It came in "waves."

Sometime between the founding of Folgers in 1850 and the introduction of vacuum packaging by Hills Bros. in 1900, coffee became America's preferred drink. Coffee's "first wave" saw an urban luxury turned into a pantry staple. By 1962, every American over ten years of age was drinking on average 3.1 cups of coffee a day. For breakfast, lunch, and even dinner, in office break rooms, at PTA meetings, and for church socials, Americans brewed it by the potful in a percolator and then, in the 1970s, an electric drip coffeemaker. Pitchman Joe DiMaggio helped move over forty thousand Mr. Coffee makers *a day* off department store shelves at the end of the 1970s.[3] While pots of coffee that sat on warmers for hours offered plentiful and free refills, the coffee wasn't always tasty, nor was that from tins of supermarket blends freshly roasted. The industry was aimed at convenience and guided by mass production rather than nuanced flavor.

---

* In 2017, the American and European bodies of the association joined to form a single entity, the Specialty Coffee Association (SCA).

In 1966, a Dutch immigrant named Alfred Peet opened a shop in Berkeley, California, that sold small batches of dark, European-style roasted beans that produced strong, almost oily brews. The son of an Amsterdam *koffiebrander* (coffee roaster), Peet had become convinced that there was a market for higher-quality beans. From his corner shop, the second wave emerged, and with it a redefining of the American coffee experience.

Among those impressed by the bold beans were three former University of San Francisco students, Jerry Baldwin, Zev Siegl, and Gordon Bowker. In 1971, the trio opened their own shop in Seattle with high-quality coffee beans and roasting equipment called Starbucks Coffee, Tea and Spices. At first they sold Peet's coffee, but then began roasting themselves, favoring similar dark, dense flavors.

In the early 1980s, with four stores, they hired Howard Schultz to direct marketing and operations. While in Milan for a trade fair, Schultz got the idea to open a series of Italian-inspired cafés ("but with seating and big cups").[4] Experiencing the interaction of people in Milan's numerous espresso bars, Schultz "had a revelation: Starbucks had missed the point—completely missed it," he wrote in his first book. "The connection to the people who loved coffee did not have to take place only in their homes . . . What we had to do was unlock the romance and mystery of coffee, first-hand, in coffee bars." It needed to include the social aspect of coffee. "I couldn't believe that Starbucks was in the coffee business, yet was overlooking so central an element of it."[5]

Unable to convince the owners of his vision that "Starbucks could be a great *experience*, and not just a great retail store,"[6] he left in 1985 to launch a small chain of Il Giornale coffee bars that served brewed Starbucks coffee. "We would take something old and tired and common—coffee—and weave a sense of romance and community around it," he wrote of his vision. "We would rediscover the mystique and charm that had swirled around coffee throughout the centuries. We would enchant customers with an atmosphere of sophistication and style and knowledge."[7]

Two years later Schultz bought Starbucks from his former employers, renamed the Il Giornale outlets, and, with investor help, mounted an aggressive campaign of expansion.

While European villages had a café to meet at on the main square, and cities one on virtually every corner, coffeehouses in 1980s America existed mostly around universities. Just as in seventeenth-century Europe, the drink was not the exclusive grounds for their popularity. Americans were, Schultz felt, eager for community, and Starbucks became a new third place, "a comfortable, sociable gathering spot away from home and work, like an extension of the front porch."[8]

In 1992, the year Starbucks went public, the *New York Times* dining correspondent reported on the burgeoning coffee scene: "Virtually every New York restaurant, from the exalted to the expedient, now serves something called espresso, strong Italian-style coffee in small cups." It was becoming part of the American experience. "Coffee is the wine of the 90's," Schultz told the newspaper.[9]

At that time, Starbucks had no plans to open a location in New York.[10] The company soon scrapped such limited expansion and set a goal of two thousand outlets by 2000. During the 1990s it opened a new one each working day, bettering the objective by a thousand. New York City alone had 220 locations by 2016, when a CUNY grad student calculated that from any point in Manhattan, the nearest Starbucks would be on average 445 yards away.[11]

The company rapidly expanded at a time when flavored coffees—with an added shot of vanilla, hazelnut, or raspberry syrup—accounted for 40 percent of the specialty coffee business.[12] For any hint of coffee taste to come through, the beans had to be a dark roast. It was also easier to calibrate on a bulk scale when the beans were like this. The style became a Starbucks hallmark. While the snarky might refer to the chain as Charbucks and compare their brewed coffee to watered-down tar, dark roasting was initially perceived to be superior, a reaction to the tepid stuff sitting on the Mr. Coffee hob.

Along, too, came a change of cup sizing. Starbucks vanquished the standard small, medium, and large, which *Frasier* brilliantly spoofed when the Seattle radio psychiatrist tried ordering in a place that wasn't his regular Café Nervosa:

> SERVER: I'm afraid we don't have large, sir. Just piccolo, macho, mucho, and mucho macho.
> FRASIER: I see. Uh, do you happen to know what size would correspond to a Nervosa grande?
> SERVER: No. But our mucho is about the same as the semi-colossal over at Don't Spill the Beans.
> FRASIER: Ah, ah, all right. I know that their colossal is comparable to a Nervosa grande, so the semi-colossal would be three

quarters of a colossal, so the mucho and the semi-colossal would
be equivalent . . . so I should have the mucho macho. But only
fill it five-eighths.[13]

In a few short decades, Starbucks achieved market domination.
Revenue for the world's largest coffee buyer is more than nineteen billion
dollars, and growth remains robust. It has around twenty-four thousand locations in seventy countries. At the 2016 annual shareholders
meeting, it announced that it would open five hundred new outlets a
year for the next five years in China, a notoriously difficult market that it
had managed to crack, and set 2017 as the date to open a Starbucks in a
country long deemed impossible, Italy, where Schultz had his "epiphany"—
"so immediate and physical that I was shaking"[14]—thirty-four years
before.

"But the price of conquest is cachet. What was once novel—the warm
décor, the gentle music, the faux-Italian lingo—has become banal," wrote
Slate columnist Will Oremus. "Today's coffee snobs would rather snort
Sanka than set foot inside a Starbucks."[15]

Yet it is impossible to go straight from a pot of Folgers in a Mr. Coffee
drip machine to a Blue Bottle pourover. That necessary middle step happened at Peet's and Starbucks, where the drink was the main attraction.
"We're not just selling a cup of coffee, we are providing an experience,"
Schultz said in 1991.[16] Starbucks introduced many Americans to a variety
of espresso-based coffees they didn't know existed and offered the first
inklings of coffee origins with an awareness that beans from Kenya are a
bit different from those from Indonesia or Guatemala.

Peet's and Starbucks also got customers used to paying more for a
cup of joe. When Alfred Peet died in 2007, Blue Bottle's James Freeman
said, "He really showed that people in America are willing to spend a
little bit more money to get a little bit better when it comes to coffee."[17]

Freeman, a coffee aficionado and concert clarinetist, founded Blue
Bottle in Oakland in 2002, roasting in an old potting shed and selling at
the farmers' market. Embracing the Japanese tradition of *kodawari*, the
obsessive and relentless pursuit of perfection, he began with cultish disci-
pline preparing exceptional coffee for a discerning clientele, striving for the
flawless cup by doing the same thing over and over, just as he had done as
a classical musician.

By Peet's death, coffee had become more than a commodity. It was an artisanal product, revered, treated with serious attention at every step of the process, and prepared one precious cup at a time. The third wave had arrived.

A few steps from the fourteenth-century basilica Santa Maria del Mar in Barcelona's El Born neighborhood is Spain's best-known specialty coffee roaster, Cafés El Magnífico, founded in 1919 by the grandfather of Salvador Sans. While a larger roasting facility a few blocks away now does much of the company's volume, Sans himself still roasts every Wednesday and Saturday mornings in the rear of the crowded shop, greeting a stream of longtime customers by name. While few are as steeped in coffee as Sans, or literally grew up in the smoke of roasting beans, third-wave roasters share a similar passion for the uniqueness of beans sourced at different origins, a respect for the labor that went into producing them, and scrupulous attention to detail in order to draw out their full potential inside the drum of the roaster. ("There is no light roast, no dark roast, there is only the perfect roast," as another roaster put it. "It's the right one or you've fucked it up.") Roasting is tactile and physical, and many delight in the heat and smells as the beans transform under their eye. Sans calls it an *oficio*, a trade or craft honed over years.

In North America, of the countless local and regional roasters that developed relationships with coffee farmers and sought to educate drinkers, Intelligentsia Coffee in Chicago, Stumptown Coffee Roasters in Portland, and Counter Culture Coffee in North Carolina emerged as the Big Three, with San Francisco's Blue Bottle the more elite, somewhat precious fourth.

Just as Peet's and Starbucks had looked to Europe, the American third wave initially looked to Scandinavia, northern Europe, and Japan before largely leading the global movement themselves. "Small Scandinavian guys were experimenting, and pushing the ball to see where you can go, and then combine with the right coffees and the right roast and then the right brewing method," said Menno Simons, founder of Amsterdam's Bocca Coffee Roasters, the 2014 European boutique roaster of the year. "It gives you something that you might never have tasted before."

Freeman has spoken about the enormous influence on him by the Japanese way of brewing coffee, from the slow, measured pouring from a particular style of kettle to creating a precise environment that completes the experience. "What they do there is stunning in their sense of meticulous execution to details, stunning in their desires. Everything about the space, this beautiful perfect bubble."[18]

Light—rather than dark—roasting was central to the movement. "Maybe because they were focused on buying real high-quality beans," Simons said. "Because these light roasts you can only do with really good beans because it will show every good but also bad element in a coffee." (Roasts can be too light, though: under-roasted beans leave a distinctive paperiness on the tongue.)

On a Saturday morning, Sans stood in his standard place beside his Vittoria roaster in the back of El Magnífico. He nibbled on a baguette filled with Iberian dry-aged *jamón* while a batch of sun-dried Ethiopian beans from Guji gradually darkened. Every minute or two he pulled a sample out of the roaster to smell their progress. Toward the quickening end of the roasting, he checked the beans every few seconds.

Tumbling in a drum roaster, beans go from a smooth olive-green color with a distinct aroma of green peas to a slightly pale color, then orangish, and tan. The first part is slow, the roasting gradual. The beans begin to exude aromas of cut grasses and hay, rising bread, and sometimes a nuttiness of popcorn. Depending on the density of the beans, around ten or twelve minutes there is the "first crack," a loud popcornlike snap, as they reach the light-roast level that brews a bright and lively cup with a natural fruitiness. The beans now smell of *coffee*. Roasting accelerates, moving the aroma quickly to nuttiness and caramel tones before the beans emit a sweet smokiness. This is a dark roast, generally used for espresso. At around sixteen or seventeen minutes, there is a second, softer crack, more akin to a crackle or light snap. The sugars in the bean become fully caramelized, with the oils burned off. The flavors are dense and charred, with ash and charcoal dominating.

Once Sans gauged the Gujis done, he opened the gate and let them tumble down into the perforated circular tray. A paddle wheeled through the beans to cool them as Sans loaded a new batch into the roaster. This was a light roast, the beans a bronzy-brown to almost milk-chocolate color that would brew a juicy, sweet cup of coffee, with hints of mango and tropical fruits.

The popularity of lighter roasts brought about a revolution in brewing methods. Aficionados stored their automatic drip coffeemakers and began using simple manual methods of brewing individual cups that date back to 1908, when a German housewife in Dresden named Melitta Bentz punched holes in the bottom of a brass pot and lined it with blotting paper from her son's schoolbook to keep the grounds out of the extracted coffee. With a patent and some start-up money, Bentz launched into business, building a company that today dominates the disposable-filter market.

Each method of brewing coffee has its distinctive utensils, filter shapes, and grind coarseness. The workhorse is the cone pourover, usually done with a Japanese Hario V60 ceramic cone, Melitta, or similarly-styled Kalita wave filter. For enthusiasts, the French press has largely been usurped by the AeroPress, an airtight plunger that forces water through the grinds. But many, even most, of the industry's elite prepare their own coffee in a Chemex. Invented in 1941 by a German immigrant in New York named Peter Schlumbohm, the hourglass-shaped decanter, with its hallmark polished-wood collar and toggled leather tie at the neck, is so gorgeous that the Museum of Modern Art in New York holds it in its design collection. Along with sleek and sexy midcentury elegance comes an accomplished functionality that ekes out maximum flavors and clarity from the grinds.

Such preparation can be precious and solemn, even serious, and done with a gravity that makes it easy to mock. The non-initiated wonder if it really requires an expensive burr (not blade!) grinder that gives a consistent, uniform grind, or a digital scale to weigh the beans, and then the water being poured from a kettle with a long, thin spout that tightly controls the flow. The outcome from such precision is unquestionably a finer cup of coffee, where the nuances of fruits, chocolates, or tangerine rise above bitterness—or its even less desirable cousin, blandness.

When Howard Schultz called coffee the wine of the nineties, he meant as a social drink, as being an integral part of life's important moments. Third-wave connoisseurs frequently use wine comparisons, too, but usually when talking about the effects of terroir and the various flavor profiles. Roasters place an importance on the direct sourcing of high-quality, single-origin beans from a specific region that yield distinct, singular-tasting brews. Dozens of variables between the picking of the cherries and the turning of the beans into a drink affect the final taste, and attention is placed on each contributing factor.

Some, though, see the movement less as one for purists and obsessives who pay zealous attention to origin and roast in pursuit of the perfect cup than as just "fancy language for the movement of artisanal coffee shops that charge you $4 for cup of coffee you waited 10 minutes to receive."[19]

On a late Sunday morning in October 2015, Simons and his brother, Tewis, pulled a handcart through the streets of Amsterdam's chic Jordaan neighborhood. Stabilized on a burlap bag of coffee beans was a hefty 1970s Probat roaster. They were taking it from the garage where the two began roasting in 2001 to its new location on Kerkstraat. A hundred customers and friends followed along the cobbled streets, helping push on the slight inclines over canals. A quartet of Togolese drummers and two stilt dancers led the procession and gave it a sense of carnival festivity. The day warmed unseasonably, and Simons was down to a sky-blue Bocca Coffee T-shirt by the time the procession reached its destination in the Spiegelkwartier (Mirror Quarter) among galleries and antique shops.

"Where the roaster is," Simons said a few days later, "that is where the magic is happening." The old Probat inaugurated the café and took up its position at the entrance as something more symbolic than decorative.* "That's what you do, if you are a coffee roaster," he said of keeping it. "That machine is basically your heart."

The café wraps around a long, angular U-shaped bar topped with three of the finest espresso machines on the market and a long pourover counter. It has a postminimalistic Scandinavian feel with clean lines accented in vibrant lichen green—a striped carpet, the back wall, retro 1950s thick-lipped coffee cups—and plenty of textured wood surfaces. Even though it immediately won a pair of important design and innovation awards, and *Esquire* named it the best new *koffiebar* in the Netherlands, Bocca's café is a one-off. "The idea was specifically to inspire our customers and not compete with our customers," said Simons. Bocca is now roasting almost half a million pounds (220,000 kilograms) of coffee a year at their main facility an hour north of Amsterdam in Flevoland, and a large number of Dutch cafés serve their roasts. Rather, the café was to be a space for events, meetings, and, importantly, to train baristas who are using Bocca coffee beans in their own establishments.

Compared to producing tea, making coffee has more steps involving more people that influence the final taste. Whereas tea is manufactured on-site just after plucking, coffee beans are dried, milled, and exported green, then generally roasted in the country where they will be brewed. Even after roasting, much can go wrong. At its final step, a cup of tea is nearly foolproof: simply pour over hot water. Wine even more so. "The wine guy just pulls out the cork," said Simons over lunch near his Amsterdam office, "but the guy at the end of the coffee chain can wreck it all."

---

* And certainly not practical. He doesn't believe in roasting inside a café: "If you want to do both properly, you shouldn't do them together."

Pulling an espresso is a perfect example. Assuming the coffee, roast (darkish), grind (fine, almost powdery), and grounds (compressed into an even, compact puck) are correct, and that the machine has the right water temperature (around 194°F) and pressure (130 psi) and has been recently cleaned, then the time of the extraction from the beans remains the kicker. The optimal length on many machines is about twenty-five seconds. If it is some seconds too short, the coffee will be weak and sour and have little of that rich layer of *crema* on top; some seconds too long and the dark, inky extraction will draw out bitter oils from the beans and give the drink a burned flavor.

"It's painful to see people messing up your coffee," Simons said, wincing at a certain memory. It is a roaster's grievance that few can do much about.

Blue Bottle Coffee might be the lone exception. The company wanted to manage every step until the last swallow, including the shape of the cup and the music. "I get nervous when we can't control the contexts, methods, and outcomes that are part of the experience of drinking our coffee," Freeman explained on the company's website when announcing his decision in 2015 to close the wholesale roasted-coffee division after a dozen years to focus on its own retail cafés.[20] Bocca is taking a different approach and trying to make that final step in bars and cafés across the country as good—or error-free—as possible.

Through obsessive attention to detail, Bocca produces much-sought-after roasts and now, in its café, divine cups of coffee. Also, it is with Bocca and a select group of other roasters continuously questioning and experimenting in their quest for perfect coffee where signs of the elusive fourth wave—predicted, despite lacking a clear definition, almost since the third wave emerged—have begun appearing.

A few years after starting Bocca, Simons founded Trabocca, a coffee importer with a focus on Ethiopia.* The probability is high that a cup of Ethiopian coffee from a specialty coffee company in North America, Europe, Japan, or Korea today comes from a batch that passed through Trabocca's cupping rooms in Addis Ababa and then in Amsterdam. In 2016, the company dispatched two hundred containers of specialty coffee

---

* Bocca is not the roasting arm of Trabocca, but a separate entity, a customer of it like Stumptown or Intelligentsia.

from Ethiopia, some 8.5 million pounds. Simons's easygoing, low-key charm, boyish grin, and standard uniform of faded jeans, T-shirt, and a Ducati motorcycle sweater somewhat masks his heavyweight status in the industry. He commands respect for his honesty and for the attentive groundwork his company does in Ethiopia. Rather than the celebrated third-wave names, it is usually Trabocca who meticulously sources the finest coffees around Ethiopia. The company has nearly every famous roaster on its books as a customer.

This work has given Simons, as a roaster, a privileged holistic view of the entire coffee chain. For more than a dozen years he has been working closely with Ethiopian farmers and cooperatives at every level, from soil analysis to honing postharvesting techniques, and spends much of the year on the road. He continues to experiment with the final steps—roasting and brewing—but also to gain a deeper understanding of the beginning ones in the field and mill that will, months later, mark the final cup.

The third wave has placed real attention on coffee and seen big steps forward in technique and appreciation for a segment of the public. The fourth wave will be a separation of "real coffee folks," Simons said. While the audience for coffee has grown, each of the waves has gotten progressively shorter and narrower, and the next will be the shortest and narrowest yet. It will have nothing to do with latte art and the ability to create a leaf or the face of Elvis in the foamy head of a cappuccino, or the surge of canned cold brews. "It will be in the actual knowledge of coffee."

That means returning to the basics, and a mastery of coffee's two ingredients, beans and water. Bakers know their wheat, Simons said, but many roasters have little in-depth knowledge of the beans they are using. Roasting requires a thorough understanding of the subtleties rather than the generalities of origin and varieties.

"This combined with the true knowledge of water," he said. "A cup of coffee is ninety-eight percent water." It's a key part of brewing, but the least considered. Bocca's experimentation with water has included significant testing with reverse osmosis, a process that removes the solids—the salts and minerals—in the water. "Good for drinking but not for making coffee," Simons said. "You need some solids to attract flavors." A controlled amount is then put back into the water. Exactly how much depends on the coffee, their cuppings have shown, making it difficult to apply the system broadly. "From the tests we found out you need different types of water for different coffee origins."

Simons is confident but also patient on the fourth wave's arrival: "It might take time. But it will bring out tastes we didn't know existed." The experiments continue. "In the end we try to understand coffee—because we don't really understand coffee."

In 2009, the *New York Times* reported the arrival in New York of Stumptown, the Portland, Oregon, artisanal coffee company "known for an intensity that's part punk, part religion."[21] Its Left Coast hipster cool was as much of Stumptown's identity as its vintage German roasters. Two years later the private equity firm TSG, noted for investing in Vitaminwater and Popchips, became Stumptown's majority controller. Bloggers and social media responded with dismay. "Duane Sorenson, the founder of Stumptown, the Che Guevara of the rock-star barista movement, sold his life's work to the highest bidder," groused Todd Carmichael, TV host and cofounder of La Colombe coffee roasters.[22]

It took TSG four years to flip Stumptown for a handsome profit, selling it to Peet's. Reaction was swift and vocal. "Thoughts on the @Peets_Tweets and @stumptowncoffee purchase? Is it death for punk rock DIY or Birth of greatness?" asked one caffeine-buzzed Southern Californian specialty coffee roaster on Twitter. "Punk's not dead—and neither is Stumptown. Long live good coffee for all!" Stumptown responded. That was one perspective: the deal would mean high-quality specialty coffee for more people. Not all agreed, and some mourned the loss of Stumptown's independence.

"Coffee is the new tech company," said Josué Morales of Mayaland Coffee in his Guatemala City roasting facility and coffee laboratory, TG-LAB. "Everyone wants to be involved in it." In the tech world, such an acquisition would have been universally celebrated. Eventually selling to Google, Amazon.com, or Microsoft is the goal of most technology start-ups: the bigger the buyer, the greater the prestige. Not so with much of the coffee world.

Yet the condemnation of the deal didn't seem to have the rancor that it might have had Starbucks been the buyer. Peet's was, after all, the anti-Starbucks, a Berkeley institution that still refers to its devotees as Peetniks. What generally went unreported and remains little publicized was that in 2012 Peet's had been acquired for around one billion dollars by JAB Holding Company, a German consumer-goods conglomerate owned by the secretive Reimann family. They hold a majority stake in Jacobs Douwe Egberts, the world's largest company dedicated solely to coffee, with more than a dozen global coffee brands (including Douwe Egberts, Moccona,

Senseo, and L'Or) and five billion euros in annual revenues. JAB also owns Caribou Coffee (the second-biggest coffee chain the United States), Einstein Bros., Noah's New York Bagels, Manhattan Bagel, and Krispy Kreme. More surprising in JAB's portfolio for many Peetniks is the array of luxury retail holdings that include Jimmy Choo, Bally, and Belstaff, and the giant beauty company Coty. With annual revenues of $4.4 billion, Coty holds the number two global market position in fragrances, with dozens of major brands, including Calvin Klein, Chloé, Marc Jacobs, Davidoff, Playboy, Guess, and Beyoncé.

JAB-Peet's was on an aggressive coffee-buying spree. In October 2015, Peet's acquired a majority stake in Intelligentsia. Then in December, JAB paid $13.9 billion for Keurig Green Mountain, which included Keurig K-Cups coffee pods as well as Tully's Coffee, Timothy's World Coffee, and Van Houtte. JAB now controlled 21 percent of the global coffee market, just a percent or two behind Nestlé.[23] Two behemoth corporations preside over nearly half of the global coffee market. In April 2017, JAB bolstered its coffee and breakfast empire with the $7.5 billion acquisition of the bakery-café chain Panera, a direct challenge to Starbucks.

Yet Stumptown, Intelligentsia, and even Peet's still quietly pretend to be small. Reading "Our Story" or "Our History" on their websites gives no indication that they have moved beyond their maverick, artisanal roots. On Peet's, a single mention of JAB is buried deep in "Investor Relations." Stumptown placed a note on its blog when it was bought by Peet's, and Intelligentsia's blog published an open letter from cofounder Doug Zell, largely pitched at employees, saying that it was sold "to Peet's Coffee, the 'Granddaddy' of specialty coffee."[24] Nothing else, and no mention at all of JAB.

Blue Bottle, in the meantime, has become the caffeinated darling of venture capitalists, the Apple of the coffee world, with Silicon Valley glitterati—Instagram's Kevin Systrom, Twitter cofounder Ev Williams, and Flickr cofounder Caterina Fake, plus Morgan Stanley, Google Ventures, and True Ventures[25]—writing tens of millions of dollars in checks. In its first three rounds of funding, Blue Bottle raised $120 million. It expanded to New York and Tokyo, acquired Handsome Coffee Roasters, converting it into Blue Bottle's Los Angeles base of operations, and began opening new locations in Southern California. It also bought the iconic artisanal San Francisco bakery Tartine.

A business model based on charging an extravagant price for a cup of coffee and making people wait for it as long as they might spend on eating lunch creates significant challenges in upscaling, in sustaining what is both unique and niche without compromising the quality so fundamental to the company's product, even its identity.

Stumptown began by focusing on cold brews, offering a trio of options, each with unique retro packaging: the Rainier-beer-like stubbies of black cold brew; the Hamm's-like cans of coffee infused with nitrogen; and cold brew flavored with coconut cream and sold in small milk cartons. Stumptown calls the last a "vegan game changer"; others see it as well-packaged, ready-to-drink Frappuccino.*

Inevitably, corporate headquarters and investors demand returns, and often the brand gets diluted: too many outlets, too many products, and lower-quality goods used to increase the margins. Third-wave coffee is about drinking the best coffee available, and that itself creates a ceiling: there is only so much of "the best"—or even so much coffee that scores over 80 on Specialty Coffee Association's scale and can even be called "specialty."

The first intimations of change took place in the supply chain. After being acquired by JAB, Peet's moved its net financing terms from the industry standard of 30 days (or less) to 120 days or more, meaning that traders had to wait 120 to 280 days to get paid.[26] The same happened after JAB purchased Tim Hortons and the Europe brands Tassimo and Senseo. With Keurig, Intelligentsia, and Stumptown, similar conditions have been enacted.[27] One of the core tenets of third-wave coffee is sourcing, often in micro-lots direct from farmers. Large suppliers and middleman may not *want* to wait 180 days to be paid, but smallholder farmers in Central America or Africa, on the other hand, *cannot*. They depend on that money. The risk is that direct buying will be replaced by larger purchases from middlemen.

The massive financial injection from maximizing cash flow, though, allows for pursuing new projects and increasing distribution and visibility. "If anything, this means we will have more muscle and resources to invest in the things that got us here," Zell wrote in his missive when Intelligentsia was acquired. Peet's "wants to provide a canvas that will allow more of the world to see the picture we are painting," he said. "Perhaps a good analogy is we've been showing our artwork at a local gallery and now have an opportunity for a spot at the Louvre."[28] He was right on increasing exposure, although a more likely scenario than his Louvre comparison would be a string of outlets in suburban American strip malls.

---

* PepsiCo has been producing Starbucks' canned Frappuccino since 1996.

The coffee industry is clearly robust. Growth is strong. Traditional markets remain solid and emerging ones growing. In the United States, millennials' thirst for coffee seems unquenchable. Those between twenty-nine and thirty-four years old account for 44 percent of America's coffee demand.[29]

But Arabica itself is in trouble. The problems are not in the final cup, where flavors have never blossomed more beautifully, or in the account books of major chains, but in the field. "We are in the middle of the biggest coffee crisis of our time, the product that we all live off, the entire industry," said Morales, one of Central America's top roasters and coffee consultants. Takeovers, barista competitions, and the new, much-publicized SCAA flavor wheel are distractions from a serious issue that is getting far too little attention.

The history of the coffee plant's spread has come back to haunt the vast industry. Combined with the way that Arabica reproduces, it led to coffee farms across the world having highly limited genetic diversity. New environmental threats have created precarious conditions. "Coffee as it is now is well-positioned for a major natural catastrophe like the potato famine," breeder and WCR executive director Tim Schilling cautioned. "It's just like a train-wreck waiting to happen."[30]

Or rather, one that is already happening. Cars are sliding off the track.

CHAPTER 11

La Roya

P ablo González drove through the gate of Finca El Valle, a coffee plantation just south of the picturesque Guatemalan city of Antigua. He parked his red Jeep Wrangler at the *vivero* (nursery), where hundreds of young coffee plants sprouted from inverted water bottles with their bottoms cut away, and set off down the dirt road that bisects the forty-hectare (one-hundred-acre) plantation. The harvest had finished; the families of pickers who had stayed in the barracks during the *cosecha* had returned to their mountain villages. The May rains were just a few weeks away, and the road was dusty and gray with volcanic ash. Shells dropped by squirrels in the high branches of the macadamia trees that lined the drive crunched underfoot. All around, beneath a lush umbrella canopy of gravilea, were fields of coffee trees with orange-fronted parakeets, woodpeckers, and a number of unseen songbirds twittering in their branches.

In his thirties, with broad shoulders, an easy smile, and his hair pulled back into a short ponytail, Pablo is a fifth-generation coffee farmer. Originally the finca formed part of a larger farm known as Los Valles (The Valleys), founded by his great-great-grandmother, a legendary local figure of will and wealth. Divided into fourths among her grandchildren, the estate broke apart. The lone quarter to remain in the family was the section called El Valle, which Pablo's mother, Cristina, inherited as a young woman in the 1970s and runs with her husband and three sons, including Pablo, the youngest.

Finca El Valle produces about 140,000 pounds of superior-quality Arabica from its heirloom Bourbon and Typica trees for a select handful of America's premier specialty-coffee roasters. "Elegantly balanced, bold, lush, and intense," Batdorf & Bronson, the Olympia, Washington, roaster, describes it. "Chocolate-infused aromatics, a heavy caramelly body and sugar-cane sweetness dominate the cup, but don't overpower the subtle nuance typical of the finest Antigua coffees—a clean spicy note that is a constant reminder of the active volcanoes that surround the region."[1]

French Jesuits carried Bourbon to Guatemala in the 1750s but, unlike their brethren in East Africa, used it largely as an ornamental plant in monastery gardens. Commercial plantations began a century later around the colonial city of Antigua, with its high-altitude sunshine, cool nights, and nearby trio of brooding volcanoes. Farming coffee came easily. "You can throw a seed and you'll have a cup of coffee in five years," said Josué Morales, whose coffee lab works with thirteen hundred growers on producing specialty coffee in Guatemala. The volcanic pumice in the soil helps retain moisture, countering the low humidity, and heavy shading protects the coffee trees from intense sun as well as insulating them against frost. It is ideal for coffee, and farms in the hills around Antigua grow some of the finest Arabica in the world.

In 2012, just after the finca exported its first coffee to the United States, the influential *Coffee Review* awarded PT's Coffee Roasting Company in Topeka, Kansas, a score of 92 for their Finca El Valle roast. "Blind Assessment: Crisp, nut-toned chocolate and raisiny fruit in aroma and cup. A touch of citrus. Soft but lively acidity; silky mouthfeel. Deep, gently flavor saturated finish."[2] Two years later, the review gave Equator Coffee's Finca El Valle roast a similar high score. That autumn at the HarVee Awards, sponsored by the Portland, Oregon, importer Sustainable Harvest, Equator's roast took first-place honors in the Central America and Mexico category.

The finca sprayed no pesticides, herbicides, or fungicides. It converted the remnants of pulped cherries into tea-bag-like natural-fertilizer infusions and recycled the wastewater from the wet mill. It was a model farm in every respect, and part of Sustainable Harvest's training program for Latin American and African growers.

At a crossroads in the center of the plantation, Pablo turned to the left, walking along a section of sickly bushes. The trees stood stripped of many of their leaves. The ones that remained had burnt yellow and orange splotches on their undersides. A few scattered beans—shriveled and bereft of flavor—clung stubbornly to the spindly latticework of branches. *"La roya,"* he said. *Roya* is the Spanish name for coffee leaf rust fungus.

At first, small pale-yellow spots appear on the upper surfaces of the leaves. These increase in size, coalesce with adjacent spots, and morph into irregular shapes. Soon after, on the underside of the leaves, circular yellow-orange dustlike spores appear. New spores develop from the lesions and pass to other plants. Coffee rust does not kill a plant outright but rather debilitates it. The leaves eventually fall, and nutrients to the beans get choked off. Yields plunge.

Starting back in the 1980s, *la roya* was on some of the finca's plants, Cristina had explained in the family home that morning. The leaves would fall and return. As they were set to begin harvesting the 2011 crop, they found it covering a whole section on the southern edge of the farm. Over the next few years *la roya* gradually spread to every part of the finca.

By the time Finca El Valle received the HarVee Award in 2014, not a plant could escape the fungus. That year the farm harvested a meager twenty-eight thousand pounds of coffee, an 80 percent drop. The 2015–16 *cosecha* that had just finished was even lower.

Pablo slowed and grew quiet as he approached a rust-ravaged section. On a field stretching a few hundred yards in each direction, the coffee trees had all been "stumped"—cut down to about knee height—and the towering shade trees trimmed back almost to their trunks. The coffee trees had been bucked up into foot-and-a-half-long pieces and stacked in neat rows along the dusty road. The farm was selling them for kindling.

Coffee rust is caused by the *Hemileia vastatrix* fungus. It developed simultaneously with coffee, coevolving with its host over millennia[3] in equatorial Africa, including Ethiopia's southwestern highlands. In Kafa, the fungus found some sort of evolutionary balance[4] and was—is—kept in check by a variety of factors. "Rust is everywhere in Ethiopia," said geneticist Philippe Lashermes, "but it is not a big problem because of diversity." It is present but not problematic in the forests around Bonga, where the fungus does not even have a specific local name. "That thing which is on the leaf" was the literal translation of what coffee collectors in the Kumpti Forest call it. "It doesn't have a name," reasoned Mesfin Tekle, "because it doesn't have an impact."

Before 1500, much of the world's coffee came from wild trees. As the global demand for coffee beans grew, cultivation was established on the Arabian Peninsula. The plant prospered on Yemen's irrigated terraces, but because of the extremely dry climate—among the most arid in the world—the fungus did not. Yemen lacked the water droplets that *H. vastatrix* needed to germinate and reproduce. The layover, according to Stuart

McCook, a Canadian environmental historian and coffee rust expert, "created an accidental but highly effective ecological filter against the rust."[5] With Yemen as the global fountainhead of cultivated coffee, it was an important sieve. The plants that spread around the world from the seventeenth century until the second half of the nineteenth century didn't come from the wild, but "descended—directly or indirectly—from a cultivated coffee zone singularly free of rust," said McCook. "The health of the world's cultivated coffee had been preserved by an accident of ecology and history."[6]

In 1861, a British explorer around Lake Victoria reported the fungus. The first major outbreak appeared in Ceylon (Sri Lanka) less than a decade later, and then, shortly after, in South India.[7]

The Dutch had introduced coffee to Ceylon in the 1600s, but systematic cultivation didn't come until the British began occupying the island in the late-eighteenth and early-nineteenth century. Despite a general lack of expertise, the industry flourished in a rush of jungle clearing and speculative planting in the island's central highlands. The bubble burst in 1845 when a financial crisis in Britain crippled credit and slashed coffee prices. Plantations were left abandoned, and monkeys, rats, squirrels, caterpillars, green scale, and other pests appeared on the feral fields.[8] Within a decade, though, confidence returned, and the industry resumed its explosive growth. In 1869, with a new railway connecting the coffee-producing center with the coast, a steady flow of cheap labor coming from south India, the right climate for the crop, and strong demand, the future of the island's industry seemed assured. That year coffee rust arrived.

Coffee farmers in Ceylon began planting elsewhere on the island, but the new fields did not stay rust-free for long. Between 1870 and 1877, production dropped nearly a third, even though planting was still increasing.[9] The average coffee estate had been producing 450 pounds of clean coffee per hectare. Within a few years it had fallen to 200 pounds, and then even lower.[10]

If the rise of the island's industry was swift—it had become the world's greatest coffee producer in just fifty years[11]—the crash came even faster. In 1870, it had exported some 118 million pounds of coffee. In 1873, as it was grappling with rust, it still managed to export 111.5 million pounds.[12] Yet within fifteen years the crop virtually disappeared from the island.

The timing and location were not completely random. European colonial expansion facilitated the spread of malaria, smallpox, plague, and the cattle disease rinderpest.[13] Direct trade routes were growing around the globe, and the increased travel made coffee plantations susceptible to pathogens, as did the shift in farming styles. Planters cut down forest belts between fields that would have acted as natural barriers, helping to check the spread of fungal spores, and switched to intense monocropping, which favored the appearance of such epidemics.[14]

How the fungus got carried across the Indian Ocean from Africa is not certain.[15] Perhaps it arrived on a shipment of plants or ivory, or on the kit of a British soldier returning from Ethiopia in the 1860s. It may have come from a small coffee farm around Kafa or Harar,[16] the country's two largest-producing areas at the time. Perhaps it simply came borne on the monsoon currents.[17]

The living spores detach into the air and can be carried by winds. They can survive for months; then, once in contact with a coffee tree under the right moisture or temperature conditions, they germinate and penetrate a leaf within a few hours.[18] Inside the tissue the mycelium grows rapidly and matures in weeks, with powdery orange bundles of spores forming on the underside of the leaves. A tree may have thousands of spots, or sori, which can each produce about 150,000 spores. The spores detach into the air and float along with the winds or rains, on fieldworkers or birds and even insects.

In early 1880, a decade after rust arrived on Ceylon, London's Royal Botanic Gardens, Kew, sent a slim twenty-five-year-old Cambridge mycologist named Harry Marshall Ward to the island. During a two-year stay, he proved the parasitic fungus *H. vastatrix* caused leaf rust and methodically worked out the pathogen's life cycle. Still, he could offer no cure, nor a means to stop the thorough destruction of the island's coffee crop.[19] Growers devised ad hoc remedies, but these did little to forestall an endgame. Losses became so steep that it quickly became economically unviable to grow coffee, and many began to forsake it altogether, planting tea,* rubber, cinchona (the source of quinine for malaria), and some cacao. By 1886, coffee exports were down 80 percent.[20] By 1890, just two decades after rust arrived on the island, 90 percent of the area under coffee had been abandoned.[21] It was an ecological calamity.

Coffee from Africa and other Asian countries began to replace Ceylon's beans on the market. But they, too, eventually succumbed. On Réunion, production fell by 75 percent in the last two decades of the nineteenth century.[22] Rust slashed yields in lowland Java and Sumatra by one third to one half in a single season.[23] By 1920, the fungus had affected most of the

---

* Tea turned out to be a wildly successful replacement. Today Sri Lanka is the world's fourth-largest tea producer.

coffee-producing countries in Central and East Africa. Ethiopia was the exception. Meanwhile, the industry in Latin America was burgeoning, and countries in the Western Hemisphere became major Arabica producers.[24]

Latin America remained isolated from outbreaks as rust continued to steadily steal across Africa. In the 1950s, it reached West Africa. The most feared coffee disease in the world—scientists consider it one of the all-time most important diseases of plants alongside potato blight, wilt of banana, and stinking smut of wheat[25]—was just a direct shot across the Atlantic on oceanic winds.

Eluding the disease could not last indefinitely for Latin America, although the fungus didn't arrive until surfacing—finally, inevitably—in 1970.

A plant pathologist discovered rust-infected leaves on an abandoned coffee farm in the eastern Brazilian state of Bahia. Experts dispatched to the area were less surprised at the fungus's arrival than at the scale of the infestation. It had already spread to plants in an area covering two hundred thousand square miles in Bahia and two other states. The rust had probably arrived years before and had by then infested such a large expanse of land that eradication was impossible.[26]

Panic swept through the industry. Coffee was central to the region's economy. It was the first or second most important export of thirteen Latin American countries. There were fears of a Ceylon-like catastrophe. The Colombian Federation of Coffee Growers predicted losses of up to 80 percent for their farmers.[27]

A plan for containment was drawn up. But before it could be enacted, the fungus had already carried onward to other Brazilian coffee areas,[28] and soon over the border.

Wind currents likely took the fungus into Paraguay and Argentina in 1972. Bolivia recorded it in 1978 and Peru a year later, possibly from infected seedlings that came out of western Brazil. From Peru, it swept windborne to Ecuador in 1981, showed up on a Colombian farm in 1983, and in Venezuela the following year.[29] In Central America, rust appeared in 1976 in Carazo, Nicaragua, brought by immigrants or perhaps a worker who had visited Brazil. Coffee pickers inadvertently took it from there to El Salvador in 1979. Honduras and Guatemala both reported it a year later, Mexican growers detected spores in 1981, and finally, in 1983, so did ones in Costa Rica.[30] In a dozen years, rust had spread to every major coffee-producing country in the Americas.

To enormous relief, no immediate region-wide meltdown of the coffee sector occurred. Farmers had some success managing its impact. Rust seemed controllable. Many held out this sanguine view—at least until the next, more virulent wave of coffee rust swept across their fields.

In the early 2000s, worldwide oversupply caused coffee prices to tumble, falling from around three dollars to under forty cents per pound, well below the cost of production. Farmers abandoned their coffee trees. At the same time, production costs rose sharply. Those struggling to survive had less money to buy fungicides, and certain maintenance measures that had helped keep rust in check were neglected. Most of the region's coffee varietals were traditional and viewed as particularly susceptible to coffee rust. With the region primed for a severe epidemic,[31] La Niña brought a wetter-than-usual winter. "It was a perfect storm," said Morales of the combination of factors. *La roya* arrived in 2008 with a powerful wallop. In Colombia, it cut the harvest by 40 percent.[32]

The outbreak lasted three years. Antigua—and Finca El Valle—escaped relatively unscathed. But then, at the end of 2011, almost immediately after the outbreak had lessened, another arrived, striking Latin America with even greater ferocity. "This time it was different," said Pablo. "It wasn't the same *roya* as before." That year, Cristina recalled wistfully, they had a superb harvest. It was the last. Production plummeted.

It was the worst outbreak the region had ever experienced. Warmer-than-average weather, heavy rainfall, and strong winds hastened its spread. It was particularly aggressive and in the heat climbed to higher elevations, attacking coffee fields once thought immune. Farmers considered coffee planted above 5,200 feet safe from rust, but found infected trees as high as 6,550 feet.[33]

Over the next few years it spread from farm to farm. In 2013, coffee rust affected 74 percent of El Salvador's crop, 70 percent of Guatemala's, and 25 percent of Honduras's, causing losses of nearly two hundred thousand jobs in the trio of countries.[34] With less developed and less diversified economies than some of their neighbors, they were unable to handle the crisis, forcing all three to declare states of emergency from the economic fallout.

The epidemic coincided with a glut of cheaper Robusta on the market from Vietnam's growing industry, and low coffee prices on the international market added to the gloom. Many smallholders switched to growing bananas, but these sold for much less. Profit margins for larger farms dropped, which meant fewer jobs and lower wages. Coffee was the livelihood for more than two million Central Americans.[35] For many of those households, it was their sole source of income, money they used to cultivate staple foods. Jobless farmworkers poured into the cities looking for employment. Gang membership increased. Violence surged. El Salvador became the world's murder capital, only to be overtaken by Honduras in 2016.[36] Parents sent their children north, often unaccompanied and entrusted with coyote smugglers, passing through a series of way stations as they tried to reach extended family in the United States. In 2011, U.S. agents caught 4,219 children from El Salvador, Honduras, and Guatemala crossing the U.S.-Mexico border. That number doubled in 2012 and doubled again in 2013. The following year, authorities apprehended nearly 55,000 unaccompanied minors.[37] The exodus didn't slow. In October and November 2015 alone, they detained more than 10,500 kids from the trio of countries.[38] As the Obama administration earmarked billions of dollars in emergency funding in response, the national debate on illegal immigration took on added rancor. While a U.S. congressional report cited coffee rust as a major factor in the surge of unaccompanied minors illegally entering the United States,[39] *la roya* remained largely out of the conversation. "To discuss the current Central American immigration crisis without talking about the coffee rust," one newspaper wrote, "is like talking about the 1845 Irish immigration without mentioning the 'potato blight.'"[40]

Overall, estates in Latin America experienced 30 to 70 percent losses. "It is basically annihilating the entire industry in the country," Morales said recently. He was referring to Guatemala, although he could have said the same of its neighbors on the isthmus. During the 2015–16 harvest,[41] El Salvador produced just 46 million pounds of coffee, down from 225 million in 2011–12.

The greater coffee industry largely ignored the rust outbreak, assuming that Brazil—by some margin the world's largest producer of coffee—could make up any global loss. But then back-to-back droughts struck Brazil, sending production down 15 percent between 2014 and 2016.

Coffee rust has no cure. It can be cared for, controlled to an extent (generally using copper-based fungicides), but not eradicated. Scientists do not fully understand the mechanisms to unlock Arabica's resistance to it.[42]

At the Institut de Recherche pour le Développement facility in Montpellier, France, Philippe Lashermes opened a small spiral notebook to illustrate a point about the complexity of rust. He held a Bic ballpoint pen for a moment, then put it down. He blew out his cheeks, shook his head, trying to figure out how to explain the problem in simple terms, and, switching to French, aimed a quick burst of frustration at a colleague across the conference table. "It's complicated," he finally said in English.

The disease is mutating, overcoming more and more natural resistances in plants and stymieing work on fungicides.[43] Besides, many plantations do not want to use them—or cannot if they are certified organic.

Rust causes not only a drop in the quantity of fruits but also in the flavor of the beans. "The cup quality of these plants is lower, sure," said Benoît Bertrand. "Why? Because the fruit is not being fed correctly. The biochemical composition of the fruits—in fact—depends on the photosynthesis capacity of the plant and on the capacity of the plant to extract the nutrients and water from the soil." Essentially, the beans are malnourished. *"Las hojas no sólo adornan la planta,"* quipped a professional taster in Antigua. The leaves don't simply decorate a tree: they have a function.

Generally, farmers are advised that if an infected tree is producing less than half of what it ought to, or if it is more than twenty-five years old, it should be dug out and replaced. If not, it can be stumped and allowed to regrow. After stumping, it takes just three years for a field to begin producing coffee again, compared to five years when replanting.

Stumping, though, creates enormous stress in the tree and carries its own risks. "If the incidence of rust has been too high, the plant is not able to recover completely. It is better to replant," Bertrand said.

After rust decimated Finca El Valle's fields, the goal was to return health to the farm by stumping the younger trees and replacing older ones. The entire plantation will eventually have to be renovated, but the work is both daunting and economically unfeasible. *La roya* has a double financial hit: the cost of replanting accompanied by the loss of income. If all goes well, it will take five to ten years for production to return to at least profitable levels.

For the González family, the labor and expense needed to deal with *la roya* struck a financially crippling blow. In another setback, one of the sons had a pair of heart attacks, and the family spent its savings on medical bills. This was the beginning of a heartbreaking string of bad luck with his health and subsequent hospital expenses.

Pablo thought the family's only option was to mortgage the finca at steep interest rates to pay for replanting. But banks are hesitant to lend money to a *roya*-infected farm. The only option is selling off a piece of the property. Finca El Valle is not that large, though, and cutting it down by more than a quarter would risk turning the farm into a hobby. *"Ya no es un negocio,"* Pablo said. "It's not a business anymore."

In spring 2014, Ted Stachura of Equator Coffees attended a meeting on the Google campus about a project using satellite imagery to analyze environmental changes. Stachura suggested a study that focused on coffee rust. The Google team liked the idea of looking at healthy, infected, and recovering farms and gave Stachura some criteria on size and accessibility.

Stachura is steeped in coffee. After toiling as a barista in college, he worked with the legendary Alfred Peet for a dozen years before joining Kenneth Davids at his coffee consultancy and powerful *Coffee Review*. Five years ago Equator hired Stachura as their director of coffee. Still, he was unable to think of one of Equator's regular partners that fit the criteria for analysis. He asked Sustainable Harvest's founder David Griswold for ideas, and Griswold recommended Finca El Valle.

The Google project didn't go ahead, but it began Equator's relationship with the farm. Stachura sampled and then bought some of their harvest.

When Finca El Valle was hit by both rust and medical misfortune, Stachura suggested a Kickstarter campaign to help fund the replanting. Sustainable Harvest facilitated it and produced a short video for the page. The goal was twenty thousand dollars. With a hundred-dollar pledge, the farm could plant twenty-five coffee trees or treat twenty rust-impacted ones. Rewards included roasted coffee from Equator and Batdorf & Bronson, beefy, rodeo-style belt buckles, and even a trip to Antigua to visit the finca.

The campaign opened in October 2104 with a few small pledges before Allegro Coffee, the specialty roaster owned by Whole Foods that had bought from Finca El Valle, made the maximum one of five thousand dollars. "This woman-owned family farm needs help to recover from illness at the farm and the devastation of roya," it wrote on its Facebook page.[44] Donations then stalled.

When Stachura heard the goal, he had worried that it was too ambitious. If the amount was not reached, none of the money would be paid. Equator decided to chip in five thousand dollars, knowing that the closer to the goal, the easier it would be to get the remaining funds. That got the momentum going, and with just a day left, the campaign crossed over its target. Griswold flew to Antigua to present Cristina with an oversize check for $21,464.

Rather than replanting with newer, hardier coffee varieties, ones that were more rust resistant or even higher yielding, the González family decided to use their own stock, raised in the farm's nursery. These are "folk selections," an unscientific collection of seeds taken from trees that perform well on the finca. It was not clear how the flavor profile would change in the cup with new varieties, and the family did not dare risk it. With its modest production even in a good year, the finca can only compete—even survive—with high-quality specialty coffee. Using heirloom Bourbon will mean significant challenges with *la roya*. "The whole world has quantity," Pablo said. "The only flag we can fly is good flavor, good quality."

The Spanish established the colonial capital Antigua in the early sixteenth century and laid it out on a grid pattern inspired by the Italian Renaissance. In 1773 an earthquake destroyed much of the city and the Spanish shifted the capital to Guatemala City, some twenty miles away. In something of a graceful time warp, powder-blue- and butterscotch-colored colonial-era mansions, patios with gurgling fountains, and baroque churches radiate out along the cobblestone streets from *el parque*, the central plaza, of Antigua. On weekend afternoons, hundreds come to stroll in the shade of blossoming jacaranda and magnolia trees, buy *helados* from the women street vendors, and sit under the arcade to chat.

Antigua has become a favorite spot for Guatemala's elite to have a second home and for North Americans to study Spanish or retire. The city's growth has become a greater long-term threat to Finca El Valle and nearby coffee farms than *la roya*. The González family has been offered money for their property. Developers are not interested in the coffee, or in building a handful of stately homes or even a picturesque resort among the old Bourbon trees. They would simply rip out the coffee. The farm is a fifteen-minute drive south of Antigua down a two-lane road flanked by large coffee and macadamia farms, a number of which have already been turned into subdivisions or substantial real estate projects. As Finca El

Valle is quite flat, a company approached with plans to convert it into a golf course.

It has rarely been easy to make a living growing coffee, and *la roya* has made it substantially more difficult. It seems to be an opportune time to sell. But the González family has been growing coffee for generations, and it is part of their identity. Employing a large number of workers brings deep satisfaction, and also a buzz of excitement during the harvest when some two hundred people move into quarters on the finca from villages in the surrounding hills. (The 2015–16 harvest required just seventy.)

If there is pride in being coffee farmers, then there is some romance, too. The well-known lines of Karen Blixen from another continent and another era ring true here: "It was hard work to keep it going; we were never rich on the farm. But a coffee-plantation is a thing that gets hold of you and does not let you go."[45]

Like other growers in the region, the González family has accepted that the fungus isn't going away. "You have to learn to live with *la roya*," Pablo said. Despite deep losses and a highly insecure future, he remained upbeat and took comfort in small signs. Standing in a field of stumped trees, he unfolded the beefy knife he carries clipped in his jeans pocket and pointed to some new shoots, fine green veins crawling up a severed trunk. The trees had been stumped less than a month beforehand and were already rejuvenating.

To the southwest, Volcán de Fuego belched a cloud of smoke and gases. It grumbles almost continually and erupts not infrequently. In February 2015, a large eruption closed the capital's airport, forced nearby residents to evacuate, and covered Antigua's cars in a layer of *ceniza*. Finca El Valle, just a dozen miles from the crater, received a dusting of ash. So fine and so heavy, ash caves in roofs. But for the coffee, it's an excellent natural fertilizer. As well, Pablo claimed, the power of *la roya* had been diminished in the light coating. "The finca was gifted a rain of ash," he said. "The minerals and sulfur in it exterminated much of the rust spores along with fertilizing the coffee. For us it was a *bendición*," a blessing.

The air had turned cool by the time he returned to his Jeep. He put on a brushed canvas bomber jacket and drove in a slow loop through the farm in the dusky light. At the edge of a stumped field, a great horned owl swept down, the long feathers at the end of its broad wingspan curled up. He stopped. It was an auspicious sight. Owls, he said, were a sign of prosperity (rather than simply wisdom) in Guatemala. "Piggy banks are always made in the shape of a *tecolote*," he said, putting the Jeep back into gear.

CHAPTER 12

Impoverished

A rabica passed out of the forests of Ethiopia to Yemen and from there across the globe. It grew easily and spread rapidly; it was uniform and stable and, in the right conditions, thrived. Allotting for nuances of terroir, the beans produced consistent, familiar cups of coffee. Arabica coffees grown in Guatemala taste, generally speaking, quite similar to ones from Kenya when dried, roasted, and brewed in the same manner. Even more remarkable are the genetic similarities of most of the world's cultivated Arabica.

"Due to its history," said agronomist Jean-Pierre Labouisse at France's Center for International Cooperation in Agricultural Research for Development* (CIRAD), "its genetic base is narrow." Arabica's diversity diminished with its spread. The first dramatic narrowing came as coffee went to Yemen, with only some surviving, and again, an even tighter narrowing, as the global crop sprung from a minute gene pool.

But that was only part of the cause. "It is also rather narrow because it is selfing," Labouisse said. Arabica is self-pollinating—its pollen can fertilize its own ovule—and pollinates itself about 95 percent of the time. This keeps diversity from entering the species.

After decades in various African field stations, Labouisse returned to an office at CIRAD. Formed in 1984 with the merging of nine institutions specializing in tropical agricultural research, the center sits at Mont-

---

* In French: Centre de Coopération Internationale en Recherche Agronomique pour le Développement.

pellier's rural northern city limits among a dozen similarly focused research institutions. Just five minutes' walk away, along a quiet road lined with tall plane trees, is IRD. Together, the two have made significant contributions to coffee research and employ many of the world's foremost coffee experts.

"It is not surprising that coffee rust was able to cause such epidemics throughout the world on such genetically uniform plantations," reads the referential textbook on coffee rust.[1] Cultivated Arabica is genetically poor. In plants, genetic poverty can be characterized as being highly vulnerable to pests, diseases, and changes in climatic conditions. They also have an inability to adapt or respond to environmental, or even market, demands, and limited potential for breeding new varieties.

Diversity is the key to any species' survival. When an entire field or even region of coffee trees is essentially identical, they are unable to pass on genetic advantages and are particularly susceptible to threats. Higher gene variety in a population of plants increases the chances to adapt, or even to excel, against evolving challenges.[2]

Coffee rust is merely a preview of what can happen to a plant rendered defenseless by its weak gene pool and battered by heat and a capricious climate.

While most of the world's Arabica is virtually uniform, with many trillions of coffee seeds produced each year,* a sudden and significant change in an offspring—a spontaneous genetic mutation—is bound to appear from time to time. One of the first advantageous mutations that farmers discovered was a tall Typica tree with unusually large "elephant" beans in Maragogipe (Bahia, Brazil) in 1870. While giant beans would seem to be an ideal trait for boosting yields, it was exactly the opposite type of mutation that turned out to be far more useful.

In the 1930s, a "dwarf" Bourbon mutation named Caturra was found in Brazil. Caturra's diminutive size meant that more trees could be packed into a field, while shorter spacing between nodes made the trees higher

---

* It takes about four thousand coffee beans to make one pound of green coffee. With Arabica production at around 11.1 billion pounds, that's over 44 trillion beans—the seeds—a year only from processed and recorded coffee.

yielding. Other dwarf mutations have appeared since, including Pacas in El Salvador and Villa Sarchi in Costa Rica.

"This was one of the keys of the green revolution," said breeder and geneticist Benoît Bertrand. Coffee's dramatic increase in productivity in the 1970s and 1980s received scant attention compared to that of staples such as rice, wheat, and maize, where raising yields helped feed a growing population and fight global hunger.

For coffee, Bertrand said, "the green revolution needed to reduce the size of the plant—to increase the density per hectare." Until then, coffee plantations generally had fifteen hundred to three thousand trees per hectare. They grew under a canopy of shade trees that protected them from too much direct sunlight or wild swings in temperatures, and they received few chemical fertilizers, pesticides, fungicides, or herbicides.[3] A tree's producing life-span was typically thirty-five to forty years.

In the 1970s, farmers were persuaded that they could substantially increase yields by cutting down shade trees and growing coffee in full sun, and using an abundance of chemical applications. New high-yielding, compact-size varieties such as Caturra allowed farmers to jam five to eight thousand trees per hectare. Yields jumped from between 150 and 500 kilograms of clean, green coffee per hectare to more than a 1,000, or even, in certain circumstances, 3,500 kilograms per hectare.[4] Such productivity requires significant chemical inputs and also takes a toll on trees, which need to be replaced in just ten or fifteen years.

Cultivating coffee in this way is referred to as technified. About 40 percent of Costa Rica's coffee grows in this manner. In Colombia, the world's second-largest Arabica producer, the amount is significantly higher. While the iconic Juan Valdez, with a white sombrero and *mulera* (poncho), was leading his burro Conchita down a narrow mountain trail with just-picked coffee cherries on advertisements, Colombia's powerful coffee growers' federation was helping transform the way the country grew coffee. In May 2017, the USDA reported that of Colombia's 940,000 hectares of planted coffee, 780,000—or 83 percent—were technified. As such farms are higher yielding, they account for a higher percent than that of the total production.[5]

Genetically, though, little has changed. A Caturra on a technified farm in Colombia is essentially the same basic strain as the Dutch presented to the Louis XIV in the early eighteenth century.[6] The world's Arabica industry largely relies on just a handful of cultivars with few genetic differences between them.

After leaf rust struck Ceylon in the 1860s, British planters replaced their coffee trees with other crops. But when it infected plantations in lowland Java and Sumatra with similar ferocity, Dutch planters didn't immediately capitulate. They tried different varieties of Arabica, even different coffee species. They found that *Coffea canephora*—Robusta—showed high resistance to the fungus, and by 1900 planters were replacing Arabica with it.[7] During the 1930s, 94 percent of all Indonesian coffee was Robusta.[8]

Discovered growing in the Belgian Congo and independently reported in Uganda by both James Augustus Grant and John Hanning Speke in their 1860s search to find the source of the Nile,* it wasn't recognized as a species of coffee until 1897. Robusta has its natural distribution in the lowlands of West and Central Africa. Reaching thirty-five feet in height, the Robusta tree is larger than its Arabica counterpart. The root system is shallow, with masses of feeders spreading through the upper layers of the soil. The leaves are broad and pale green, with generous bunches of fragrant white flowers. While the cherries are smaller than Arabica ones, they grow in fuller clusters, of eighty or even more.

For a grower, Robusta has a number of highly desirable traits. It's easier to cultivate than Arabica, begins bearing in its second year (compared to Arabica's fourth), and fruits more heavily. Robusta is hardier, with a high tolerance for leaf rust and many pests, and can be grown at lower and more humid elevations. The coffee is less expensive to produce compared to Arabica.

While Arabica is self-pollinating, Robusta needs to be cross-pollinated. This creates an almost unlimited number of genotypes. Unlike Arabica, each tree is inherently different, which means Robusta can better succeed and adapt to changes in growing conditions. It is naturally more resistant to a broader spectrum of threats, as surviving plants can pass on their genetic advantages.

---

* "The natives do not make use of [coffee] as we do, but refresh themselves on a journey by throwing two or three beans, husks and all, into their mouths," Grant recorded near Lake Victoria. They "chew it as a sailor does tobacco," he noted: "It is pleasant, inducing saliva, and leaving a comfortable flavor in the mouth." Grant, *Walk Across Africa*, 160–61.

Perhaps part of Robusta's tropical durability derives from its elevated caffeine content, nearly double that of Arabica. A trio of theories explain why caffeine evolved in coffee and other plants, and all three may be correct. The first is that the caffeine, which accumulates in the leaves, acts as a natural pesticide that repels insects and deters herbivores. Second, when the leaves fall to the ground, the caffeine leaches into the soil and contaminates it,[9] limiting, stunting, or even killing off competing species.[10] And third, the caffeine-laden nectar might encourage pollinators to return and spread the pollen,[11] diversifying the species even further. Perhaps remembering the buzz, they keep coming back for more—just like people.

With its lower price and higher caffeine content, Robusta is commonly used for instant coffee, the large and fast-growing "soluble coffee" market. It goes into many supermarket blends and strengthens certain espresso ones. Brazil, Indonesia, India, and West Africa grow significant amounts of Robusta, while Vietnam, shooting up from a 0.1 percent market share to 20 percent in just thirty years,[12] has become the world's largest producer of Robusta and the second-largest producer of coffee after Brazil.

But one key trait keeps Robusta from completely dominating the coffee market: flavor. Less refined and less subtle than Arabica, it is marked by bitterness and woody, burnt-rubber notes. The New York Coffee Exchange banned Robusta for nearly fifty years because of its low quality,[13] and it only significantly hit the global market after World War II. Nevertheless, since then it has grown immensely, especially in the last few years. In 2016, Robusta accounted for 40 percent of all coffee.

Ever since leaf rust appeared on fields in the nineteenth century, coffee growers were aware that Arabica needed to be reinvigorated with traits from another coffee species. Thus, soon after the Dutch found success against the fungus in Java with Robusta, they tried to breed it with Arabica. The hope of a hybrid is that the offspring from parents with distinct traits will take the best of each. In this case it meant the smooth, complex flavors of Arabica with the fungal and pest resistance of Robusta.

But breeders had little success in crossing them. Robusta is a diploid, with two copies of every gene, while Arabica is a tetraploid, with four copies. Robusta has twenty-two chromosomes to Arabica's forty-four.*

---

* Between forty thousand and two hundred thousand years ago, or even further back, somewhere in Central Africa—perhaps in Uganda, perhaps near the Ethiopian border

At the core of Ethiopian life is the traditional coffee ceremony. ALL PHOTOGRAPHS © JEFF KOEHLER

LEFT: A cup of traditional Ethiopian coffee with butter and a sprig of rue.
RIGHT: Simple stalls preparing traditional *buna* (coffee) are commonplace across Ethiopia.

In Bonga's popular Kofi Laande Hoteelo (aka Coffeeland), coffee beans are roasted, ground, and then brewed in a large jebena pot over embers.

FACING PAGE: A muddy trail winds up through Kafa's Gela coffee forest.

Foraging for wild coffee in the Mankira Forest.

TOP: Ripe coffee cherries in the Kafa's Ufa Coffee Forest.
BOTTOM: A branch of ripening wild coffee in Kafa's Boginda Coffee Forest.

TOP LEFT: Coffee takes about two weeks to dry on traditional beds.
TOP RIGHT: A tiny wild coffee plant emerges through the floor of the Mankira Forest.
BOTTOM: A handful of drying wild coffee cherries in a Mankira Forest hamlet.

TOP LEFT: Woldegiorgis Shawo holds a handful of drying coffee in a hamlet of the Mankira Forest.
TOP RIGHT: Carrying collected coffee out of the forest to the nearby hamlet to be dried.
BOTTOM: Foragers take not only the perfectly ripe wild coffee fruits but others as well.

TOP LEFT: A man sells dried wild coffee in the large weekly market of Kafa's capital, Bonga.
TOP RIGHT: Measuring out wild beans by the cup in Bonga's Saturday market.
BOTTOM: A basket of wild cherries in the Mankira Forest.

TOP LEFT: One of Kafa's important spiritual leaders, Gepetato Haile Michael.

TOP RIGHT: Most rural homes in Kafa have a bed for drying coffee in their compounds.

BOTTOM: Plowing a piece of land of a *gepetato* (spiritual leader) in Kafa.

TOP: Every morning clouds smother Kafa's montane rainforests.
BOTTOM: A man stands guard in the Gela Forest watching that a troop of monkeys does not stray into his garden.

TOP: The only way to transport coffee from Mankira to the regional capital, Bonga, is by horse or mule.

BOTTOM: Mesfin Tekle, the preeminent expert on Kafa's forests, inside the biosphere reserve with leaves infected by coffee rust.

TOP: A traditional home in southwestern Ethiopia surrounded by enset.

BOTTOM: Jimma, the coffee-producing region that neighbors Kafa, has a significant Muslim population.

TOP: Sheki Kedir Sedik, the imam of Tengola mosque in Kafa.
BOTTOM: The mosque in Tengola was once part of an import trade link.

TOP: Bags of coffee beans in a vast Addis Ababa warehouse.
BOTTOM: Sorting beans at the coffee exporting company MOPLACO in Dire Dawa, eastern Ethiopia.

TOP LEFT: Haddis Teka Gebremariam cups recent samples in Trabocca's Addis Ababa office.
TOP RIGHT: Abdela Mume stands in front of an old coffee tree on his farm a few hours outside Harar.
BOTTOM: A table of coffees ready to be tasted in Trabocca's Addis Ababa office.

TOP LEFT: Coffee husks—the dried peel of the coffee fruit known as cascara in some countries—sold by the can in a Harar market.
TOP RIGHT: Grinding coffee in the ancient city of Harar.
BOTTOM: Dried coffee beans offered by a merchant in Harar, a key city in the history of Ethiopian coffee.

"Even if they have the same common ancestor, if you try to cross the two species you have this genomic shock," said Bertrand, resulting in "a wide rearrangement" of the genome. "The main consequence of this genomic shock is the reproductive genes." The offspring are sterile.

A breakthrough in crossing came not from science but nature. In 1927 (or, some claim, 1917) a spontaneous hybrid appeared growing in a field of Typica trees on the Southeast Asian island of Timor. The Híbrido de Timor* possessed some of the vigor, disease resistance, and large root system of Robusta, and some of the cup qualities of Arabica. What made it unique, and from a breeding perspective so important, was that it had the same number of chromosomes as Arabica. The hybrid could be crossed with other Arabica varieties. It ignited a breeding revolution and has been widely used as a parent since.

In 1959 breeders first crossed the Timor hybrid with the dwarf mutation Caturra to produce a cultivar called Catimor. Dozens of versions of Catimor followed. When coffee leaf rust swept across Latin America, many national research institutes bred local variations suited for their own growing conditions. While the trees needed heavy fertilizer inputs and tended to have short life-spans, requiring replacement after five to ten years, they were productive, resistant to rust, and gave good yields.

One major problem soon became apparent: Catimor generally lacked cup quality. Even after multiple generations of "backcrossing"—repeated recrossing of the new generation with Arabica to try to dilute the flavors of the Timor hybrid—the bitter woodiness, rubbery aromas, and salty aftertaste tended to still come through. Stumptown Coffee's scribes note the frequent low acidity and high bitterness of this "problematic coffee bean" and describe the flavors of the finest Catimor that the roaster offers as delivering "piquant herbal and fruit-rind flavors."[14] *Serious Eats'* exotic description captures its often-curious flavor: "Catimor tends to have a bit of a cherry-like sparkle on top of the mushroomy savory qualities."[15]

While Catimor commonly goes into commercial blends and gives

---

with Kenya—two species of the *Coffea* family crossed in a spontaneous, singular event that created Arabica: Eugenia (*Coffea eugenioides*), a small and narrow-leafed species, and Robusta (*Coffea canephora*). The cross was extraordinary because rather than getting half of each parent's genes, they doubled. Of all the *Coffea* species, Arabica is the only tetraploid.

* Spellings vary. It is also known by its acronym HdT or just HT; Latin American farmers often call it Tim Tim.

body and some cream to espresso ones, the specialty coffee industry stridently avoids the Catimor family and its hybrid siblings. They might be immune to the effects of coffee rust, but farmers have had difficulty in getting good prices for them, and some have chosen to rip them out and replant with purer Arabica varieties. At least where they could.

In the second half of the twentieth century, the dwarf Caturra gradually replaced Typica and Bourbon as Colombia's most popular cultivar.[16] Yields increased, but the trees tended to be susceptible to disease. In the 1960s, Colombia's National Coffee Research Center, Cenicafé, started breeding dwarf mutations with the Timor hybrid and, by the end of the sixties, were working on their own Catimor lines.

Conventional breeding is slow. It is hand-done by taking the pollen from one plant (the father) and placing it on the stigma of another (the mother). "The idea is to get all those desirable traits that you're working for into one single, uniform plant," said American coffee breeder Tim Schilling. Researchers assess its robustness against diseases, pests, and climatic variables, and experts, through protocol-driven cuppings, the flavors. With backcrossing generally done over five generations, it takes twenty-five to thirty years to create a stable new strain and ensure that the desired characteristics have been assimilated in the offspring.

In 1982, after honing generations of Catimor lines, Cenicafé created the Colombia cultivar. Work continued, and in 2005 it released a further fine-tuned version named Castillo (for researcher Jaime Castillo), with improved disease resistance, productivity, and, Cenicafé said, cup quality.[17] Colombian breeders tailored more than a half dozen variations for the country's main growing regions.

After the 2008 outbreak of *la roya*, Colombia's coffee authorities mounted a massive campaign to replant with Castillo. They tore out infected bushes but also many healthy ones.[18] (The soil, though, remains unaffected and does not need to be replaced.) In 2009, when rust wiped out 40 percent of the crop,[19] some six hundred thousand hectares (one and a half million acres) had susceptible cultivars. The country's coffee planters' union spent one billion dollars replanting with *roya*-resistant coffee.[20] By 2013, when the outbreak eased, more than three hundred thousand hectares had been replaced with Castillo. That year, rust occurrence plummeted to just 3 percent.[21]

Colombian authorities heavily promoted the new hybrid and offered subsidies and public financing for farmers to plant Castillo. Private lenders meanwhile balked at offering loans for traditional varieties viewed as higher risk. By mid-2015, Castillo accounted for nearly 40 percent of Colombia's coffee.[22]

Resistance to rust is at the moment based exclusively on certain genes from Robusta—in Robusta itself or with cultivars having hybrid parentage. "This work started in 1950," said Bertrand, writing the date on the dry-erase board in his office. "And today we are . . ." He finished his sentence by writing *2016*. "So all of the new main varieties"—he wrote a list of popular rust-resistance hybrids including Catimor and Castillo—"are all made with the same genes.

"A resistant gene for a plant is a gene able to recognize a pathogen." These are called R-genes. "Coffee has more or less nine known R-genes able to recognize the different races of rust."

He drew the analogy of humans and influenza—the flu—where people are resistant to some strains but susceptible to others. "Coffee rust is the same: you have resistant genes able to identify and fight against some rust strains. But the coffee plant does not have all the genes, so it can be susceptible to *some* strains and resistant to *other* ones." There are more than fifty distinct races of rust. A single field of coffee might have a dozen of them present simultaneously,[23] although the norm is just one or two.

That is one problem. The other is that the fungus is quickly evolving to overcome the resistant genes. "We know, for example, that some varieties, good varieties, are now susceptible. So we know that rust is evolving. The presence of rust is higher and higher each year." Bertrand pointed to coffee being grown in China. "It seems that plants that have a huge number of resistant genes are now susceptible."

Insusceptibility will not last forever. Or even much longer. "*When* rust *will* overcome this ultimate gene of resistance, we have no more options. All plants will be susceptible to it." Exactly when that might happen remains unknown. "No one wants to say for sure. In five years, in one year, in ten years." Bertrand spoke with assuredness and authority. "But we know it is a question of time. No more."

Coffee breeders such as Bertrand recently gained a potentially powerful new tool. In September 2014, a group of scientists successfully sequenced the genome of a Robusta plant. Coordinated by IRD in Montpellier, the French National Sequencing Center (Genoscope) in Évry, south of Paris, and the University at Buffalo, this large, collaborative effort published a paper in the prestigious journal *Science*, listing sixty-four authors (including Bertrand) from around the world.

For breeding work on any plant today, said Philippe Lashermes, who led the project, "having the genome sequence is the starting point." He sat in a warm, glass conference room among labs at IRD.

As Arabica's genome is much more complex than Robusta's, initially sequencing the latter was obvious.* Work took a year, but understanding the results required two more, he said.

"The challenge now is to translate these decoded genomes into new and improved tools for plant breeding," Dani Zamir of the Hebrew University of Jerusalem wrote in a *Science* editorial accompanying the findings.[24]

New varieties take decades to create, and few public institutions have budgets to sustain such long projects. While seemingly economically important enough to warrant full government support, coffee is grown largely in poor, tropical countries. Even large private coffee companies generally lack the necessary resources. Nestlé might be the exception, but it is secretive about its work.

One of the key outcomes from the sequencing, Lashermes said, will be speed, allowing certain characteristics to be linked to a precise function of a gene. But while traits such as caffeine levels might be easier to identify, ones that make a plant more resistant to drought, for instance, are more complex. That means breeders, Lashermes said, "can make better choices, be more efficient." It will take significantly less time to get the seedlings to farmers, a key point in the face of more aggressive challenges.

While the technology might give an edge, and lab work remains vital, breeders depend on the raw materials found in the fields and forests. "The worldwide production of Arabica coffee relies on a small number of cultivars with very little genomic and phenotypic diversity between them, relative to those available in Africa, the center of origin," Zamir wrote. "The key for ensuring that coffee can survive as an affordable crop lies in the genetic variation found in African species. This variation will help to mitigate the effects of unstable climate and plant diseases, as well as modify the wealth of health-related chemicals present in the coffee seeds (e.g., naturally de-caffeinated Arabica coffee)."[25]

---

* In January 2017, researchers at the University of California, Davis, announced that they had sequenced the Arabica gene.

According to Surendra Kotecha, a coffee adviser to the World Bank, the European Union, the United Nations International Fund for Agricultural Development, and the International Coffee Organization, Ethiopia possesses 99.8 percent of world's genetic diversity of Arabica. This is particularly important as Arabica is almost exclusively self-pollinating. "To achieve results in future breeding programmes, the coffee world needs the existing diversity in Ethiopia."[26]

"In Ethiopia," Labouisse said, "diversity is higher than anywhere else, especially in the forest area." Genetic variation is highest at its origin.

The coffee industry has a history of going back to the wild to salvage its industry.[27] After the first outbreaks of coffee rust in Asia, the Dutch went to the Congo and took Robusta, planting it in Java, beginning a large and important part of today's coffee industry.

"When you have a problem, where do you go?" Jenny Williams, a coffee specialist at the Royal Botanic Gardens, Kew, said of Arabica. "To Ethiopia, where it all started."[28]

Eduardo Somarriba, a researcher at Costa Rica's Center for Tropical Agricultural Research and Education, the most important institute for coffee in the Americas, agreed: "We have to really go back to the forest, capture what is in the wild, bring them into the science, to somehow save this genetic variability."[29]

The montane rain forests of Kafa hold not only the origins of Arabica but also a unique and critical key to the industry's future.

PART THREE

Back into the Forest

Collecting

The first showers in early February trigger a blossoming of fragrant creamy-white flowers on the coffee trees that, for a few short weeks, leaves the forest redolent of jasmine. The rains steady and increase over the new few months, steeping Kafa's valleys in charcoal blues and indigos as tiny green nubs of berries form on the branches. Cooking smoke mixed with the damp smell of poverty hangs over the forest hamlets. The clay trails turn gummy and swampy, streams swell, becoming treacherous to cross, and rising waters sweep away temporary bamboo bridges. Only a few of the region's roads are paved, and unsealed ones become riddled with potholes and puddles. By May, even the most rugged Land Cruisers get mired in muck.

From a rural stretch of road, the trail into the Gela Forest on a drizzly mid-June afternoon first skirted a knee-deep boggy morass and then crossed a grassy expanse, where an elderly man in a tattered three-piece suit—no shirt but a striped vest and a newsboy's soft cap, which he tipped in a greeting—watched a cow leisurely graze. The path meandered under a canopy of trees as it climbed up a sodden hill. A dozen grivet monkeys, their inquisitive black faces framed in a parka of whiskery white, darted around. One gave a harsh staccato bark as it swung up into a tree, where it perched above on a branch.

Standing off the path watching them was a tall farmer. He wore a fishmonger's high-cut white rubber boots muddied rusty red and carried a long, deep-bellied panga with a deadly upturned tip. He was protecting his nearby crops, he said, his eyes remaining on the monkeys confidently bounding among the branches. Baboons are a problem, wild pigs come at night, and he had dug trenches around his garden to keep out the porcupines. Farther up the trail sat his hut, a mesh of thin bamboo poles coated in a mixture of mud and teff chaff. Cook smoke seeped up through its newly thatched roof.

The narrow trail curled up into a dense patch of wild coffee encrusted with silvery-green mosses. Whippy trees arched overhead, and remnants of the morning's rain shower dripped from the broad leaves above. A silvery-cheeked hornbill cried out in a nasally, huffing *quark, quark, quark* from a buttressed old fig tree. Not far off, a troop of black-and-white colobus monkeys sat looking bored along a high branch chewing leaves. A thin layer of bright clouds pushed down from above, giving a steely, shadowless light that made the array of greens inside the forest particularly vibrant. Wet ferns soaked pant legs at every step, and brambles prevented walking with any ease.

What is most striking about being inside a coffee forest such as Gela is its chaos. Far from the organized rows of cultivated coffee, with their pleasing aesthetic unity of neat, evenly spaced trees, wild Arabica splayed out in every direction. Branches had been bent down from foraging pickers. Older trees leaned to the side. Limbs, snapped from the weight of baboons climbing to gather ripe cherries in past harvests, remained suspended in tangles of vines and climbers. Harvesting was still four or five months away, and the asymmetry of wild coffee's ripening was pronounced: Most of the coffee fruits were green and the size of peppercorns, but a scattered few had already matured and turned crimson. Many trees, though, had no fruits at all. Or just a few cherries high up and out of the way.

This untamed, rather than picturesque, woodland was a throwback to the time when great forests dominated the land. It felt utterly unknown, undiscovered even, a place confined within its own seclusion and uniqueness: long off-limits, still rarely reached, and almost never spoken about.

Until a few centuries ago, the natural history of coffee was virtually unknown. Gaps were filled—gradually but only partially—as hearsay gave way to secondhand reports and eventually firsthand ones. Initial samples of coffee specimens were taken from trees in Europe, then India, Yemen, and lastly Ethiopia, the inverse of its spread.

The first botanical clues to the coffee plant in Ethiopia came from the French physician Charles-Jacques Poncet. During his time at the court of Emperor Iyasu I in Gondar from 1699 to 1700, Poncet examined the plant closely and offered this detailed description: "The Coffee-Plant resembles very much the Myrtle, its Leaves are always green, but larger, and more tufted; it bears a Fruit such as the Pistacho-nut, and on the Top a Husk, in which are contain'd two Beans, and this is what they call Coffee. The Husk is green at the Beginnings, but as it grows more ripe becomes of a darker Colour."[1] While well schooled in botany, and having an interested, excellent eye for it, Poncet appears not to have collected a coffee sample, or any other plants, during his time in the country.

Botanical exploration began in Ethiopia on a limited scale with the adventurous James Bruce, the only European to gather specimens there during the eighteenth century.[2] During his nearly disastrous desert crossing in Sudan on the way home, he was forced to abandon all of his luggage, collections, and copious notes on the flora and fauna. Almost miraculously, he managed to retrieve them. In Marseille en route to Scotland he

Joining James Bruce on the expedition was the Italian painter Luigi Balugani, who died in Ethiopia. YALE CENTER FOR BRITISH ART, PAUL MELLON COLLECTION.

presented Comte de Buffon, the celebrated collector and author of the thirty-six-volume *Histoire Naturelle*, with giraffe skins and plant seeds, and in Paris, Bruce gave King Louis XV seeds for his garden in Versailles as well as cuttings held in glass bulbs that had remarkably survived the long journey.[*3] While Bruce saw coffee growing, and later mentioned it in his multivolume travelogue, and the Italian painter Luigi Balugani, who accompanied him for part of the journey, drew a coffee branch, the Scot carried none back among his known samples.

Twice traveling to Ethiopia in the early 1800s, the British artist and diplomat Henry Salt made numerous drawings and exquisite engravings. While—curiously—none are botanical, he did assemble an ample collection of dried plants, the first from the country.

Collecting plants dates back to at least the fifteenth century B.C., when the beard-wearing Egyptian pharaoh Queen Hatshepsut dispatched five ships to the Land of Punt (most likely the area around Eritrea and Ethiopia) to gather exotic goods. A relief in her temple in the Valley of the Kings shows a pair of vessels being loaded with apes, ebony, panther skins, and myrrh trees. The ships arrived back in Egypt carrying thirty-one incense trees.[4]

During the eighteenth and nineteenth centuries, hearty, driven individuals tramped around the globe taking notes, making detailed drawings, and collecting exotic specimens. Adventurers such as Lewis and Clark on their expedition across North America, Alexander von Humboldt in South America, and Joseph Banks, botanist on Captain James Cook's first voyage to the Pacific, enhanced an understanding of the world's natural history. The British in particular were keen plant hunters. They scoured the Amazon, Far East, and Himalayas, returning with waxy, jewel-like orchids for wealthy collectors and easy-growing perennials to plant in flowerbeds. The East India Company sent Captain William Bligh to Tahiti for breadfruit plants (to feed slaves) and Robert Fortune to China to smuggle out tea (to soothe British addiction), introduced rubber to Malay, and planted cinchona in Ceylon. These were not just ornaments but keys to a burgeoning colonial domain.

The botanical heart of that empire was the Royal Botanic Gardens, Kew, along the River Thames in west London. Opening in 1759 on land

---

* Bruce was showing his gratitude. He had been shipwrecked en route to Ethiopia, and Louis XV, at Buffon's urging, replaced the instruments necessary for the Scot to accurately record and map his journey to find the source of the Nile.

that belonged to Prince Frederick and Princess Augusta, parents of the future King George III, it had the grand ambition to "contain all the plants known on Earth." A century later, along the edge of the fan-shaped Kew Green, it added a three-story herbarium. A new wing has been added to the herbarium every twenty-five years or so since its founding to house a continually expanding collection of dried plants and fungi. With more than seven million specimens, it is the largest in the world today. But its earliest coffee samples are relatively recent and date only to the mid-nineteenth century.

On the ground floor of Kew's herbarium, Aaron Davis pulled open a tall, hinged cupboard door and scanned the shelves of bulging folders. He slid out a stack, set them down on the long wooden table, and opened the one marked with a wide red band. It held two folio sheets of archival paper, each with a coffee twig affixed to it.

The top one had been preserved by Georg Wilhelm Schimper. With permission from the local Ras, the German naturalist had settled in northern Ethiopia in the mid-1830s and spent more than forty years in the country, marrying a local woman, having three children, and acting for a time as governor.[5] "That's probably the earliest," Davis said, holding the sheet horizontal. A couple of fine strips of strapping tape had been placed over the tips of the brittle, tobacco-brown leaves glued to the sheet. Schimper had collected it on April 6, 1840, at an elevation, the caption noted in Latin, between six thousand and sixty-five hundred feet.

Drying and mounting plants on sheets began in the sixteenth century with a professor of botany at the University of Bologna, Luca Ghini. The legendary botanist Joseph Pitton de Tournefort at the Jardin du Roi in Paris first used the term *herbarium* around 1700, and Carl Linnaeus took it up.[6] By the time Schimper was collecting in Ethiopia, preparing herbarium sheets had become quite commonplace.

Davis leaned in to read the fine, spidery handwriting on a pair of attached notes. Originally gas lamps and even candles had not been allowed inside Kew's herbarium because of the fire hazard to its precious dried samples. The building design reflects this, with a series of minigalleries studding a broad, open oval plan and skylight, each minigallery with a long table and window wedged between hinged-cased archives built specifically for herbarium sheets. Even on this dusky January morning, the cribbed writing could be clearly read in the natural light.

"Mount Aber," Davis said after a moment. "Definitively not wild. That'd be cultivated." Peering over his thick-rimmed reading glasses, he added, "There isn't an awful lot here. It was so inaccessible at the time."

Davis set the sheet alongside the folder and picked up the other stiff page, also from cultivated coffee but striking for the dozens of dried coffee fruits still attached to the nodes. It came from the expedition in the late 1830s and early 1840s of two Frenchmen, Richard Quartin-Dillon and Antonio Petit. Arriving at Kew in 1867, it was among the oldest coffee samples in Kew's herbarium.

"This is from the north," Davis said of the sheet. "Nothing from the southwest." He placed it back in the folder. "To get down to the southwest would have been monumentally difficult, mainly because there's no river transportation." He stored the folder. That was a geographical impediment. The local king had also forbidden foreigners to enter Kafa and ringed it with defensive ditches.

All of the early botanical collectors in Ethiopia missed wild Arabica in the montane forests. Kafa's first explorers—Antonio Cecchi and Alexander Bulatovich at the end of the nineteenth century, Friedrich Bieber and Max Grühl at the beginning of the twentieth—collected many objects, but not, it seems, coffee seeds or cuttings. Their reports of coffee growing wild remained scientifically unverified. In 1922, William Ukers, coffee's supreme authority, could only speculate about its existence in Kafa in his comprehensive *All About Coffee*: "It is said that in southwestern Abyssinia there are immense forests of it that have never been encroached upon except at the outskirts, where the natives lazily pick up the beans that have fallen to the ground." Coffee trees, he ventured, "grow in such profusion that the possible supply, at the minimum of labor in gathering, is practically unlimited."[7] Experts considered their existence largely unconfirmed rumor.

Italian botanists did some collecting in the area during their country's brief occupation in the late 1930s, but incredibly, the cloud forests with wild Arabica remained virtually botanically unknown to the outside world until the 1950s.

Standing on an office swivel chair, Davis scanned the labels on the dozens of cabinet doors that reached to the high ceiling. Some held Davis's own herbarium sheets. He is one of the great contemporary plant hunters, having named around two hundred species. He completed his Ph.D. at the University of Reading in botany, then held various postdoctoral positions in Europe before joining Kew in 1997. During nearly fifteen years of rigorous fieldwork in Madagascar, Tanzania, and West Africa that followed, he discovered 35 previously unknown species of coffee, bringing the *Coffea* total to 124. "We found all of the ones that had been fully recorded on the island"—about forty species—"and a whole lot more as well," he said of Madagascar, where he teamed up with a local botanist. "And we found things that were really profoundly different than anything else, I mean, really wacky stuff." One species had beans twice the size of any other Arabica tree, and another produced winged yellow fruits. A third species, *Coffea toshii*, stood just twenty-four to thirty-two inches high.

Spotting the cabinet he wanted, Davis pulled a wheeled ladder over and climbed up five rungs. "The Meyer collection," he said, bringing down an armload of folders. Frederick Meyer was an American taxonomist and botanist from the U.S. National Arboretum in Washington, D.C. "Fairly recent. Nineteen sixty-four."

In the top folder he found a herbarium sheet prepared by Meyer himself. Jewel-like drops of glue secured the browned leaves, and a pale string threaded through the folio page to hold a single dried fruit in place, with another pair of loops stitched around the stem. The specimen had been collected on December 10, 1964, a typewritten note informed, some five miles east of Tepi, a village west of Bonga now known for its eponymous coffee plantation. It was one of the first *wild* Arabica samples in Kew's herbarium.

Meyer had come to the coffee forests with more than just curiosity or scholarly intentions. "Apart from the desire to document the wild plant botanically," he wrote at the time, "a practical need exists to introduce germ plasm from the wild for use in coffee breeding research."[8]

By the 1960s some were aware of the importance of the genetic richness in the little-explored southwest corner of Ethiopia, and that the habitat was coming under threat from ax and bulldozer.[9] Collecting now also meant conserving. Meyer took cuttings to mount herbarium sheets but also gathered seeds that could be propagated.

The most convenient way to store seeds for future use is to dry them. Rice remains viable for a decade, some cereals a few years, and certain crops for significantly longer. Recently Native Americans successfully grew bright orange squash from seeds found in an eight-hundred-year-old pot, while a researcher in Israel germinated a two-thousand-year-old Judean date-palm seed unearthed during an excavation of Masada, the ancient mountain-top fortress. But mango, coconut, avocado, and many tropical fruits cannot be dried in such a manner. Nor can cacao, tea, or, alas, coffee.

Coffee seeds—the beans—are recalcitrant, or nonorthodox. They do not survive drying, making long-term preservation in seed banks impossible. In the right conditions, they can remain viable for up to two years, but to be stored for longer, they must be planted out in a field gene bank. Conserving a plant outside its original home like this is called ex situ.[10]

The first collecting of living coffee material in Ethiopia for ex situ sites began in 1929. The British, through their consul in Harar and then later the one in Maji, in the far southwest, sent seeds to their colonial agricultural stations in Kenya.[11] This was short-lived, though, and halted when Italy occupied the country in the mid-1930s. In 1941, an English botanist from the Department of Agricultural in Kampala named A. S. Thomas took wild coffee samples from across the border in Sudan, on the Boma Plateau, but in Ethiopia, no systematic collecting was done until the mid-1950s.

When Pierre Sylvain arrived in southwestern Ethiopia in 1954 under the auspices of the United Nation's Food and Agriculture Organization, he was exploring fresh territory. He had come to offer technical assistance to Ethiopia's growing coffee industry, but also to study Arabica in its native habitat. From his research he published a pair of groundbreaking papers. The previous ones on Arabica had been, he wryly noted, "written by investigators who apparently never visited Ethiopia."[12]

While the early plant hunters had largely been European, Sylvain was a lanky Haitian whose father was a noted poet, diplomat, and key figure in the Haitian resistance against American occupation that lasted from 1915 to 1934. Sylvain received his Ph.D. from Iowa State in 1944, and spent most of his career at a Pan-American research center in Costa Rica, rising to principal horticulturist emeritus.

Battling tropical illnesses, dangerous animals, and difficult terrain, Sylvain collected hundreds of accessions in Ethiopia. An accession is a gathered plant sample. For coffee, this refers to a single specimen that has not been taken close to another and is usually in seed form. The accessions Sylvain collected came from trees with a range of leaf shapes, sizes, and colorings, and different bean sizes.

"It is of interest that coffee horticulturists are now starting to work with more than [Typica or Bourbon strains]," wrote author Frederick Wellman. "They"—he was writing grandly but really speaking of

Sylvain—"are going back to Ethiopia and the region of its nativity, to secure better, stronger, more resistant strains from among the countless thousands of wild trees of the coffee forests."[13]

Seeds gathered for ex situ sites are ideally pulped in the field by peeling away the fruit but leaving the fine, silvery parchment. After rubbing away the mucilage, the beans are cleaned and dried with a cloth and placed in a cool spot with high humidity. Collectors stored the seeds in a box with a moistened piece of cotton or wool in the bottom and a perforated layer to separate the cloth and the seeds. On lengthy expeditions, they dusted them with ground charcoal to keep away mold and fungus. The methods are similar to traditional ones still used in Kafa and Yemen to store seeds for future planting.

At the end of 1961, Frederick Meyer arrived in Ethiopia and spent nearly four months collecting, including in Kafa and its neighboring province to the north, Illubabor. He was working at the behest of the U.S. Agency for International Development (USAID), created that very autumn by President John F. Kennedy.

Meyer's journey turned out to be an exploratory trip. The FAO had been leading a series of conferences that looked at the wild relatives of cultivated crops such as wheat, rice, and coconuts. It mounted a large-scale campaign to gather as much of the coffee heritage as possible,[14] a proposal surprising in its novelty considering that coffee was, the organization said at the time, "the most valuable single agricultural commodity in world trade, just ahead of raw cotton, raw wool, and wheat."[15] The lack of knowledge about the plant in its original habitat was shocking.

The FAO tapped Meyer to lead its 1964–65 Coffee Mission to Ethiopia, which included specialists from the world's top research centers, including a breeder from Tanzania and another from India, a geneticist from Brazil, and an entomologist from Uganda. Ethiopia sent five representatives from the Coffee Board, the Ministry of Agriculture, and the new agricultural college in Jimma.

Meyer and his international crew came with five objectives: to document the coffee plant botanically; to collect seeds for breeding and selection; to collect insect pests; to gather seeds for screening against leaf rust; and to collect rust spores to identify races.[16]

Haile Selassie was decades into his lengthy rule of the country, and at a peak of his power. His attention was expanding internationally—critics say to deflect internal turmoil—as a prominent Pan-African leader. The previous year had seen the founding of the Organization of African Unity in Addis Ababa, and Selassie giving his famous "War" speech about African independence and freedom in front of the United Nations General Assembly.

The FAO expedition was international, with the goal of supporting the global coffee industry, including Ethiopia's. The emperor welcomed the mission.

Even to a nonbotanist's eye, the diversity among wild Arabica in the montane forests is obvious. In a dense, natural patch of coffee trees, the range of their sizes and shapes is striking: There are thick trunks as well as slender ones, trees that shoot straight upward and fork into perfect *V*'s, others that slouch. One tree has few branches and few leaves, while foliage plasters its neighbor. The leaves might curl or have tinges of silver or bronze or maybe elongated tips like the nibs of antique fountain pens. Among a cluster of barren neighbors, a lone tree holds dozens of fruits. The fruits themselves vary slightly in size and even shape—some are more elongated, others plumper—across the patch. The number of riches appears to be nearly infinite, and it seems simple to gather seeds from a tree with desirable characteristics such as bearing a generous amount of fruit or being more resistant to pests.

But it is a fool's errand to try to select something specific based on its phenotype, the characteristics that the tree is exhibiting in that specific forest environment. That tells only part of the story, and often little of its potential. It is impossible to guess how a tree will respond when transplanted down the trail beside a small hut, much less out of the region or across the ocean on a coffee plantation among thousands of trees produced from the same seed. Will it retain its vigor when cultivated in a different climate, elevation, and soil? Which ones are more resistant to heat or drought? Coffee rust? How will it grow in full sun? Or respond to diseases or pests that are either not present in these forests or else kept in check by the forest's diversity? Will it give good yields? Until the seeds have been taken out of the forest, raised, and observed, often for generations of offspring, it is impossible to answer those questions and see which genetic traits ultimately manifest themselves in a plant's new home.

With this in mind, Meyer's crew chose broadly, even promiscuously. The goal was to collect as many types of coffee from as many areas as possible. "Whether the coffee plant is truly wild, escaped, abandoned, exploited or cultivated matters little when a collection of Ethiopian coffee types is being compiled," the final FAO report noted.[17] Meyer found trees with the known Arabica characteristics, but also new types. There was an assortment of coloring and considerable size differences in the leaves, and in the shape of the fruits, which ranged from flattish to almost spherical and from just under a half inch to over an inch long.[18] The men took them all. They gathered 621 Arabica accessions from across Ethiopia. The largest number came from Kafa.

"He was the first in modern times to collect the genetic resources of native wild coffee from southern Ethiopia," Meyer's 2006 obituary read.[19] But this was a side note. Meyer is best known for his achievements in identifying plants that were blooming in the gardens of Pompeii when Mount Vesuvius erupted in A.D. 79. While this came from botanical sleuthing and is of historical interest, the progeny of his collected coffees, still growing in ex situ fields, continue to be crucial for the industry.

"Since 1961 I have made two trips to Ethiopia to collect seeds and other botanical materials in an effort to introduce new germ plasm and to document *Coffea arabica* botanically," Meyer told a conference in Honduras the year after he returned. "These collections of the 1960s are the most important since the 1700s when a few seedlings were brought to tropical America,"[20] he said, referring to the plants that had essentially begot the global industry.

Among those not present to hear him speak were two botanists from the French government's research institute in Montpellier, ORSTOM.* Following closely behind the FAO expedition, the pair were gathering coffee germplasm from seventy different sites[21] in Ethiopia's southwestern highlands with a specific focus on wild coffees.[22]

While confident in the importance of his efforts in Ethiopia, Meyer could have had no idea of the value that these two collections would have fifty years later.

---

* Office de la Recherche Scientifique et Technique Outre-Mer. In 1998, it became IRD.

CHAPTER 14

Ex Situ

O utside Jimma on the road to Bonga is the turnoff for the Jimma Agricultural Research Center, usually called by its acronym, JARC. The road runs behind the airport, where herds of bohor reedbuck, nimble antelope with lyre-shaped horns, graze in the tall grasses surrounding the runway, and then, after three miles, reaches JARC's main entrance. Inside the guarded gate, painted rockery and flowers line the drive. Scientists in white lab coats move among low-slung yellow buildings with shiny corrugated roofs. A wall of tall trees hems in the compound. Behind it are the orderly ex situ fields of coffee, which fill much of center's 450-acre site.

JARC began as an agricultural and technical school in the 1950s. Pierre Sylvain passed 140 accessions—unique samples taken from different parts of Ethiopia—to the nascent institute.[1] Between 1954 and 1956, workers raised them in seed beds and then planted them out in fields near the school. Technicians recorded data on the trees' yields for several years, but the collection was ultimately not conserved.[2] A decade later, Frederick Meyer's FAO mission gave the largest number of accessions—some 433 of them—to the school, which had two members on the expedition. Unfortunately, the seeds were not planted and were lost as well.

With funding from Ethiopia's National Coffee Board and a FAO Special Fund,[3] the agricultural college converted into the country's first coffee-research station. Established in October 1967, JARC had a national mandate to improve coffee quality and productivity, work on disease resistance, and increase income for coffee growers. It received seventy-eight coffee accessions from the ORSTOM collection and 123 varieties of

Arabica from research stations abroad to start its ex situ fields.[4] Workers cleared land and planted the trees out in blocks—five trees per accession—on a neat grid interspersed with Egyptian pea trees that shaded the coffee with their fernlike leaflets.

In 1971, Ethiopia had an outbreak of coffee berry disease (CBD). Caused by the fungus *Colletotrichum kahawae*, it attacks Arabica trees, causing blacked and mummified cherries within days and a significant drop in production, up to 80 percent in wet years. First reported in Kenya in 1922, it slowly spread across Africa and remains the greatest disease threat to Ethiopia's coffee industry.

Following the outbreak, JARC launched a program to breed more-CBD-resistant plants. The first accessions came from the forests in Jimma and Kafa. They were raised, tested, and evaluated at JARC, then planted out around Ethiopia. "But they found that selections would not adapt to every area," said agronomist Jean-Pierre Labouisse in his office. Labouisse spent from 2004 to 2006 working at JARC as a technical adviser on the management of genetic resources and breeding. "It's a problem of adaptation. We don't exactly know the reason. Sometimes they do not develop, or rapidly they die, or some are very bad yielders. Sometimes they express very high susceptibility to disease because the conditions of environment are different."

JARC began bringing in seeds from around the country. But not all would grow successfully in Jimma's ex situ fields, especially ones from the dry eastern hills around Harar. Labouisse opened a bound file of maps that had a jigsawlike breakdown of Ethiopia's regions by *woreda* (district). Printed in the center of each was the number of accessions JARC held from that district, making the pages look like a paint-by-numbers activity. He traced a finger along a colored band that denoted high-elevation coffee areas to the west of Harar. The topography, soil, and climate were distinct, and the trees had difficulty adapting to the unfamiliar conditions. "The amount of rain, the humidity, these are very different from Harar." And temperature. "Temperature is a complex factor. It is not only the average temperature, it is the difference between the night and the day."

To tackle the problem, the center expanded its CBD program to collect genetic material from gardens, fields, and forests in Ethiopia's different coffee-growing areas. They opened nine regional substations to plant and observe the locally taken seeds, then pass the most promising offspring to smallholders in the same area. The goal was to get CBD-resistant varieties that would smoothly adapt to local conditions. Coffee is also sensitive to the influences of terroir, and seeds taken from one area and planted in another can give a different final taste. As a secondary consequence of this strategy, then, Ethiopia's coffees retained their distinctive regional profiles—the winey notes and delicate sweetness of Limu; the deep blueberries, plums, and florals of Yirgacheffe; a certain amount of spice and berriness of Sidamo and citrus of Guji; the mocha of Harar; and the fruitiness of Wellega.

Over the last fifty years, JARC has aided and supported the Ethiopian coffee industry as it has grown from producing 180 million pounds of coffee at the end of the 1950s[5] to 1 billion pounds today, a 400 percent increase that has been, excepting deep dips during years of drought, fairly steady. With a current annual budget of around $3.5 million,[6] JARC runs facilities for plant pathology, coffee processing and quality, soil and plant analysis, breeding and seed technology, coffee physiology, and plant biotechnology.

Fundamental to its work are the twenty-five thousand trees in its ex situ fields, an astonishing five thousand different Arabica genotypes. "I counted them one by one," Labouisse said. During his stint working at JARC, he prepared the inventory by cross-checking the catalog of introductions with plants in the fields to see what was actually still growing. Considering the relatively limited resources, the center's ex situ collection is well preserved.

"It is the most diverse collection in the world," Labouisse said emphatically. Like many scientists, he speaks with precision but rarely complete certainty. *Probably, maybe,* and *possibly* stud his sentences, not because an idea is only partly understood, but rather because it has not yet been conclusively proven. "We can say this," he said of JARC. "I am sure of it."

On the large dry-erase board in his office, Bertrand drew a horizontal line with tick marks along it. Above the leftmost one he wrote *Thomas 1941*, referring to the British botanist who collected on Sudan's Boma Plateau. Over the other ticks he wrote *Sylvain, FAO, ORSTOM,* and *JARC/Ethiopia*. "For breeding purposes we cannot do anything with that," he said, making a bold *X* through *JARC/Ethiopia*, "because they don't want to share genetic resources. So we have this and this and this," he said, circling the others.

Ethiopia guards its treasured resources carefully, even zealously, and accessing genetic material in the collection by non-Ethiopians is essentially impossible. While keen to capitalize on the country's coffee heritage, the government understands the value of what JARC and the coffee forests, uniquely, possess. It is not obliged to share them, either. No less than seven international conventions legally forbid the taking, transfer, or use of genetic resources without an agreement, including the important Convention of Biodiversity. Ratified at the 1992 Rio de Janeiro Earth Summit, its aim is clear: "the conservation of biological diversity, the sustainable use of its components, and the fair and equitable sharing of the benefits arising from commercial and other utilization of genetic resources."[7]

"I don't blame them for saying, 'We're not going to give you any of these resources,'" Aaron Davis said in the Orangery at Kew. "If you look at the history of coffee, people have just taken what they wanted and made a huge amount of money. If Ethiopia got a penny for every sack of coffee that ever traveled, it would probably be one of the richest countries." Behind Davis, palm trees and a pair of statues of Roman deities bookended an elegant arched window: Diana, goddess of nature, wild animals, and the woodlands; and Flora, goddess of flowering plants. "The problem is, how far do you take it? Where does that money come from? The Americas. So you could take it to its logical conclusion. 'So, okay, why aren't we charging you for our maize?' And if you look around the world, every country is using resources from another country for their main agricultural purposes, if not their main staple. So it's a complicated dialogue, isn't it?"

There is a way to use traceable genetic markers with Ethiopia receiving compensation, or even royalties, for any commercialization of its coffee progeny that breeders use to generate new cultivars with higher yields, rust or coffee berry disease resistance, or the particularly valuable trait of being naturally decaffeinated. The initiative would need to include scientists from the global community and have strict guidelines in place. "If you set up something that was regulated, then the Ethiopians wouldn't be afraid of it being stolen. At the moment they are accusing anybody and everybody of piracy of their genetic material," said Surendra Kotecha, the highly regarded international coffee adviser who has done substantial work in Ethiopia. "That would be more sustainable, I think, rather than what is going on right now. At the moment they think they've got it all in a safe and they've locked it up."

He was referring to JARC but also the coffee forests. "And the argument is they'll lose it. They are going to lose it," he repeated emphatically. "In thirty, forty, fifty, sixty years' time it's all going to go away. Because the coffee forests have been dwindling, the population clusters are getting all mixed up. For the moment they still have the chance."

The coffee forests remain as much out of bounds for the international community as the ex situ gardens in Jimma. Breeders such as Bertrand cannot not even consider material from JARC and certainly cannot come and whisk away genetic resources from forests.

"So, we don't have access to the genetic resources of Ethiopia. The only ex situ site we have access is CATIE," Bertrand said, referring to the research facility in Costa Rica.

Along with financing expeditions to collect coffee resources in the 1950s and 1960s, the international community also established a number of field gene banks to plant, study, and reproduce the collections. Accessions from the early collecting missions went to stations in Costa Rica, Cameroon, Ivory Coast, Tanzania, Madagascar, Colombia, Kenya, and Peru. The Inter-American Institute of Agricultural Sciences in Turrialba, Costa Rica, some forty miles east of the capital, San José, received the most generous selection.

Founded in 1942 at the initiative and vision of Henry Wallace, past U.S. secretary of agriculture, and Ernesto Molestina, Ecuador's director general of agriculture, it sought under the aegis of the Pan American Union (now the Organization of American States) to bolster regional agricultural development. The first coffee accessions arrived in 1949,[8] and over the next few decades, dozens of new ones were added each year to its expanding fields. Under a canopy of tall *poró*—coral trees, with spectacular blossoms the color of boiled lobster claws—and, for wild accessions, eucalyptus, the coffee follows a spacing pattern of 2 meters by 2.5 meters (roughly 6.5 feet by 8.25 feet). The early introductions of bushy Robusta have more room, and some of the dwarf Arabica mutations less. The FAO and ORSTOM expeditions sent hundreds of accessions, and more followed.

In 1973, the institute split off its education and research activities into a separate unit named Centro Agronómico Tropical de Investigación y Enseñanza (Tropical Agricultural Research and Higher Education Center), better known by its acronym, CATIE. The extensive ex situ gene bank, with its world-class coffee collection, became CATIE's responsibility. Today it contains around ten thousand coffee trees representing two thousand accessions and nine *Coffea* species. It's half the size of JARC, but less regionally focused, comprising a broad selection of wild and semiwild coffees, mutants, hybrids, and cultivars from around the globe.

In early 2010, Volcán Turrialba, visible from CATIE's fields, erupted for the first time since 1866. "The wind carried the ash northwestward," said William Solano, a researcher of genetic resources and biotechnology responsible for CATIE's ex situ coffee collection, "which is fortunately in the opposite direction of CATIE, just twenty-six kilometers in a straight line from the crater." Volcanologists consider the eruption ongoing. Seismic activity continues, with eruptions in May 2015 and again in May 2016, and frequent quakes, tremors, and bursts of ash. "When there are no clouds, we can see the imposing volcano releasing gases."

While the most dramatic threat to the collection is being smothered in hot ash or carried away by flooding or an earthquake, it is hardly the only one. Field gene banks are consistently exposed to pests, diseases, and the vagaries of climate. Storms blow through, sometimes violent ones; a cyclone in Madagascar nearly wiped out one station. There is human error and vandalism, encroaching cities, and pressures from population growth. Trees age and need to be replaced. In the last five years CATIE has rescued about two hundred coffee accessions whose numbers had dwindled from the standard five to eight trees per accession to just one or two, replanting about a thousand trees. Gene banks require considerable resources—money, land, labor—even for simple upkeep. Long-term commitments necessitate political and economic stability.

Many important stations, particularly in the Congo, Madagascar, and the Ivory Coast, have confronted severely challenging conditions and were at times not adequately maintained, data was not kept up or was lost, or the collection was simply wrecked at the end of colonial rule or during fighting that followed. (Surviving stations have largely become off-limits to breeders outside their own national programs.)

Despite Ethiopia's turbulent modern history, JARC has remained in excellent shape. Not all of the country's regional research stations fared so well, though. In 1998, one in Harar was destroyed, most likely over a land dispute. Its collection of 592 accessions, gathered in 1986 from an area that has experienced high levels of genetic erosion, was completely lost.[9]

While Costa Rica has stayed remarkably stable over the years, and CATIE's fields continually well maintained—the coffee collection has been under the care of the most renowned figures in the field, including J. B. H. Lejeune, Sylvain, Frederick Wellman, François Anthony, Philippe Lashermes, and Bertrand—it, too, has its weaknesses.

The fields contain more than thirty-five thousand accessions representing hundreds of different plant species from around the globe. Its singular geographic setting can hardly be ideal for each of them, or even all those in its coffee collection. Each type of coffee should ideally be kept in conditions similar to its original microclimate. CATIE might be well suited for lowland Robusta, but much less so for Arabica. Wild accessions from Kafa crave dense, almost permanent shade, while those taken from Yemen's luminous terraces should be growing in dry conditions in near-full sun.

CATIE's location is significantly lower and more humid than is usual for Arabica. While JARC is at a near-ideal 5,750 feet (1,753 meters) above sea level, CATIE's fields sit significantly lower, at 1,975 feet (602 meters). For Arabica, this is considered, in the center's own scientific parlance, "suboptimal." "Quite low. Very low. For that the conservation is not good," said Bertrand, who spent more than a dozen years as a breeder at CATIE. It has an average daytime temperature of 22.5°C (72.5°F), annual rainfall of 2,600 mm (102 inches), and no marked dry season. "So the plants are suffering from an excess of water and an excess of temperature. There is a lot of mortality in trees. It is impossible to do a good evaluation of quality, and to do a good evaluation of productivity." These are crucial when selecting plants to use in breeding.*

"It's not a coffee landscape. All that coffee can be compromised," Davis said at Kew. "What you see from genetic studies is a lot of—because it isn't from an ideal environment—a lot of compromise in the collection, a lot of cross-pollination. The diversity is still there," he said, raising his pitch sharply at the end of his sentence, implying a strong *but.* The age of the trees, he added after a moment, is another issue. "Collections tend to degrade over time."

Coffee is what researchers call an orphan crop. Unlike wheat and rice, it grows almost exclusively in poorer, tropical countries that have generally not had adequate resources for substantial research and development. "Richer countries buy it, roast it, and drink it, but have not paid for the agronomy. Only now is the industry waking up and seeing the need for

---

* To deal with this problem, WCR identified a core collection of one hundred accessions and planted them in two higher locations, in El Salvador and on a farm owned by Starbucks in Costa Rica's Central Valley.

it," Tim Schilling, executive director of World Coffee Research, told the BBC in 2015. This was a motivating force behind launching WCR, a collaborative research organization based at Texas A&M University, in 2012.

In the past ten or fifteen years, awareness has grown of the perilous state of the genetic resources in ex situ sites as well as in Arabica's natural habitat, which faces rampant deforestation. These are the raw materials that breeders rely on to improve and create coffee varieties. "People started to understand there is really a huge problem," said Bertrand, head of breeding at WCR.

One of WCR's first tasks was to assess CATIE's coffee collection. "We took every one of those strains and sequenced the DNA strands and matched them one by one to see what diversity there was," Schilling said to the BBC. "We got the results back and there was amazingly little diversity. It was a big shock. We knew it was small, but not that small."[10]

The results still astonish Schilling and, he recently said, "show how outrageously narrow the diversity base is for Arabica coffee."

The closer to the source, the more diversity can be found among Arabica, and breeders are anxious to tap into the wild coffees growing in the southwestern forests of Ethiopia. "These populations, whose genetic makeup is very diverse," Davis recently told a seminar in Addis Ababa, "include varieties naturally resistant to many pathologies, or having other interesting traits for coffee producers."[11]

One of those "other interesting traits" is taste. Breeding work has historically been for disease resistance or increased yield—not in improving aromas and flavors. That is reflected in the elevation of CATIE's coffee collection, the only gene bank available for Central American and Caribbean countries, which is better suited for gauging a tree's tolerance to various funguses than in brewing a delicious cup of coffee. The bulk of JARC's ex situ collection was gathered in the mid-1970s[12] for work against coffee berry disease, and little assessment has been done on the trees apart from their resistance to that fungus.

Cultivated Ethiopian coffee is generally considered the finest in the world, with explosive flavors and unmatched floral and fruity notes. Unlike Latin America's plantation coffees, with rows of almost genetically identical bushes, most Ethiopian coffees come from small gardens with a range of different trees, a blend of "heirloom" Arabica varieties that get further mixed at the local cooperative. Just imagine how good a coffee might be if the very finest—the most floral, the most intensely fruity, the juiciest in the mouth—was isolated from that mélange back in the field, cultivated in optimal conditions, and processed with the utmost care.

That possibility fires the imagination of coffee aficionados around the globe. Especially because it has happened—spectacularly—once before.

CHAPTER 15

Geisha

Fourteen judges worked through the dozens of cups grouped on round tables, methodically sniffing, slurping, and spitting back out the tepid brews. The coffees had reached the finals of the 2004 Best of Panama competition by progressing through a series of qualifying rounds at the *beneficio* (wet mill) owned by Panama's ex-president Mireya Moscoso. Those judging were largely elite specialty-coffee buyers who had been nearly begged to come to the low-key event.

With depressed international prices but a rising interest in specialty coffee, a small group of producers around Boquete, a coffee-rich valley in the western highlands near the border with Costa Rica, founded the competition in the mid-1990s as a way to promote Panama's fine but overlooked and underrated coffee.

In A. E. Haarer's heavy, referential 1956 volume on coffee, the country received just a single sentence: "Panama does not have much land suitable for successful coffee cultivation and the little that is grown is sold and consumed locally."[1] Four decades later, the country's coffees remained, in sharp contrast to those of its more acclaimed Latin American neighbors, virtually unknown on the world market.

Coffee plants had arrived in Panama at the beginning of the nineteenth century, brought by European settlers, who established the first farms along the coast and after around Boquete. The narrow, lazy-S-shaped isthmus gets climatic influences from both oceans: rain from the Pacific between May and December and the Atlantic between December and March. The strong wind patterns create numerous microclimates with varying degrees of rainfall. Winds blow over the mountains, creating a misty, hovering fog known as *la bajareque* (and double, even triple, rainbows). The numerous deep valleys that twine through the highlands around Boquete create ideal pockets for growing coffee, giving a "sweet, nice body, mild aromatic taste," according to one grower. "A very pleasant cup." At their finest, the high-elevation coffees from Boquete can be bright, somewhat fruity, and a touch floral and carry notes ranging from winey to caramels and white chocolate, flavors that the entrants in the Best of Panama competition were showing that year.

"Amongst the 25+ finalist coffees we tasted, all of which were of very high caliber, there was one that had us all simultaneously delighted and befuddled," one of the judges, Geoff Watts of Intelligentsia Coffee, later wrote. "You could smell it from across the table—beautiful jasmine, lemongrass, coffee-blossom, sweet lime and white peach aromas drifting through the room. At first we thought someone was playing a trick on us—had they slipped an Ethiopian coffee onto the table? Had someone doctored a sample? All of us had cupped thousands of coffees from Central America and not once had tasted anything quite like this."[2]

He was referring to a wildly different entrant among the Bourbons and Catuais,* an unknown variety from Hacienda La Esmeralda that had the coy name of Geisha.

"In an instant I tasted the overwhelming aftertaste of jasmine, papaya, lime and honeysuckle," recalled another judge, the San Francisco–based Willem Boot, a renowned consultant to coffee growers, exporters, roasters, and governments across the globe. "Never in my coffee career had I tasted such an otherworldly beautiful coffee."[3] It came at the judges "like a thunderbolt."[4]

Hacienda La Esmeralda sits above Boquete on the highland slopes of the dormant Volcán Barú, at 11,398 feet above sea level (3,474 meters) the tallest peak in Panama. In 1967, Rudolph Peterson, a Swedish-born Californian who at the time was president and CEO of the Bank of America, purchased the farm. His son, Price, a neurochemist, left his position at the University of Pennsylvania in the early 1970s to run the hacienda. "We were dedicated to dairy," explained Price's daughter, Rachel. "We had some coffee but it was not a big part of our organization."[5] In the mid-1980s, as

---

* A semidwarf cultivar resulting from a cross between Caturra and the popular, high-yielding Brazilian variety Mundo Novo.

coffee "started becoming more interesting," they planted more trees and, in 1994, built a *beneficio* to process the farm's coffee. Two years later the Petersons purchased an abandoned coffee farm across the Boquete valley in an area known as Jaramillo.

"We were going to plant some areas that hadn't been planted and replant some other areas," Rachel recalled. "On the lower part of the farm there were some coffee trees and it was a bad year for funguses."[6] *La roya* had yet to arrive with much force in the valley, but in spring different fungi—including *ojo de gallo* (rooster's eye)—attacked the trees. "The Catuai were losing all their leaves and were looking pretty ugly. So my dad decided to take seeds from one of the trees that was looking pretty well. So we replanted the higher altitude part of the farm with that."[7]

In January 2004, Price's son Daniel began cupping coffees from the entire estate, methodically working section by section, "testing the notion that rather than a general good cup, there might be an area with an intensely fine cup which was flavoring all the output of the farm when it was all mixed together," according to Price. "It turned out he was right."[8]

At the upper extreme of the Jaramillo farm, at the end of a small valley some fifty-three hundred feet in elevation[9] in "a cold thrashing wind," Daniel found ten hectares of trees later named Geisha. A third of them had simply died, a third were limping along, and a third were doing well. The trees were unusually tall and unruly, with angled branches and elegant leaves that curled slightly upward.

Even more striking were the flavors of its long thin beans. "A couple weeks before the competition it came out on a cupping table on the farm. And I had never tasted something like that. And not having much experience with coffees outside of Panama, I thought that it was a defect, honestly," Daniel later admitted at a coffee conference in Paris, drawing a knowing laugh from the audience. "It was not at all a traditional flavor from Panama. In a good Panama you always expect a nice, clean, balanced cup. You did not get blueberries, aromatics. You did not get bergamots and this pronounced jasmine, which is the trademark of the Geisha that makes it unique."[10]

The family called it Jaramillo Special and decided to give Geisha its world premier in the upcoming Best of Panama. They had no idea how it would be received and wondered if the judges would assume, as Daniel initially had, that it was an error in the postharvest processing, perhaps its excessive fruitiness deriving from too much time in the fermentation tanks.

To the Petersons' surprise and delight, the judges awarded it an average score of 95.6 out of 100. One gave it a perfect mark. Of the things that Daniel most remembers about that day was something almost as rare as that: "another judge (Danny O'Neill) sitting on a table and picking up a cup of the cool Geisha which he had already scored, and just enjoyed drinking the rest of it."

The unusual coffee easily won the competition, earning it a spot in the special online auction held a few months later. While coffee generally fetched decent prices at the Best of Panama auction, Hacienda La Esmeralda wasn't sure how the Geisha would sell. Yet even before the auction began, a number of the judges were plotting to buy the lot themselves.

In July, the Specialty Coffee Association of America hosted an online auction of nearly twenty thousand pounds of high-scoring coffees from the competition. The lowest lot fetched $1.25 per pound—the commodity market was trading commercial-grade Arabica for seventy-three cents at the time.

Hacienda La Esmeralda offered seven sixty-kilogram bags of Geisha, about a thousand pounds of green coffee. Bidding climbed past $2.50 and kept rising. When it hit $15, Price Peterson called the auction organizer. Suspecting a hacker had broken into the system, they shut down the auction until the bids could be verified. Once restarted, offers continued to ascend, and the lot eventually sold for a staggering $21 a pound, shattering the online record for bulk unroasted beans. (That day, the second-highest lot went for $2.53.)

Seven buyers split the Geisha, including Intelligentsia, Stumptown, and Sweet Maria's, which specializes in selling green beans to home roasters. Sweet Maria's divided up its allotment into 131 one-pound bags and strictly limited customers to a single one. ("The idea is to get the coffee spread around to as many people as possible!" the website nobly reasoned.) "The cup character of this coffee is not only unique among Panamas, it is unique among all Central American coffees," Sweet Maria's founder, Thompson Owen, wrote in a review, "with floral aromatics, a fresh citrus flower brightness, light body, herbal and honeyed cup."[11]

"What is the 'Geisha' variety? Is it a type of Typica? Where did it come from?" an interviewer and broker asked Price Peterson after the auction. No one was sure, not even Price. "We are still puzzling that out," he responded. "It is probably a Bourbon derivative full-sized tree. Probably came from Ethiopia, although the Ethiopians I've asked have never heard of it!"[12]

Like all Arabica, it originated in Ethiopia. But it would take a decade to work out Geisha's circuitous route to the Petersons' farm.

The name Geisha was not a demure wink at the exotic, but the name of an area and a mountain to the southwest of Bonga, about thirty miles from Maji. Nineteenth-century Swahili ivory traders and hunters following herds of elephants north used the spot, some eight thousand feet up on the edge of a plateau near the Kibish River, as a halting place and named it Maji, Swahili for "water."[13] After Menelik II conquered the region and established a fortified garrison at Maji,[14] the British opened a consul in an effort to halt ivory poaching and the slave trade. By the time the last British consul, Captain Richard Whalley, arrived at his isolated posting in 1930, the area had been practically denuded of its inhabitants, with, he wrote to his superior in Addis, "scarcely more than about 10 to 20% of the original population left."[15]

Geisha fell within Whalley's territory, and during his posting the eponymous variety started its journey to Panama. Jean-Pierre Labouisse, the CIRAD agronomist, began piecing together the route. On a shelf in his Montpellier office is a thick sheaf of bound mimeographed pages with hand-drawn and hand-colored maps, an unpublished 1969 report prepared by F. Millor* titled "Inventory of the Coffee Varieties and Selections Imported Into and Growing Within East-Africa." The Geisha entry quotes the notes of a British botanist based in Kenya named T. W. D. Blore: "Seeds were imported from Geisha forest, S.W. Abissinia, in about 1931. 50 to 70 inches rainfall at altitude of 5500 to 6500 feet. Long drooping primaries, prolific secondary growth, small narrow leaves and bronze tips."[†16]

The coffee nursery at Kitale in British East Africa (Kenya) received and planted out some seeds in its ex situ field. It was one of the many coffee selections sent on to various international experimental agricultural stations for use in breeding. In 1936, seeds, perhaps from the first or second harvest, were planted in two agricultural research stations, Kawanda, just

---

* No details can be found on Millor.

† Whalley, Millor, and Blore all spelled it Geisha, as do the Petersons and Labouisse, although some American specialty-coffee roasters now spell it Gesha.

north of Kampala, Uganda, and Lyamungu, on the slopes of Mount Kilimanjaro, outside Moshi, Tanzania.*

Earlier that same year, Whalley went to Geisha himself. "The Director of Agriculture, Kenya, asked me to collect some 10 lbs of coffee seed from these parts to enable him to carry out experimental work in the Colony," Whalley wrote to his boss at the British Legation in Addis Ababa on January 29, 1936, upon returning under heavy Amhara escort from the area inhabited by the Tishana tribe. The trip had been delayed and Whalley feared missing ripe coffee fruits.

> I had always imagined that the Geisha coffee (the best in these parts) was cultivated. Imagine my surprise and interest to find that it was wild coffee growing in an old and aged rain forest under the shade of enormous trees. The season was almost over and at one time I was afraid that Zaude's delay would not allow me to get even 10 lbs of seed. I wandered about the forest and after 3 days had only collected about two or three pounds of seed. Thereupon I got hold of the Tishana and gave them some good presents in money and after another two days they brought in coffee in the berry which allowed me to obtain what I wanted.[17]

The journey took Whalley two weeks. Once back, he sent the seeds off to an isolated colonial post across the Kenya border. Within months, he closed the Maji station because of the Italian invasion and crossed over the Sudan border to Boma.†

In 1953, Geisha seeds from Lyamungu arrived in Costa Rica at CATIE's forerunner as a disease-resistant strain.[18] The center received numerous other introductions of Geisha from different research centers, including the Congo (1954), Tanzania (1955), Puerto Rico (1957), Oeiras, Portugal (1965 and 1971), Colombia (1972), and Brazil (1974).‡ The variety

---

* In the 1980s, a CIRAD botanist, Pierre Charmetant, saw the original growing strong in Lyamungu. According to the current program manager for crop improvement, Deusdedit Kilambo, it continues to grow on-site along with its progenies.

† Whalley remained in Boma during the Italian occupation, then led a group of British and local partisans across the border to liberate the area.

‡ In December 1964, Meyer's FAO mission also obtained some seeds from Geisha. These were not collected by members of the expedition themselves but by contacts "sending out messengers." *FAO Coffee Mission to Ethiopia*, 18.

showed good rust resistance and was sent to and from various agricultural stations. A 1958–59 report on field trials in the British protectorate of Nyasaland (later Malawi) noted that among "well-foliated low yielding varieties" Geisha was least affected.[19] Such assessments were not fully complimentary, though, and Millor's overall evaluation was critical: "It is not a high-yielding variety; it has often an undesirable type of bean (long and thin) and generally a liquor of poor quality, but, because of its resistance to leaf-rust, it has been used for hybridizations."[20]

Finally, in 1963, Geisha arrived in Panama, when a coffee farmer and Ministry of Agriculture employee named Francisco "Pachi" Serracin brought some from Costa Rica. He planted them among other new and potentially disease-resistant varieties on his Boquete farm, Finca Don Pachi.

Serracin shared Geisha seeds with some neighbors in the valley, including one who planted them on an estate in Jaramillo. There they would languish in anonymity for decades.

Up in that high valley on the Peterson farm, though, something extraordinary happened. After years of negative reports on its taste in the cup, Boquete's terroir unlocked Geisha's flavor potential.

Until the Best of Panama auction, essentially all of the Arabica produced in the Americas had originally come from cultivators based on either Typica or Bourbon, and the novelty of Geisha's flavors made valuing it a challenge. "It is difficult to price this sort of cup character, and when it is as exotic . . . no, extraterrestrial . . . as The Esmeralda Gesha, it is even more hard to quantify," Thompson Owen wrote of the 2006 crop. "A basket of fruit, a bouquet of flowers; no description seems too sappy, sentimental or ridiculous for a coffee that is so obviously unique."[21] Others were even more effusive. "I am the least religious person here and when I tasted this coffee I saw the face of God in a cup," said Don Holly of Green Mountain Coffee in Vermont, one of the judges of the 2006 Best of Panama.[22]

That year Esmeralda's Geisha hit an auction high of $50.25, fifty times the price of commercial-grade coffee. It took ten hours of bidding before the Small Axe Coffee Alliance—Intelligentsia, Stumptown, Sweet Maria's, Groundwork Coffee Company, and the Norwegian roaster Kaffa—placed the final offer. After roasting their allotted share, Intelligentsia sold eight-ounce bags for $51.95 each.

The 2004 auction had made the front page of the main Panama newspaper, but garnered only a few brief mentions elsewhere. Even Kenneth

Davids, in his online *Coffee Review*, buried the news in the middle of a piece about international competitions published some months later.[23] The 2006 auction was different. Reuters, *Forbes*, and *Wine Spectator* (which called Geisha "a Yirgacheffe on Central American acid")[24] were among the many publications that reported the new record.

The 2007 auction arrived with considerable anticipation, and the five-hundred-pound lot of Hacienda La Esmeralda's Geisha floored the previous record, selling for $130 per pound to a consortium of North American roasters.

While the Geisha variety made Hacienda La Esmeralda famous, it accounted for just 3 percent of its total crop. That has gradually changed, though it was still only a quarter of the 2015–16 harvest. Geisha is not an easy variety to grow. It hasn't been bred over the years to increase production. Long growth times from the high altitude necessary to eke out its flavor potential, and the trees' sizable gaps between the nodules where the cherries form, contribute to yields that, according to Daniel Peterson, are only one half to one third of the farm's Catuai and Caturra trees.

After such success in the Best of Panama auctions, the Petersons gave Esmeralda's Geisha its own dedicated bidding platform as well as continuing to participate in the larger auction. The first solo one, in 2008, highlighted the keen difference between the best and the rest of the Geishas. Of the five lots on offer, one sold for $110 per pound but another just $5.[25]

The best, though, is exactly that, and the finca's mantel of trophies is crowded. The estate's high-grown Geishas have repeatedly taken the industry's top awards and crushed their own market records. The 2010 auction reached a staggering $170 per pound.[26] The following year, the Specialty Coffee Association finally created a separated category for the variety in the Best of Panama competition to give Bourbons, Typicas, and fruity Caturras a chance to shine.[27]

Along with the delicious uniqueness of the coffee, skillful marketing, extremely limited quantities, high expectations, and fame helped drive up the price. Yet the quality of the coffee was nearly incomparable. Every step in the process at Esmeralda is precisely managed, from farming in deep 40 to 50 percent shade and picking only the most perfectly ripe cherries, to postharvesting techniques, storage, and even transportation. Rather than sending by shipping container, in which the beans may linger in a steamy port for weeks, Esmeralda airfreights them, adding as much as seven dollars per pound to the cost of the coffee for a Bay Area roaster, more than the wholesale price of many of the world's other finest coffees.

During the 2013 Best of Panama auction, as coffee prices were declining and Arabica was fetching on average about $1.50 per pound, the opening bids for Geisha came in at $4 and then $4.10. "Chocolate, grapes, juicy, high acidity, strong strawberry notes," read the brief, almost generic description. Yet a buyer's counteroffer of $50.10 made it clear that the auction would be extraordinary. The one-hundred-pound lot came from the Cañas Verdes section of the farm and had been naturally (dry) processed, a relatively new style for the finca. The auction finished in the afternoon with Saza Coffee (Japan) and Haaya Gourmet Coffee (Taiwan) sharing the prize, paying a staggering $350.25 per pound.[28] All of the previous records seemed like quaint bargains. At the July 2017 auction it topped even that astronomical figure when Korea's Kew Specialty Coffee Co. shattered the record by paying $601.00 a pound for a 100-pound lot of Esmeralda's natural Geisha.

Without a doubt, Geisha is the reigning rock star of the specialty coffee world, the darling of the third wave, and the industry's most outstanding success story. Yet while Geisha might be the winner at cupping competitions, tops auctions, and is considered the most distinguished varietal by coffee aficionados, it remains a rarity to actually drink. North America's most elite specialty coffee roasters—Rocanini in Vancouver, B.C., Batdorf & Bronson's tasting room at its Olympia headquarters, Stumptown in Portland, Fourbarrel in San Francisco, and even the counter at Blue Bottle's roasting facility in Oakland—have no brewed Geisha on the menu, much less do any of the numerous Peet's or Starbucks outlets nearby. Cafés El Magnífico in Barcelona sometimes sells the beans in the shop but not as a drink in its high-end MAG café nearby. Bocca's café in Amsterdam doesn't even do that. The Monmouth Coffee Company's flagship behind Neal's Yard in London serves over a dozen top, carefully sourced coffees of origin and offers a four-page printout lavishing paragraphs of details on each. "We had one Geisha a few years ago," one of the its baristas said recently.

Geisha beans favor lighter roasts, which bring out their unique fruity citruses. It needs a simple, clean way of brewing, such as Chemex or another hand-drip pourover method. Espresso-based drinks, though, dominate even third-wave-style cafés. "An espresso with Geisha is a waste," said Salvador Sans, the owner of El Magnífico. The nuances disappear. And adding milk swamps the delicate and unique flavors. Just as an aged single-malt whiskey *can* be used as a blender, there is little point in making a caramel macchiato with Geisha. Yet even those angling for the pourover counter of a high-end coffee shop are largely unwilling to spend five times more for a Geisha than a cup brewed from, say, the cult-level Ninety Plus Coffee's Ethiopian beans from American roaster Joseph Brodsky.

My own first taste of Geisha came in the back room of El Magnífico. The lead cupper, a tall young Brazilian named Cássia Martinez de Carvalho, had set out five leading Latin American coffees that had arrived. Half a dozen of us ran down the line with cupping spoons, breaking the crusts and quickly inhaling the aromas that were bursting up. Once the cups had cooled, we began tasting, calling out flavors that our palates caught: "café con leche," "chocolate and cinnamon," "like that crust on a cheesecake," "chocolate and some lacteos."

But Hacienda La Esmeralda's Geisha was completely different. Rather than crisp chocolaty tones, nuttiness, and the slight cream in the mouth that Latin American Arabicas tend to express, it was closer to floral and berry-rich Ethiopian-grown coffees, with heady, aromatic notes of stone fruits, orange marmalade, rose petals, and bergamot. "Pure apricot," Salvador Sans said, taking in the aromas. A sharp slurp of liquid off his spoon flooded his palate. "Apricot and mango," he said a moment later with deep pleasure.

The Geisha had everything so delightful in Ethiopian coffees, but with more elegance and subtle emphasis. It was lighter, brighter, and fruitier. More refined. Effusive, but gently so: it teased rather than gave a straight-up smack of flavors. Beside four of Latin America's most elite other coffees, all top scorers at cuppings and winners of major competitions, it had a particular airiness to it, a spring.

"Geisha is here," Sans said, holding his palm flat out at chest level. He lowered his hand slightly. "And Yirgacheffe here." Ethiopia's Yirgacheffe is made from a collection of heirloom varieties. "Because it's a mix," he said. "Not exactly the same, but it has elements."

Geisha's flavors continued to evolve as it cooled to lukewarm, with notes of rose petals and tangerines concentrating until tangerine became the single dominant flavor. It was uncanny and mysterious, even spooky, to have a coffee taste so overwhelming of the sweet citruses just beginning to arrive in Barcelona's food markets.

The success of Geisha led to a rush of growing it elsewhere around Panama, then Latin America, and soon beyond. Costa Rica, Guatemala, Colombia,

Brazil, Tanzania, and even Ethiopia are among the dozen or so countries that have now planted the variety. A number of top American and European roasters are making their first forays into coffee farming and are planting hillsides with a single variety, Geisha.

Results have been deeply mixed. The impact of terroir is strong, with the environment heavily informing the final quality: the composition of the soil and nutrients, temperature, rainfall, and elevation, the directional aspect of the slope.

Geishas from Colombia's Valle del Cauca were the highest-scoring coffees in the SCAA's 2011 and 2012 Coffee of the Year competitions. But this was an exception. The finest continue to largely come from high Panamanian slopes around Boquete. *Coffee Review*'s number one coffee of 2015 was a Geisha from Finca La Mula, a recently established farm owned by Boot, one of the judges of the variety's maiden auction. At the 2016 World Brewers Cup, three finalists, including the winner, used Panamanian Geishas.

Elsewhere they can elicit blahs. "There are a lot of mediocre Geishas," said Sans, a past Best of Panama judge, "even those from the lower slopes around Boquete."

While acknowledging that microclimates vary from valley to valley, the cutoff for planting Geisha on Hacienda La Esmeralda is fourteen hundred meters (forty-six hundred feet). "That is the very minimum altitude I would plant Geisha and expect it to start showing character," said Daniel Peterson. He credits elevation for the elegant expressiveness in Geisha on his hacienda. "Same as other Arabicas, where good attributes seem to pronounce themselves as you go higher and cooler—higher acidity, more aromatics." The cool nights slow down the maturation of the cherries and stimulate the complexity of aroma- and flavor-producing oils in the beans. But growing too high has risks: UV radiation can burn the leaves, wind and cold can cause certain plant diseases, and frost will kill the trees.

The variety's success has also set off a hunt for another Geisha in Ethiopia's southwestern cloud forests. Third-wave producers are scrambling to find the next princely varietal, a yet-to-be-discovered coffee that will be even more dramatic in the cup. Some have taken to mounting expeditions into the montane rain forests to collect seeds.

Such surreptitious forays are risky—Ethiopia levies heavy punishment on those trying to spirit out coffee germplasm—but also futile. That's not because sublime and unknown varieties don't exist in the forest—certainly many do—but because any search needs to be widespread, systematic, and patient, knowing that it will take decades of careful evaluation before tasting any conclusive results.

The appearance of Geisha in coffee cups was both random and accidental and took seventy-five years to be noticed. From the beginning, the variety had been planted for its disease resistance and never its flavor, even in the decisive final move to a high valley on Hacienda La Esmeralda. The Panamanian Geisha came from numerous generations of trees grown in various research stations before it reached Boquete. Along the meandering route to the Petersons' farm, the chances of its not being mixed, mislabeled, or cross-pollinated were slim. For Sans, the variety is specifically Panamanian Geisha, rather than simply Geisha.

The original seeds were imported from the Geisha Forest in southwest Ethiopia in 1931,[29] though who gathered the coffee is unknown. Clearly something in that first collection showed enough promise for the director of agricultural in Kenya to specifically request ten pounds of seeds from the same isolated region.

Prospectors for Ethiopia's black gold tend to focus on the area around Geisha. However, three villages in the area have a name that might phonetically match, including Gecha near Meji (rather than Geisha near Maji). Perhaps the original seeds came from a regional weekly market dozens of miles away. "Firstly the Geisha cultivar, and in particular the Lyamungu breeding program selection VC: 496 which has been used so extensively in the Lyamungu breeding program, reputedly originated either on Geisha mountain or possibly in the Maji market," wrote L. M. Fernie,[30] who worked in that program and had also accompanied the FAO mission to Ethiopia in the 1960s.

While Geisha's provenance is highly questionable, so is even its status as a single variety. Blore, writing later about hybrid work with the Lyamungu Geisha (VC: 496) in Kenya, made a curious comment: "Now Geisha is not a variety in the sense that it is a genetic entity; there is much variation in trees which are called Geisha and all that they have in common is that they came originally from near Geisha Mountain in Ethiopia."[31]

"There are so many gaps," admitted Labouisse of Geisha's journey.

The search continues, though, in the coffee forests around Kafa. But the time frame to discover that elusive new coffee is limited. Wild Arabica might not be around for much longer.

CHAPTER 16

A Matter of Degrees

A aron Davis at Kew Gardens came to public prominence in 2012 when he published a study that used computer modeling to understand climate change and its effects on wild Arabica in Ethiopia. The results forecasted that the number of possible locations where it could grow by 2080 could decrease by 65 percent. That was the best-cast scenario. The worst case was 99.7 percent reduction. Of the populations of wild coffee trees themselves, the modeling predicted between a 40 and 99 percent decline.[1] Climate changes could lead to the extinction of wild Arabica within the next sixty-five years.[2]

Since the 1960s, the mean annual temperature in Ethiopia has risen 1.3°C, an average increase of 0.28°C per decade,[3] and .30°C in the southwest. The increase is accelerating. "But it has been accelerating for a long time," Davis said.

The southwestern highland forests offer a relatively cool and stable climate for the coffee trees. The optimal mean annual temperature for Arabica is 18° to 22°C (roughly 64° to 72°F). As the temperature increases, the development and ripening of the coffee fruit quickens, with a loss of quality. The beans cannot accumulate the correct blend of chemical compounds that give coffee its unique flavors. As the temperature climbs, yields begin to break down, and soon the plant's survival is at risk. "Move up a degree, you affect taste," Davis told a 2013 SCAA symposium in Boston. "Move up two degrees, you affect production. Three degrees, mortality: your plants are dead."[4]

In London he pulled back from such a straightforward formula, acknowledging slight regional deviations from certain physical factors.

Ethiopia's topography is varied, and the shifting seasonality of the rainfall plays a large role, he said, making predictions complicated. Still, Arabica is a remarkably sensitive plant and can survive only in a thin strand of environmental conditions.

Wild-coffee collectors around Kafa have already noticed changes in the climate. The weather is more extreme and more erratic, and less predictable than it has been for generations. It's warmer and wetter, Woldegiorgis Shawo said in Mankira, standing on the heavily canopied slope deep in the forest where his family has been gathering coffee for generations. Ripe cherries knocked down during the previous evenings' heavy showers were scattered across the ground. Such rain wasn't normal during harvesttime, he said. The coffee is ripening later, and drying the cherries on raised beds beside his home is more difficult with the rain. "They get moldy," he said, and are spending too much time under an orange plastic tarp as showers pass. In the Saturday Bonga market, coffee pods being sold had a musty smell and even splotches of whitish mold.

Davis drew a bell curve showing the traditional rainfall pattern in Kafa, carefully filling in the months and numbers on the sides of the graph. "You have the same rain over the year, but it's falling in a very short period. So your dry season is extended," he said. "The dry season is getting longer, the wet season is getting shorter."

Over the curve he drew a second one showing the current rainfall pattern, which arched both higher and narrower. "People say, 'It's getting wetter, the temperature is fine.' But it's getting wetter here," he said, crosshatching in the gap between the high points of the two curves. "All that rainfall comes in the wet season when you've already got enough rain." The problem is during the shoulder seasons, he said, shading in the gaps where adequate rain was no longer falling.

In the Ufa Forest south of Bonga, a community leader named Kero Misho said, "We should be harvesting now." It was the penultimate day of October. He walked among dozens of coffee trees to gather a scant handful of nearly ripe berries more scarlet or candy-apple red than crimson. Ufa's harvest was weeks later than usual. The onset of the main rains has shifted. The same happened the previous year. "Climate change," he said with a shrug, a gesture that could be interpreted either as not being fully certain of the reason, or as meek acceptance of it.

• • •

The situation is even more dire for the only population of wild Arabica outside Ethiopia, the coffee growing on the Boma Plateau some forty miles across the border in South Sudan.

In 1938, the botanical adviser to the Anglo-Egyptian Sudan government found wild coffee on the forested patches of the plateau, the highest part of a ridge of hills that run for about a hundred miles above the Blue Nile floodplain. (On a clear day, Geisha Mountain is visible from Boma.) He returned with the British botanist A. S. Thomas in 1941 to document and gather samples. The harvesting season was winding down, and most of the coffee had already been collected. Thomas took as much fruit as he could, prepared the seeds, and managed to get them to coffee research stations in Tanzania, Uganda, and Kenya.[5] One of the varieties, named Rume Sudan, has been extensively used over the decades in breeding for its quality. (Being a low yielder, it is rarely grown as a pure strain.)

In April 2012, World Coffee Research organized a return expedition to the Boma Plateau. Led by its executive director, Tim Schilling, the group numbered a dozen or so and included Davis. They flew first to Juba, capital of freshly independent South Sudan, where they chartered a small plane to drop them in the remote Lower Boma. Not given permission to camp on the plateau itself—those living in the forest were somewhat hostile to their presence—they had to make a difficult three- to four-hour hike each day to reach it.

They located some wild Arabica, but the populations were far fewer and far less remarkable than Thomas had observed. "We were kinda blown away in Boma," Schilling said. "We had Thomas's writings going in there, and when we got in there, we were going, 'Jesus Christ, this is completely different!'" In his journal Thomas had noted the presence of numerous Arabica trees with seven-inch trunks. "We were looking for all these old coffee trees and we didn't find any of them." Thomas had also recorded incredible diversity among the Arabica, in the ages of trees, in their coloring and sizes of leaves. The group found nothing of the sort.

"I wasn't a hundred percent sure where some of the localities [Thomas mentioned] were," Davis said of the forest's dramatic changes. Some was from climate—locals told them that the big canopy trees began dying in the 1980s—and some man-made. Moving aside the crispy, dry leaves with his boot, Davis found bits of charcoal. Each year locals burn the fields to get rid of the long grasses and generate tender shoots that make better grazing fodder. These fires eat away at the forests.

Traveling during the flowering—not fruiting—season, the WCR expedition wasn't able to collect any seeds. Instead, they drove stakes, took GPS readings, and marked trees. "We know where the plants are," Schilling said. "The hard work was finding them." The plan was to go back when the trees had fruit. WCR is keen to get material for its breeding program. Boma sits 500 or 600 meters on average lower than Kafa, and with a maximum elevation of 1,600 meters (5,250 feet). "Given the climate degradation over the past hundred years, surviving plants could possess desirable climate-resiliency traits," Schilling said.*

Five years on, though, they have still not been able to return. Not long after their trip, a South Sudanese rebel group took over the strategically important plateau. Insecurity has rendered the area far too dangerous for a coffee-collecting expedition.

"We can't just sit around for years and years and years waiting," said Schilling. His impatience to salvage some of the germplasm was palpable, even if his wording belied the more urgent reality. *Years and years and years* generally indicates decades. But modeling done by Davis and his team at Kew shows a 99 percent probability that wild Arabica will be extinct on the Boma Plateau from the effects of climate change by 2020, just a few years away.[6] Between the climate and deforestation, the forest itself won't last much longer. "It won't be there in twenty years," Davis said.

Davis was surprised by the kind of attention that the 2012 study on wild coffee received. It is rare for a scientific paper to be reported in mainstream media and even rarer to trend on Twitter. A number of respected news outlets, though, widely misread it. "Coffee Beans in Danger of Extinction," ran a Canadian Broadcasting Corporation headline. "Climate change could kill off prized Arabica plants by 2080," it warned, missing the distinction between wild and cultivated. "Rising global temperatures and subtle changes in seasonal conditions could make 99.7 percent of Arabica-growing areas unsuitable for the plant by 2080, according to a new study by researchers from Kew Gardens," the *Telegraph* reported. The *Daily Mail's* headline went a (mis)step further: "How Caffeine Could Become a Has-Been."

Such misreading contained some truth, as climate change is equally implicating cultivated Arabica. Latin America, which produces nearly seven

---

* On this, Davis disagrees. He has seen no sign of any climate-resilient Arabica in Ethiopia, where there is wild coffee growing at similar low elevations, or in Boma.

eighths of the world's Arabica, has deeply felt climate change's effects in the spread and aggressiveness of coffee leaf rust, significantly dragging down production and quality. In Central America, coffee exports fell in 2016 for the third consecutive year to their lowest level since 1974.[7] Even lower numbers are almost certainly ahead.

A 2° to 2.5°C increase in temperature would significantly trim the amount of suitable land for growing coffee across the world, perhaps halving it by 2050, according to a report by the Intergovernmental Panel on Climate Change.[8] In Brazil, which produces half of the world's Arabica and a third of its total coffee, a rise of 3°C would cut areas adequate for coffee production in the principal growing states of Minas Gerais and São Paulo by a staggering two thirds and extinguish it elsewhere.[9] Even forgoing flavor and massively replacing Arabica with sturdier Robusta is not a viable solution for Brazil. While Robusta can better withstand heat and diseases, it requires more water than Arabica—water that will not be available, as aridification will stalk the country in the years ahead.

So dire are climate predictions for Brazil's substantial coffee industry that some experts have begun suggesting, in private at least, that the country should consider switching from farming *café* to other, less drought-sensitive crops. Paradoxically, surging demand means that by 2030 coffee production will have to increase by a third, or precisely the amount that Brazil is currently producing.[10] Rather than decreasing production, coffee's global titan will be pushed to increase it.

While all of the major producing countries would maintain at least some suitable regions for growing Arabica in the predicted climate-change models, only a handful with extensive high-elevation areas that receive sufficient rainfall—Colombia, Guatemala, Mexico, Indonesia, Ethiopia— could temper the overall impact by shifting coffee production upward. "An important proviso is that the areas at higher elevation are available for conversion to coffee farms, are accessible, have suitable soil conditions, and whose current or future inhabitants are willing to grow Arabica coffee rather than other crops," the first major global climate report on Arabica recently stated. These conditions, it acknowledged with scientific understatement, "may not all come together, with the consequence that Arabica coffee production may locally decline."[11]

Even in countries that do have higher areas, shifting production upward is not an option for most smallholders, who make up the majority of the globe's coffee growers: they can't simply move their fields uphill. Besides, the hills will soon run out.

"So," Benoît Bertrand said, "we have to invent a new system of production." He calls it Agro-Forestry System, or AFS.

Agro-Forestry System is a style of farming coffee under a luxurious canopy of shade trees. It's far more similar to how coffee grows wild in Ethiopian forests than it does on highly mechanized Latin American fincas. "We are fighting against the consequences of the green revolution," Bertrand said: soil depletion, excessive use of water, too much fertilizer. "Today we have to introduce a different way to farm." One of the foremost coffee geneticists and perhaps its leading breeder, he calls it a double green revolution.

On the dry-erase board hanging on his office wall, he wrote Arabica's three biggest threats: rust, temperature, and drought. "We can decrease rust, we can decrease temperature, and we can defer the effects of drought with Agro-Forestry System," he said. "But the problem with Agro-Forestry System is you decrease your productivity and your profitability, more or less twenty to thirty percent." Farmers, he acknowledged, will not accept being told to change to a style of farming that significantly slashes their revenue without being compensated for the loss. Farmers, he suggested with skepticism, could be paid a subsidy for protecting the environment and increasing biodiversity. "But"—he paused—"today there is no good price for environmental services. Nobody is ready to pay for that. So my opinion is that we have to change quickly and seek a *profitable* Agro-Forestry System."

At the heart of AFS are the so-called F1 hybrids. (F1 denotes a first filial generation.) "The F1s are good for that because they are producing forty percent more than traditional shade-grown varieties," Bertrand said. These are made by crossing what he calls "American varieties"—such as Caturra and Catuai, which have been bred over the years in the Americas for full-sun-style farming—with wild Ethiopian. The American parent gives yield while the Ethiopian one, which grows naturally under deep forest cover, offers adaptability to the heavily shaded growing style.

Such disparate parentage also gives the offspring hybrid vigor, a concept, Bertrand said, that has two definitions: "when the hybrid is better than *either* of the two parents, or when the hybrid is better than the *best* of the two parents." His F1 work has aimed for the latter. "When you cross an American variety that's very well adapted toward a full-sun system with an Ethiopian, we have a hybrid that is better than the American variety in the full-sun system, and better than the Ethiopian one in the shade system."

In plant breeding, the greater the genetic distance between the parents, the greater the hybrid vigor. "You define these in terms of vigor, but [with coffee] more in terms of productivity or yielding. Quality is another thing. In terms of quality," Bertrand said, "some effects are not so easy to understand." By that he meant what gives the best flavors to the cup. Yet, when asked about choosing the wild Ethiopia parent, he had initially said, "Why? Because this gives you good flavor."

The F1s are building upon decades of work that began in the 1990s while Bertrand was a breeder at CATIE in Costa Rica. The latest phase has the support of WCR, which is helping to create a seed industry. Coffee has no behemoth global agribusiness such as Monsanto, Syngenta, or DuPont, and many national coffee institutes have become largely seed suppliers and marketing bodies. Out of around fifty coffee-producing countries today, only Brazil and Colombia have robust breeding programs actively developing new varieties rather than selecting and choosing from work done decades before. "The other countries that have research facilities don't have any money and really haven't had money since the 1950s," said Schilling, WCR's head. "The only two countries that really have decent research facilities are Brazil and Colombia, and those two countries are all about Brazil and Colombia and not about the rest of the world."

"So," said Bertrand, "WCR has to replace for the disappearance of national institutions that in the past were able—more or less—to produce varieties. As those institutes have disappeared the WCR appeared as a solution."

One key element to the F1s is that they are completely uniform first-generation progeny, a departure from standard breeding methods that generally require five generations until a new variety is ready. This means getting a plant to a farmer in a handful of years rather than twenty-five.

"That's the main reason we are putting our money on the F1 hybrid approach," said Schilling. "It just allows us to produce things in a more accelerated fashion and respond to more direct effects of climate or environment or disease." Speed and flexibility are keys to dealing with the rapidly changing climate, and to whatever surprises from it lie ahead. The traditional decades' lag time is simply no longer realistic. "We are able to be nimble, we're able to jump, to do something," he said. "We could produce a variety, you know, if we had to, in five years. In twenty years, in this kind of environment, we're going to be screwed."

Schilling, himself a breeder, said, "When we see something is probably pretty good, then we can immediately go in and do microcuttings and scale it up to a much-higher level to thousands of plants to test." The scaling up happens in laboratories using single-cell cultures.*

The cutting-edge method uses somatic embryogenesis, an in vitro culture technique that makes it possible to regenerate vast numbers of plantlets using just a fragment of the mother plant. However, this technology remains expensive. To address this issue, CIRAD developed an efficient horticultural technique to multiply *ex vitro* plantlets that have been previously regenerated by somatic embryogenesis, Bertrand explained. The method is called rooted mini-cuttings, and it can yield thirty to forty hybrid plants per year from one somatic-embryogenesis-derived plantlet, drastically reducing production costs to less than thirty cents per Arabica plant ready for planting out in the field.

The impact of the F1s has thus far been limited. By 2016, some fifty lines had been created; only three had been released to growers. Even though one million plantlets were produced last year, a seemingly large amount, Bertrand's back-of-the-envelope estimate of the need of the seed market is eighty million a year.

Other elements in AFS beyond the coffee plants themselves can help growers compensate for their loss of yield, including using varieties of shade trees that can be harvested, earning an estate income from the timber. A farm could bring up the value of its harvest by offering different styles of coffee—along with standard washed coffees, say, also using a natural, sun-dried method or "honey processed," where the skin and pulp are removed but not all of the sweet mucilage—and by improving postharvest processing techniques. "Because we know that the quality of a coffee depends on the variety and on the system of producing it," Bertrand said, "but it also depends on the postharvest—if you do some fermentation or not, if you dry the coffee in the shade or not, et cetera, et cetera."

The success of AFS hinges on profitability. The loss in production a farmer faces has to be recuperated to make the shift to growing coffee under heavy shade viable. Bertrand sees AFS as the only course ahead. "F1 hybrids are the best way in the future to adapt to climate change, to fight against rust, and to conserve the quality of coffee, and to avoid that coffee disappears in Central America—but not only Central America but also East

---

* "We are doing cloning because," said Bertrand, unlike maize "it is very difficult to create seeds from coffee." Hand-pollinating a coffee flower yields a pair, while doing the same to an ear of maize can give eight hundred kernels. Kraft, "Coffee Hybrids and a Frank Talk About Breeding Coffee."

Africa and in other countries." Drawing circles on the board around *rust*, *temperature*, and *drought*, he said, "AFS is the only option we have today to fight, in ten years or in fifteen years or in thirty years, against these."

Rust might be combated with heavy does of chemicals and hybrid varieties based on Híbrido de Timor—at least for now, until the fungus overcomes their R-genes. "But you have climate change," Bertrand said. "Climate change is inevitable."

While climate change doesn't mean an immediate end to a morning cup of joe or to multiple daily trips to Starbucks, it will make finding pure Arabica more difficult, and likely more expensive. Robusta and Timor hybrids, with their coarser flavors, are already becoming more prevalent and used in increasingly greater percentages in supermarket blends. Colombia, a country once synonymous with 100 percent traditional Arabica, is a prime example of the growing reliance on hybrids, which now account for at least 40 percent of its plantings.[12]

Just a handful of years ago few would have noticed. No longer. Coffee has gone from being a simple hot, black, and caffeinated drink to a daily delicacy. The specialty and gourmet coffee market is the industry's fastest-growing sector.

Yet climatic repercussions for coffee go beyond the less refined taste in the cup or even a price increase of a Starbucks run. Most of the world's coffee is grown by smallholders with less than a hectare of land.[13] Coffee is the livelihood of twenty-five million farming families across the globe, involving well over one hundred million people.

And those are only the producers. Coffee's true global importance can be understood only by following the entire chain, from exporters, shippers, and roasters to coffee shops and supermarkets, and even to researchers such as Davis.

No place is more reliant on its coffee than Ethiopia. It is the backbone of the economy, with four million smallholder coffee farms.[14] A quarter of the population—nearly twenty-five million people—depend directly or indirectly on coffee for their livelihood.[15] In Kafa, that number is around 85 percent, said Mesfin Tekle. "Those who are not collecting or growing coffee are buying or selling it."

After Davis published his 2012 study, he and his team of specialists shifted their focus from wild to cultivated coffee and embarked on a highly ambitious project called Building a Climate Resilient Coffee Economy for

Ethiopia. They returned a dozen times over the next three years, logging nearly twenty thousand miles on some of the country's roughest roads to install mini-climate stations with data logs, to download information from them, and to talk to coffee farmers to gather anecdotal information. "To know what *will* happen [with the climate], you have to know what is happening *now*," Davis said. He couldn't rely on old data, or even just data. Being on the ground was fundamental to the project.

In a good year, Ethiopian farmers can just about survive from coffee. Yet by the standards of even the poorest coffee farmers in Latin America, they live in deep poverty: most have no running water, no electricity, and extremely limited access to even the most basic health care, and they frequently face food shortages. The lucky have a mule or donkey; a vehicle is all but unthinkable. The average Ethiopian earns less than two dollars a day, while a single gallon of petrol costs twice that, and a vehicle sells for double what it does in the West.

"How does a family of five," Davis said, "have the ability to make an investment in their farm or their crop?" Particularly, he stressed, "if that return on the investment is so uncertain." With climate change, success in farming is no longer simply a matter of hard work, and the outcome of any investment is uncertain. "That guy could lose everything."

"The climate is my biggest challenge," said Woldegiorgis in Mankira. ("Then baboons! They eat the ripe cherries!") Even for him, considered well-off by standards in his area, the line between survival and abject poverty is thin.

Using an enormously complex series of modeling—two thousand simulations using six modeling techniques spread across four different time frames and four different climate-change scenarios—Davis's group pinpointed land suitable for growing coffee in Ethiopia until 2099 to within thirty meters on a highly detailed "coffee atlas," information that will help farmers make better decisions. "It gives a dozen concrete recommendations for policy makers on what needs to be done, what *can* be done. But the potential is enormous. *If* you start making the right decisions and managing it properly. The main thread is that, actually, you *can* adapt if you do the right things. It's not going to be easy"—he gave the word a lilt for emphasis—"but the potential is massive." Pausing a half beat, he added, "In Ethiopia."

That isn't the case for every country, and it isn't even the case for all of Ethiopia. While areas in the southwest show good potential, those east of the Rift Valley—Bale Mountain, Arsi, anywhere around Harar—have already become unsuitable for coffee production and will soon be rendered impossible.

The future of cultivated coffee in Ethiopia will come down to good government and good agroforestry, Davis maintained. "You'd have to reestablish forests, you'd have to conserve forests, good land management . . ." Steps, he said, were already being taken by authorities.

Just as the potential is enormous if the right course is taken, so are the consequences if they are not. On its own, Davis insisted, "Arabica does not have enough to overcome climate change. There's diversity there, but there's not enough diversity to overcome climate change."

Before entering the Kombo Forest, Mesfin called out a greeting to a guard sitting on a low hill across the road at the base of an isolated telecommunication tower. "A lion is passing through the forest," the man yelled back. A lion was not a rare sighting in this spot. The previous year Mesfin had come upon one eating a horse. "Take care!" the guard added as Mesfin set off down the slim animal trail into the woods. He made his way cautiously, bending at the waist looking for tracks and inhaling for any scents. Immediately he caught the strong glandular smell of the lion.

It was a late weekend morning and Mesfin wore a white dress shirt, blue slacks, and Sunday loafers. He grew up at the edge of Bonga and is particularly at ease in the woods. "I spent much of my childhood in the forest," he said, "foraging for food, playing, hiding." Ducking under dangling lianas and scrappy coffee branches, and wheeling around thorny plants, he walked deeper inside the forest, moving with a silent, feline grace.

Twice he had moved away from Bonga, first to study agricultural engineering at the highly regarded Haramaya University near Harar, and then later to Europe, with a grant to do a master's degree in forestry from the University of Reading, Britain's leading institution in the field. Mostly he has remained in Kafa, focused on the local forests and their conservation as the head of agriculture for the regional government, and then with a variety of NGOs, including Farm Africa, the FAO, and the German development agency GIZ (now GTZ).

Mesfin has read the studies on climate change. He knows the statistics and predictions and had even taken Davis into the forest looking at its local effects. Mesfin has personally witnessed the changes in Kafa's forests that he knows so intimately. Yet, he insisted, this didn't mean that all of the coffee would disappear. He had stopped at a slight clearing where, some years before, a tall tree had fallen, creating an opening of light. Coffee trees and seedlings shot up all around. His sentences came in a steady, soft patter in the eerily still forest. No monkeys, nor even birds, moved. The lion was still nearby.

He touched the branch of a stout coffee tree encased in moss and inch-long tree ferns. "It adapted," he said of the tree. "It also competed, and it succeeded to continue as a living plant." It was not the only seed that fell here, he said. Many had. He had made this point on different forest walks. The tree was here because it—not another—had survived. "This is survival of the fittest. This one seed survived, irrespective of all the unfavorable conditions, all the suppressions, all the competition."

A bird began to hoot, deep and repetitive, and then Mesfin caught a slight movement up in a heavily buttressed fig tree. "A monkey. There are so many monkeys here. One of my worries is that if there are no monkeys, that means that there is something around here," he said, referring to the lion. A black-and-white colobus moved tentatively along a high branch. "If there are monkeys, then we are safe."

This forest has changed over the last decades and centuries, he said. Previous generations of trees have adapted, but adapted differently—to different challenges. "We relate only to the last fifty or hundred years. Recent. We don't know what was happening two thousand years ago," he said. "There was a change. Even though it wasn't as abrupt as what we feel. There was a change in this natural state. That change was adapted to by the coffee trees that are still existing here. This is the second, fourth, fifteenth, twentieth, fiftieth generation of coffee."

Eventually Mesfin turned and began walking back out of the forest that was, because of the lion, cautiously reawakening. Birds flitted around the branches, offering a growing cacophony of chirps and calls. "For me, I think nature does have the power of accumulation. It's not like us." He had stopped on the trail. A troop of vervets clamored above. "When we are hot, we go to the cold shower, and when cold, to a warm one. The plants have the responsibility of taking the change and accepting or adapting."

Later, back in Bonga, he said, "There will be some trees which adapt. And with coffee because of the variability—there is a wide genetic variability of coffee—if there is a variability, there is a hope also, for some of which are resistant for the characteristics they have." In Komba, Mankira, Boginda, or any of the other southwestern coffee forests, the richness of diversity is immediately evident.

Davis had made a similar point in his SCAA symposium talk: "If you look at the genetic data . . . the diversity [of Arabica] in those forests is enormous, absolutely enormous. Each forest area has its own distinct range of genetic variations. But also there's good evidence to show that those populations have mixed, there's been some gene exchange among populations. The other key thing is there are lots of seedlings, and those seedlings supply standing genetic variation, and that standing variation enables adaptation, and that is very important."[16]

In London, asked if wild Arabica has the ability to adapt fast enough, before climate changes overwhelm it, Davis responded, "Well, it has its limits. Because you have physiological, biochemical limits within the species. I think there's probably a certain amount of adaptivity, a certain amount of natural migrating, but . . ." He trailed off, hesitating to push the idea any further.

Trees don't move, but they can migrate by spreading their seeds, in this case higher up a slope, effectively shifting upward to more favorable conditions. "They will [migrate]," Davis finally said, "if they're left alone, or if there is enough thick forest. If there's forest, yeah, they'll move into the forest. But if there's no forest, then you have to wait for that forest to be established before the coffee can enter it. Coffee is not a pioneer species. It's not going to sit out there in the open and wait for the forest to catch up." Birds and wild animals will also carry the seeds into new forests and higher valleys.

For Mesfin, wild coffee, with such a diversity of seeds in the forests, could not possibly disappear. "The natural forest has old plants, young plants. You can see all the successions. If one dies, others will adapt." Seedlings were sprouting up beneath moss-covered trees. Coffee plants of every age were growing. Tender shoots, their leaves as supple as baby salad greens, poked through the loamy floor. "Because it adapted. Because of variability." Mesfin had shown Davis coffee still growing in places where the forest had become extremely dry. "I think [wild Arabica] can continue. The forest has adapted. And it is still adapting."

In Kombo, Mesfin underscored his confidence in the forest's ability to adjust. "We don't know the time of adaptation of nature. It is difficult to observe—because we are still feeling that change. You don't know what level of change is there. It will not happen all at once."

"It's subtle," Davis said of climate change. "It's not about decades, it's about generations."

The other great threat to Ethiopia's coffee forests, though, is less subtle, and not about generations, or even decades. It is about years.

CHAPTER 17

In Situ

The Gumi River curves around the bottom of the Mankira Forest, marking its western boundary and cutting off the route to Bonga. For nearly half the year, rains swell the river and isolate its inhabitants. During the short dryish season, the water can still be treacherous, rising rapidly after a storm and being subject to flash floods. Every year it sweeps people, even whole families, to their death as they attempt to wade across. Using a horse or mule is an option for some, but a dozen animals drown each year when they stumble on the rocky bottom and get pulled down by the swift current.

Some fifteen years ago, Ethiopia's most powerful entrepreneur offered to build a bridge across the river. It was a welcome proposal. There was, of course, a catch.

"Al Amoudi came looking for a forest to plant coffee," a Kafa resident recalled, referring to the Ethiopian-born Saudi billionaire Sheikh Mohammed Al Amoudi, one of the world's richest individuals* and the country's largest investor, with dozens of companies in Ethiopia. In return for the bridge, Mankira's forest would be converted into a coffee estate. The fertile, virgin soil, ideal Arabica growing conditions, and the cachet of a name so closely associated with the origins of coffee formed an incomparable trifecta that could create perhaps Ethiopia's most spectacular coffee farm.

"It sounded very tempting," the head of Mankira's coffee cooperative told the German magazine *GEO*, "but just as fish cannot live out of water,

---

* Al Amoudi is the second-richest Saudi on the *Forbes* list. Falling oil prices dropped him from number 61 on the 2014 global rankings to 138 in 2016.

we cannot live without the forest."[1] Wild coffee harvested in the 2,250-acre forest is the community's main source of income.

A group from Mankira approached the Kafa Forest Coffee Farmers' Cooperative Union in Bonga for help. Mankira is one of more than forty cooperatives under the umbrella of the ten-thousand-member organization. The Mankira group wanted to put into place the type of Participatory Forest Management (PFM) agreement that had recently been established in a few other places in Kafa.

The land in Ethiopia is owned by the government, and the legally binding PFM agreement transfers the right to manage and exploit the forest's renewable resources to a community-managed group. With rights come responsibilities. The contract would allow residents of Mankira to collect wild coffee but also force them to conserve the forest where it grows. This would be a ground-up approach to managing the land around them. While Kafa's governmental forestry services would monitor the woodland's condition and offer support, technical advice, and legal backing, the local community itself would be responsible for policing, conservation, and responsible use.

"If we cut the forests we will lose everything they provide," said Frehiwet Getahun, the general manager of the cooperative union. While wild coffee is the most important product from Kafa's forests, it isn't the only one at stake. "Also spices like cardamom and long pepper,* honey, bamboo, medicinal plants." He spread his hands. "If we will lose the forests, we will lose everything."

Mankira eventually signed a PFM agreement, thwarting any outside development of their forest.

Beyond the communities that depend on the coffee forests for their livelihoods, their disappearance also deeply concerns the greater coffee industry. A key to improving Arabica's flavors, yield, and resistance to certain diseases and climatic changes resides in the largely untapped gene pools growing wild. The threat of their loss haunts agronomists and breeders and motivates conservation efforts.

As coffee seeds do not store well, they have been largely conserved in ex situ field collections. New techniques such as cryopreservation, DNA, and storing coffee pollen under vacuum at ultralow temperatures are

---

* While hotter than black pepper, *Piper capense* has an earthiness to it, even a touch of sweetness, and is a favorite in local spice blends. The plant grows in the deep shade of Kafa's forests.

improving but still have significant limitations for widespread use. One way to safeguard coffee's genetic resources is in situ—in its original place.

When Mankira sought to halt the development of its forest, the concept of conserving genetic resources in their own natural environment had only been broached. In 1998, the Coffee Improvement Project floated the idea to create three gene reserves in the southwest,[2] much in the manner of a national park that protects certain endangered animal species. The sites were selected, but the program stalled, largely due to lack of funding.[3] Money, though, wasn't the only reason, according to Mesfin Tekle. "It excluded communities," he said of the plan. "It didn't interact with people. Because of that it failed."

While largely overlooked, in situ conservation is a vital long-term strategy. It isn't an alternative to ex situ—which offers better accessibility and documentation; evaluating plants for potentially useful characteristics is easier in a field gene bank than deep in the forest—but is complementary to it.

In situ conservation, though, requires maintaining coffee forests in their natural state.

Ethiopia was once heavily forested, with perhaps 40 percent of the country covered in the sixteenth century.[4] By the end of the nineteenth century the percentage was around 30. In the early 1950s, high forests still covered 16 percent of it.[5] Now it's under 4 percent forested.

"Already seven-eighths of the forest cover of Ethiopia has vanished," observed Frederick Meyer in the mid-1960s on the FAO's coffee-collecting mission to Ethiopia, "leaving only a fragment in the southern and south-western provinces still in semi-pristine condition."[6] Kafa contains some of the last patches, though even these are rapidly disappearing, too.

Over the last fifteen years, growth rates in Ethiopia have been among the highest in the world.* The exploding population, currently around one hundred million, has put an enormous strain on the land. More than 80 percent of Ethiopians are considered rural. (In the Kafa Zone it's 88 percent.)[7] With most of the population engaged in subsistence farming, the reliance on agriculture, grazing (reputedly the largest livestock population in Africa), and forest resources is intense. Wood and charcoal are

---

* The population has increased 46 percent since 2000, and 83 percent since 1990. *FAO Statistical Pocketbook, 2015.*

the main sources of household fuel, even in Addis Ababa. In the morning, a haze of blue cooking smoke floats over the capital. From the higher hills of the city it is a lovely but discouraging sight, testimony of the woodlands being slowly eaten away.

Since Meyer's visit fifty years ago, deforestation in the southwest has been severe. Plundered by charcoal burners and loggers and cleared by farmers for crops and grazing, the forests have been reduced to a fraction of what they were just a generation or two ago. "Preservation of forest loss is a key issue, especially in the South West and South East coffee zones where recent deforestation rates are high," reported Aaron Davis's 2016 paper, "and could have a more significant impact than climate change at least in the short to medium term."[8]

From 1973 to 1987, when the southwest's forest cover was shrinking significantly, a quarter of the loss came from its conversion to modern coffee plantations. Ethiopia's three largest are a couple of hours west of Bonga. Bebeka Coffee Plantation and Limu Coffee Farm were established in 1975 and remained state property until November 2013, when Horizon Plantations, one of the many companies under Al Amoudi's MIDROC conglomerate, acquired them for eighty million dollars during a wave of privatization. Limu consists of six farms with four thousand permanent workers and more than twelve thousand hectares (thirty thousand acres) of land, nearly three fourths of it planted out with Arabica. Bebeka, to its south near Mizan Teferi on the way to Geisha, is a grand, singular expanse of ten thousand hectares, more than half planted out with varieties of Arabica (including, now, Panamanian Geisha). Horizon proudly touts Bebeka as "the biggest non-fragmented coffee plantation in the world."[9] Thirty miles north of it is the ten-thousand-hectare Tepi Coffee Plantation.

Ethiopia has begun an aggressive push to significantly bolster its coffee output. Planting has shot up from 250,000 hectares in 2000 to 520,000 hectares in 2014,[10] and production has nearly tripled since 1990. The country wants to be a coffee giant, even the next Brazil.

Some of the increase has happened in Kafa. In 2008, it produced about twenty-five million kilograms (fifty-five million pounds). "At the time," according to Kassahun Taye, the manager of Kafa's regional agriculture office in Bonga, "a political decision was taken to turn this area into a market center, and the government has been providing training to farmers on how to implement new technology in addition to providing seeds and extension services on farming practices."[11]

Training, technology, and supplying seeds are ways to buoy yields. So is something he didn't mention: vastly increasing the amount of land available to plant. In just three years, from 2012 to 2015, the amount of land cultivated with coffee in the Kafa Zone jumped 45 percent.[12]

In referring to plans on raising coffee and tea outputs, Horizon Plantations managing director, Jemal Ahmed, recently told Reuters, "Ethiopia is one of the very few countries which has opportunities to invest in virgin land."[13] He was referring to the southwestern forests.

During the twentieth century, those living in Kafa had many of their forest privileges usurped. After Menelik II's armies conquered the kingdom in 1897, the forests were largely left open for people to use. "The coffee forests, however, were taken over by the Governor of Kaffa, the Ras Wolde Giorgis," wrote Friedrich Bieber. "The right of collecting coffee was given away by him as fief to followers according to rank and status."[14] Along the edges of the forest, plantings increased, and feudal landlords paid a tribute to the emperor in coffee.[15] In Kafa, providing beans to a ruler was not a new concept.

Emperor Haile Selassie encouraged agricultural development during his feudal reign and squeezed smallholders for tax revenue. In 1974 a Soviet-backed military junta known as the Derg ("committee") overthrew Selassie and attempted one of the most radical land reforms ever seen in Africa. Its rise can be partially attributed to Selassie's denial and concealing of the 1972–73 famine in the north of the country, the government's belated response to it, and the insensitivity of much of the elite ruling classes toward those suffering. The Derg began under the shadow of an ecological catastrophe and awareness in the public of the need for better management of Ethiopia's natural resources.[16]

In Kafa, district officials had been in charge of assigning agricultural land and forest rights in return for payment.[17] The Derg stripped them of their role, and new grassroots Peasant Associations oversaw the allotment of land in a communist-inspired tenure system. Foreign plantations, farmland, and feudal-owned coffee tracts were nationalized without compensation. Proclamation 31—"Public Ownership of Rural Lands"—issued in April 1975 forbade private land ownership; the sale, lease, or transfer of land; or employing others to work it. Everyone over eighteen years of age was entitled to a parcel, with up to ten hectares allocated to support a family. "But no person may use hired labor to cultivate his holding," the proclamation stipulated.

The impact on coffee production in Ethiopia was immediate, even for wild coffee.

"Everything became illegal when it came to forest products," said Mulugeta Lemenih, head of forestry and natural resources management for Farm Africa. People around the forest couldn't go and collect coffee, cardamom, and honey. "Even getting into the forest itself was illegal. There were guards that were hired by the government." It was impossible to watch all of the forests, though, and people slipped into the woods to surreptitiously gather wild coffee when they could.

After the Derg regime fell in 1991, no effective infrastructure was in place, nor sufficient funds, to ensure protection of the woodlands.[18] The new government retreated from the role of custodian of the forest with nothing to step into its place.[19] "Everything," Mesfin said of Kafa's forests, "was so open."

Into this vacuum came Participatory Forest Management programs. Farm Africa, a nongovernmental organization (NGO) working with smallholders in East Africa, helped set one up in Bonga in 1996, the first in Ethiopia. Dozens of countries in sub-Saharan Africa, Asia, and Latin America were establishing similar schemes that offered an innovative way of putting local communities in charge. The underpinning of PFM's success is that the more a community feels invested in the land, and the stronger the sense of ownership it has, the more incentive and responsibility it will take to manage it productively. The goal is both preservation and effective utilization of the forest to maximize its renewable benefits. Implemented and often financed by a NGO, sites receive local and legal governmental support. (Ethiopia's federal government recognizes PFM agreements.)

The goal, said Mulugeta, was "to motivate local people that live in and around the forest to engage in the management of the forest. That means that they would take the responsibility to protect the forest, to also improve the productivity, but also get the rights for sustainable use. Because it's not fair to ask people to just protect it, there must be something to reward them." Mulugeta's office is in a glass high-rise in central Addis Ababa. A sleek tram passed quietly below on the new Chinese-built line that crosses the city. "It's not about giving them a fine but also an incentive that can motivate them to conserve. That is why we combine the conservation with sustainable use." In other words, more carrot than stick. "The three R's, we call it. The first one is right: right of control of the forest, right of use of the forest. The second one is revenue: generate income or revenue from the forest from sustainable use." That included coffee. "And the last is responsibility." The local people are held accountable; the forest becomes *their* responsibility.

Along with Kafa's swelling population, the interest shown in the southwestern forests by deep-pocketed investors such as Al Amoudi caused concern. Farm Africa called for partners to help expand the reach of PFM coverage. The German charity GEO Rainforest Conservation began funding PFM measures in 2001, and in 2006, the Nature and Biodiversity Conservation Union (NABU), a large, 115-year-old German environmental association, joined the effort. Around 40 percent of the country's remaining forests are currently under some form of PFM program, according to Mulugeta. Coffee forests have even more widespread coverage. "I can say most of the forests where you can really find coffee genetic resources are more or less under PFM."

By 2016, GEO alone was helping fund thirty-two different PFM sites around Kafa, totaling 24,500 hectares and some 11,813 "user" members. One of those sites is the Ufa Coffee Forest, a few hours south of Bonga. Walking down the path from the small hamlet at its edge, cutting across a field of maize and past a few tukuls hidden behind enset and coffee trees, the PFM leader Kero Misho explained that each agreement has its own bylaws. There is a blueprint, but communities include their own specific ordinances. One of Ufa's stipulates that collecting is done simultaneously as a community: none of the few hundred members can begin until it has been agreed. Kero called it "team controlling." It was a way to avoid people taking from trees from which another had the right to collect cherries.

It took about fifteen minutes to reach the first coffee trees. Kero stepped over fresh buffalo scat. Animal life was rich in Ufa. "Hyena, buffalo, pig, baboon, bushbuck," he said, naming some of the species he had recently seen in the forest. His own section was another forty-five minutes deeper into the forest. Overall, he said, Ufa's members harvest about sixty-five thousand pounds of clean green coffee annually.

The first PFM sites each took about two years to set up, but the process has since been streamlined down to four or so months. Once the parties sign the agreement, there is a ceremony, said Mesfin, past head of Farm

Africa's PFM program in Kafa, "a popularization of the management plans and the popularization of the rights." The PFM committee presents to the community what they have done. An ox is slaughtered, women roast and prepare coffee in large jebenas, and there is dancing.

"Deforestation has slowed," said Mesfin, as PFMs have become prevalent. "In the last years there has been a big improvement." Illegal cutting of timber is no longer considered taking from a rich individual or the government, but from a specific community, which has an invested interest in stopping any logging. "The cutters know that there are eyes watching them." The mobile phone is a simple but highly effective policing tool for the community. If someone spots a suspicious truck used by loggers, he or she can call others, Mesfin said. In the past there was little faith in reporting to authorities. "The PFM has given them confidence. They feel empowered."

"If PFM had not been introduced in Kafa," said Frehiwet at the cooperative union, "then many of the forests would not be here now."

In 2006, Svane Bender, head of NABU's Africa Program, visited Kafa. The PFM scheme was showing success, but she saw the possibility of taking it a step further, toward something grander that would ensure longer-term protection for Kafa's unique coffee forests. She envisioned them becoming part of UNESCO's network of biosphere reserves. Designation as a biosphere, which has some overlapping aims with PFM, would give the forest official recognition by a powerful international body. And raising Kafa's profile would bring marketing possibilities for its wild coffee and other local products as well as tourism.

Concrete work on the biosphere proposal began in July 2008 when NABU hired Mesfin to coordinate the project. With his ample experience working with a range of international, governmental, and community groups, as well as his deep knowledge of the local forests, Mesfin was the ideal candidate.

Using an office at the Kafa Forest Coffee Farmers' Cooperative Union, he swiftly took the proposal through the various phases of planning, zoning, and agreements. At the end of September 2009, it went to Ethiopia's Ministry of Science and Technology, which formally submitted it to UNESCO's Paris headquarters. The application fully met the requirements. Recognizing the significance of the shrinking forests, UNESCO designated 760,144 hectares (1.9 million acres, about 3,000 square miles) as the

Kafa Biosphere Reserve in the summer of 2010, one of the first two in Ethiopia.*

The biosphere, though, is not a solid, unbroken mass of forest but rather a patchwork of farmland, hamlets, and woodlands. Just over 55 percent of the land is densely forested; coffee forests account for a quarter of that. "The biosphere is man in the biosphere, it is not only biosphere," Mesfin said, walking through the reserve's Kombo Forest. "*Man* in the biosphere," he repeated. Some 650,000 people live within its boundaries. The reserve covers two thirds of Kafa.

The biosphere has three types of "zones," each with its own rules of use and access. "Core zones" of primeval forest form the heart of the reserve, untouchable areas that only researchers can enter. These virgin expanses total 41,391 hectares, just over 5 percent of the biosphere. Surrounding and protecting the core areas are "buffer zones," which account for about one fifth of the biosphere (161,427 hectares). Restrictions in buffer zones are looser, and locals can collect coffee and spices, hang bee hives for wax and honey, and do certain types of farming that don't harm forest cover, including tending semiforest coffee. An additional 219,441 hectares are considered "candidate core zones," areas that contain highly endangered habitats but still lack a defined conservation status. While Mesfin hopes to see these gain legal protection, for the moment they are treated as either core or buffer zones. The last category is "transition zones," which makes up the remainder of the biosphere, some 45 percent of the total (337,885 hectares). Already largely stripped of trees, transition zones consist of agricultural land with teff, maize, cultivated coffee, and, around Wush Wush, tea, and grazing areas for livestock. Transition zones are home to the bulk of the population.

The biodiversity—biological diversity, the variability of species—in the biosphere is profuse, and animal life is among the richest in Ethiopia. Lurking here are sixty species of mammals, including leopards, honey badgers, numerous primates, and spotted civet, nocturnal cats rarely spotted but rather detected by their musky odors. Hyenas are common— their eerie *WHHHHooop!* echoes from the forest at night—and lions are present but more spectral. Dark-headed forest orioles, yellow-fronted

---

* UNESCO added the Yayu Coffee Forest Biosphere Reserve the same year. Two others in Ethiopia have since joined the list. As of 2017, there were 669 biosphere reserves in 120 countries.

parrots, Abyssinian catbirds, and over two hundred other species chatter in the brush.

Nature and people interact, said Mesfin, climbing a steep, forested slope of buffer zone an hour outside Bonga. "Even the proportional amount of core compared to buffer and transition is low. From three to ten percent is allowed as core," he said, winding effortlessly up the narrow path. Over the canopy coasted a heavy hornbill. "If it is more than that, then UNESCO will argue, because it is pushing out people."

The biosphere reverts PFM's bottom-up management of the forest to a top-down structure, unhitching outright responsibility from individual communities. While there was certainly pride in the UNESCO designation, some of those living around the forest felt a shift in their sense of proprietorship, according to Mulugeta. "PFM has given the forest to the community," he said at Farm Africa's Addis office. "That was taken away from them [in the biosphere], and they are not happy about that." Some farmers complained of the stringent regulations. While around forty thousand hectares are under PFM management inside the reserve, including sixteen thousand sponsored by NABU and added after the biosphere's designation, core-zone areas remain strictly off-limits, and communities aren't allowed to enter them, even to gather wild coffee. "No. Nothing. *Nothing*," he said. "It's totally excluding many people from their life-being."

Responding to such criticism, Mesfin didn't point out that core zones are largely far from hamlets and generally quite inaccessible, or that they make up less than 5 percent of the biosphere. Instead, he focused on one of PFM's requirements. He acknowledged the importance of the program that he has long supported, but honed in on one shortcoming.

The reward for conserving a forest is the right to sustainably capitalize on it. As part of the planning, sample plots must be assessed for available resources and potential revenue. A hash of trails get cut through the forest on a hundred-meter grid, Mesfin explained in his NABU office. On a scrap of paper he drew an amoebic shape that symbolized a forest, with a small piece marked out as a hamlet. He filled the outline with a lattice of dots showing how the new trails convert once unreachable areas of forest into accessible ones. "PFM exposes the *whole* forest for use," said Mesfin, who helped set up many of the region's first PFMs. "We know we are opening the forest which has never been touched by the community." This was the compromise, the trade-off for greater overall protection.

Kafa's biosphere positions itself between a PFM and an exclusive gene reserve. It might be man in the biosphere, but the natural world also requires its own exclusive territory. "You need some space for nature to dominate the system," Mesfin said quietly: nature without man.

Variability comes from nature, not from human interference, he stressed. Selecting and breeding coffee leads toward uniformity, he said, "uniform look, uniform taste." In the wild, instead, there is variability. "For that the core zones are the central bank for future generations."

Left undisturbed in their natural habitat, Arabica will continue to evolve and adapt. "[In situ] is dynamic in the sense that it allows intimate interaction between species and biotic as well as abiotic factors thus creating conditions ideal for the evolutionary process for various traits including pest/disease resistance and general adaptation," wrote a group of the coffee industry's leading scientists from CATIE, JARC, IRD, and CIRAD.[20]

Although good resources exist ex situ, and even in garden coffee with generations of varieties taken from the forests and planted around homes, preserving the original forests of wild coffee remains critical. Those ex situ gene banks might not be as genetically diverse as thought, as the analysis of CATIE's Arabica collection demonstrated. "That in itself makes the in situ more valuable," said international coffee consultant Surendra Kotecha.

For agronomist Jean-Pierre Labouisse the importance of intact in situ areas is more basic. "We don't know what is in the forest," he said in his Montpellier office. "We don't know exactly." The shelf above a pair of computer monitors on his desk held a row of thick binders containing decades' worth of scientific articles on coffee by researchers around the globe. "We know nothing."

While that is an overstatement, much basic knowledge about wild Arabica remains to be fully understood. "We don't know exactly how coffee reproduces in the forest," said Labouisse, "or how many trees we need to have to collect to get a different genotype." The structure of the population of trees, or the relationship between them, is not clear, or even the actual rate of self-fertilization. Answers remain largely educated guesses. The work required to find out is daunting.

If some worry about missing out on those answers before the forest can give them up, then others fear the loss of potential—of flavors and aromas that are now impossible to imagine. "How many strange, delicious coffees are growing wild in Ethiopia? We will never know. Just when we're ready to appreciate the unfamiliar—this generation of tastemakers is fascinated by the peculiar, the mind-blowing—it looks like coffee's most diverse catalogue of flavours will steadily diminish, and probably disappear," Oliver Strand wrote after Davis published his Kew report.[21] While Strand was specifically referring to the fallout from climate change, it is also a fitting elegy for deforestation. The dual threats of a warming climate and the conversion of natural forest to use for crops or for grazing cattle are acting together antagonistically.[22] "The loss of tonnage will be made up elsewhere, but the loss of possibility will be absolute."[23]

For coffee's precious genetic resources, securing the vestiges of untouched forest has been crucial, and the protection now afforded to the dense woodlands that contain these irreplaceable riches with the UNESCO biosphere designation and core-zone restrictions are a lifeline for the coffee industry. Even if the greater international coffee community has not yet been able to negotiate access to them, and climate change haunts their future, the safeguarding of these spots has been an unparalleled and propitious step in conserving genetic resources.

When Mesfin called them the "central bank" for future generations, he was being metaphorical. Others see real dollar values in what the forests hold. In 2006, the year that NABU first broached the biosphere idea, two agricultural economists valued the genetic resources of wild Arabica in the southwestern highlands for use in breeding programs for enhanced cultivars at $1.458 billion over the next thirty years.[24] They considered only those with increased pest and disease resistance, low caffeine contents, and increased yields, not flavor or the value of another Geisha. While the number is highly speculative, "prone to considerable uncertainty," as the authors acknowledge, and even abstract ("If your treasure is not on the market, it has no real value," quipped one specialist), it demonstrates the immense potential worth of the forests' genetic resources to the coffee community.

The forests also offer the local Kafecho something that can never have a price tag. Walking in Kombo, Mesfin said, "There is value which is not extractable value but spiritual value."

CHAPTER 18

Sacrifices

he climb to the lofty and elegant juniper tree crowning the hill took fifteen minutes. Sixty or so head of humped oxen patiently grazed along the slope, and toward the knoll, more than a dozen men were cutting hay with scythes. A couple of trees that had been trimmed into three-pronged cradles held bundles of drying fodder. The breezy afternoon sky was more post- than pre-storm blue, and the views out over the surrounding forests were the clearest they had been all week. Unbroken hills of dense green rolled away toward the horizon.

The juniper was fulsome, with long lateral branches that jutted straight out like wings. Sitting under it on a thick saddle blanket doubled over— an ornate saddle hung in the branches above—was Gepetato Haile Michael, one of the area's most revered traditional religious leaders. He wore a gray suit, sturdy black leather shoes, and, wrapped around his shoulders, a fine woven cotton shawl edged in gold embroidery. A horsetail fly whisk with smooth-worn braided-leather handle rested in his lap, and beside him, a five-foot-long pike with a silver knob and sleek iron tip had been stuck into the ground. He was the thirteenth-generation *gepetato* in his family, and these emblems of his position had been passed down. (He also has a lion-skin robe for special ceremonies.)

Literally king (*tato*) of the hill (or mountain, *gepe*), the *gepe* in the name refers to a place for leading sacrifices rather than domain. In Haile Michael's case, though, the latter was also accurate. He has five wives—he had recently taken the fifth, a woman of twenty or so—and five homes, with land scattered around a narrow, fertile valley near a highly regarded coffee cooperative and washing station, about an hour north of Bonga. After lunch, he had ridden his horse to the field where some of his followers were working.

A *gepetato* traditionally holds both sacred and secular roles,[1] acting as spiritual leader and as an elder who arbitrates or mediates issues in the community. In the past he could raise a local army during a time of emergency and collect taxes in his area.[2] Seventy years old, with a strong jaw and broad, infectious smile, Haile Michael exuded both regal authority and a calming presence.

Leaning against the trunk, he sat with his knees drawn up, revealing forest-green socks with the image of the Grand Ethiopian Renaissance Dam and the Amharic words for "Nile" and "green" stitched in lime-green thread. A man silently approached as Haile Michael spoke, set down his panga, prostrated himself before the leader, and stretched forward, kissing the boot of the *gepetato*, who didn't acknowledge the man or even break his conversation. The follower, eyes remaining downcast, crawled back away.

For the people in Kafa, the importance of the forest exceeded even coffee, the *gepetato* was saying. "Because the lives of all Kafa people depend on the forest."

"*Kubbo aallegaata, Kafachoch kashoo aalle,*" I said, offering a Kafa proverb. "Without forests, no life for Kafa." The *gepetato* laughed, repeated it with the correct pronunciation, and nodded earnestly, tugging on his wispy white chin beard.

"The forest is life for the Kafa people," he said. "Not only food, not only building materials, not only shelter, but more."

He stopped there. The "more" was obvious and did not need to be named.

The forests hold deep spiritual and cultural significance for the Kafa people. Local beliefs have been powerfully linked to them from the beginning. Origin stories tell of the Kafecho being born not of a woman but from a stone.[3] Or from a river. Or emerging, like plants, from a hole the earth.[4]

Three figures generally appear in these folktales, each representing one of Kafa's major clans of the same name: Manjo, Mingo, and Matto. "At the beginning of creations, the earth was pregnant," goes one legend, recorded by an Italian anthropologist in the late 1920s:

> As the time of parturition [giving birth] neared, the earth opened itself and out came Mantscho [Manjo], who carried a net used

for monkey-hunting on his shoulders. Mantscho hardly had come out of the earth as a monkey was caught in his net; hence, the occupation of all his descendants was determined: hunting. Shortly thereafter, Mindscho [Mingo], carrying a horn-container used to collect milk after milking, came out of the earth; he became the owner of the cattle and the king. The earth opened a third time and Matto came out carrying a drum on his shoulder. Hardly had Matto come out, as a calf neared him; he grabbed it and killed it at the foot of a tree in honour of the sky-god. This was the first sacrifice and from this time Matto and his descendants were priests.[5]

Traditional practices in Kafa center around two core elements. The first is *eqqo*, elemental spirits that live in the undisturbed parts of the forest. There is not a single spirit but various, and each family, clan, or village might have different ones that they worship.

"A spirit is appeasing, trying to serve people to do good," offered one Kafecho explaining the nuances of *eqqo*. "A kind of command mechanism to connect with god." Casting about for an analogy, he said, "Like Christ. It is invisible. You can feel it, but you cannot see it."

Certain priests are able to coax *eqqo* spirits from their usual forest dwelling places among the trees, rocks, and streams to take up temporary residence in their bodies. The spirits speak through their human host, making prophetic utterances or answering prayers. The spirits live in the *eqqo* holder and communicate directly with other spirits within the forest.

Gepetato Haile Michael is a medium. He has thousands of followers ("from as far as Addis," one of them said a bit breathlessly), and on Wednesdays and Sundays in a long shed in the compound of his main home, the *gepetato* receives those seeking advice, blessings, or help with problems such as infertility. The house sits back about ten minutes from the gravel road along a wide grid of grassy trails among swept-dirt compounds with thatch-roofed huts, enset trees, and coffee bushes. During the coffee harvest, each hut has a raised bamboo bed with drying cherries. Inside the prayer house, coffee is prepared and then drunk by the *gepetato* and others present. If prayers are answered, the petitioners return bearing gifts, which might include coffee beans, roosters, goats, sheep, or even cattle.

The second, and not unconnected, central component is *dejjo*, offering a sacrifice to the spirits. "*Dejjo* means thanksgiving," said Mesfin Tekle, "a giving for the good things given to them." The first took place almost immediately after the Kafechos' arrival on the earth—in the parturition story, Matto sacrifices a calf moments after appearing—and the sacrifices have been happening since to benefit the community. When writing about the realm of Kafa's supernatural, the anthropologist Amnon Orent quoted a fitting passage from the nineteenth-century Scottish scholar William Robertson Smith: "Religion is not an arbitrary relation to the individual man to a supernatural power, it is a relation of all the members of a community to a power that has the good of the community at heart, and protects its law and moral order."[6] People in Kafa offer crops, animals, and libations of coffee and *tej* in thanks for getting safely from year to year, for keeping pigs, baboons, and other pests away from gardens and fields, and for having bountiful harvests.

A handful of important celebrations throughout the year are essentially harvest rites. In past times, the king led important sacrifices on sacred sites, often beside a river. Assistants held the legs of three oxen—a black one, a red one, and a white one—and the king himself slit their throats. Some of their blood along with milk and honey was poured into the water, from where it would flow symbolically throughout Kafa. Along with items from the harvest, the remainder of the blood went around the base of a tree. The king said a prayer and tossed pieces of meat from the oxen as well as some grains into the river.[7] In other important sacrifices, the blood, collected in a horn cup, was poured over a sacrificial stone. Such sacred celebrations lasted for days.

Today such sacrificial celebrations continue to take place during the harvest times of teff, maize, and coffee. Coffee, though, the *gepetato* said, was different. It was wild.

We don't know where it has come from, or why it is here, goes the traditional attitude of people in Kafa's forests toward wild coffee. We did not ask for it or cultivate it, yet every season, year after year, the fruits appear. "Coffee is a gift from God because we did not plant it," the *gepetato* explained. "God gave it to the people. For this we give offerings."

He had just celebrated the coffee *dejjo* with some of his followers. They had gone to the sacred place in the dense forest and ritually sacrificed an animal at the base of a large tree for Showe Kollo, the spirit of the land. He walked barefoot into the woods with a shawl wrapped around his shoulders. His followers brought with them other items that they had harvested—maize, teff, enset—plus injera and jugs that held home-brewed *tella* (beer made from teff) and *tej*. They also carried the animal that they were going to offer. "A chicken is minimum," said the *gepetato*. "Goat, sheep, even oxen." It depended on the size of the celebration.

Around a thick tree, the men erected a simple fence, setting off an area to place the offerings. The *gepetato* slit the animal's throat with a knife reserved only for sacrifices, an old piece with a double-edged blade and bone handle capped by a nineteenth-century silver Maria Theresa thaler coin. An assistant held a wide bowl—wood now, but once folded from an enset leaf—to catch the blood, then poured it at the base of the tree. In the past, he said, the whole animal was left. Now it is just representative pieces, "the best of each part," which he cuts away and places on the ground. The recent ceremony lasted under an hour, and the celebration that followed away from the site for a couple more. They roasted the remainder of the animal and ate it along with the other provision carried into the forest.

The afternoon light was mellowing, the colors on the hill deepening. Recent thunderstorms had etched the soil with sharp runoff gullies that stood out on the exposed ocher soil like gashes. The day's work for his followers was nearly done, and most had put down their tools to listen to their leader. Every home in the hamlet has at least some coffee trees, and the men had celebrated individual *dejjos* among their families and neighbors in the days that followed the larger one led by the *gepetato*.

Such offerings are traditional across Kafa, although with slight differences from place to place, explained Alemayu Gabrielmicheal, one of two *dejjo* leaders (though not a *gepetato*) in the Kumpti Forest, a few hours away. Wearing a bright blue Samsung T-shirt, he stood at the base of a vast fig tree and probed the soft soil between buttressed roots with his panga, indicating where a shallow hole would be dug and an animal bled into the soil. On the wide blade of an enset leaf, he sets out the different foods that he and his neighbors had harvested. "That is the center," he said. "When we sacrifice the chicken, the right side is always for the *kollo*. We cut it into four pieces." These are placed in the four directions, like compass points. "To the south, to the east, to the west, to the north."

Alemayu says a prayer thanking the forest for staying calm, for being without conflict, and giving coffee each year. After, the group of men then move away from the sacrificial spot to celebrate.

At dawn they return to the site. "In early morning, before anybody is awake or the wild animals are starting to move, we come, we see," Alemayu said. He rested a hand against the gnarled, dull yellowish bark. The ancient tree rose up a hundred feet, with a crown of fat, oblong leaves spreading out just as wide. On another tall tree nearby, a couple of colobus monkeys scampered about the stout branches. "If the offering is taken, then we consider it is accepted," he said. The coffee harvest will be good. "If it is not taken, then we consider that Showe Kollo is not happy."

When this happens, Alemayu goes to an *alamo*, a spiritual leader and medium, who can communicate with the forest spirits and ask what needs to be done "to reconcile this unhappiness."

Christianity was not imported to Ethiopia by European missionaries as elsewhere in sub-Saharan Africa. Ethiopia sat along the ancient trade route linking the Roman Empire and India, and it likely arrived with merchants by the fourth century. The conversion of the Aksumite king in A.D. 330 marks the formal beginning of Orthodox Christianity as the state religion. Except for a decade during the seventeenth century when the emperor converted to Roman Catholicism, Orthodox has dominated every level of society.*

At least in the north of Ethiopia this was the case. In the sixteenth century, the Ethiopian emperor convinced the Kafa king to officially accept Christianity in his kingdom.[8] Kafa's two oldest churches—one near Andiracha, the other at Baha, an hour and a half south of Bonga on a ridgeline looking down over untouched core-zone forests—both date from that century.[9] The influence of the north waned, though, and Christianity largely disappeared from the kingdom until Menelik's troops conquered it in 1897. Ras Wolde Giorgis supposedly brought seventy priests to the area after taking control[10] and during his dozen years as governor founded a number of Orthodox churches. He ordered one built directly on top of the traditional temple in Andiracha.

In Kafa today a high percentage of the population practices a form of animism, or folk religion, in which the natural world possesses special powers and the forests are places where spirits dwell. (One study found that in Bonga, Kafa's most populous district, half practiced animism.)[11] Yet the majority identify themselves as Orthodox, even *dejjo* leaders such as Alemayu. This isn't necessarily incongruent.

---

* Until 1959, it was part of the Coptic Orthodox Church of Alexandria. It is now the independent Ethiopian Orthodox Tewahedo Church.

"Even if he is a Christian," said village elder Tetera Mekonen Yemer in Andiracha, "he has some other belief." By "other" he meant animistic.

"When you get to the rural areas," said Mesfin, "in the Orthodox believers at least twenty-five percent of their beliefs—what they think is linked to Orthodox—is actually the traditional belief." When a cow's first calf is born, the owner collects milk from the mother, churns it to butter, and takes it to the church, smearing it around the compound fence or door-frame. "That is related to the local religion," Mesfin said, "not Orthodox."

The faithful in Kafa also bring giant fern trees to the church. Mesfin explained, "In the traditional beliefs, they do the same. When they come to the traditional leader's house, they bring ferns," placing the feathery, six-foot-tall plants around the compound fence. "They are bringing them as a gift from nature." It is an offering from the forest.

Such practices remain deep-seated, and the surfacing of such rites is not unusual in parts of Africa. In his book on traditional beliefs V. S. Naipaul quoted a West African: "The new religions, Islam and Christianity, are just on the top. Inside us is the forest."[12]

Under Menelik II, the local religion was relegated in favor of Orthodox Christianity. "Gaki Sherocho was punished by Menelik, so I don't want to talk about Menelik," Gepetato Haile Michael said in a steely tone, brushing away the era because of the wrongs perpetrated upon Kafa's last king. "Haile Selassie was better—and better than the Derg."

During Selassie's long rule, there was more freedom to practice. That ended under the Marxist rule of the Derg, a violent, bloody period associated with its leader Mengistu Haile Mariam. "During the time of the Derg, our religion and our culture almost died," the *gepetato* said. It was the low point. Since the ousting of the Marxist regime in 1991, he has seen a thawing in tolerant attitudes. "Now our religion is respected."

Relatively so, at least. While traditional practices remain widespread in Kafa, they are not universally accepted or always even tolerated. "There is a difference between God and god," a young official in Kafa's education department said in Bonga. He wrote *God* and then *god* on a slip of paper. Jabbing the lowercase one with the pen, he said, "This is bad religion, bad belief."

A local accountant working for a European NGO in Bonga agreed: "There is the holy spirit and there are evil spirits, and those practicing traditional religion are worshipping the evil spirits." He was an evangelical Protestant, a growing denomination in Ethiopia that now accounts for perhaps 20 percent of the population. In his church on Sundays, he said, such evil spirits can be seen in the possessed. "Those people cannot resist the holy spirit and start shouting." He vigorously disapproved of traditional beliefs and was dismissive of leaders such as Gepetato Haile Michael. "With people bowing before him, kissing his feet, he is becoming god."

For some, it is not enough to brand traditional beliefs as backward or ignorant. "Sometimes they clear a sacred forest just to make the point," Mesfin said. Or they try to prove that certain beliefs are merely superstitions. "They cut the tree [and say], 'Nothing happens, you see. That [belief] is false.' "

Undisturbed woodlands are fundamental to traditional beliefs. Animism requires the presence of dense forests for the spirits to dwell in.

At the end of the nineteenth century, when the last king of Kafa was deposed and the kingdom absorbed into Ethiopia, montane rain forests almost completely covered the southwestern highlands where coffee grows wild.[13] The dense forests were under the jurisdiction of the king and were preserved for spiritual reasons and ritual sacrifices.[14] People revered, valued, and conserved them, refraining from cutting trees, or even entering the densest parts, home to the *eqqo* spirits. Large sections of the forest were taboo for *gepetatos* or even the region's head spiritual leader to enter, and they performed *dejjo* sacrifices along their edges. The local religion thus acted as a natural conservation mechanism for Kafa's coffee forests.

"Almost all homegrown African belief systems are, or were, based on a reverence for local ecosystems—a belief that the forests and rivers are sacred—and this helped persuade people to preserve them, alive and intact," wrote Johann Hari. "But when the colonialists arrived, they dismissed such notions as mumbo-jumbo and forcibly imposed religions that originated in the desert and had nothing to say about the African environment. The old taboos were stamped out, and before long the forests began to be systematically destroyed. It's an eco-catastrophe from which Africa has never recovered, and which many Africans have picked up and are continuing to perpetrate today."[15]

In Kafa, the colonists were not Arabs or Europeans but Amharas from the north of Ethiopia.* The shunting aside of traditional beliefs hastened deforestation.

---

* If *Galla* was imprecise shorthand for conquered ones outside the Ethiopian core, *Amhara* was also ethnically imprecise and meant those from the north who held the power.

As one way to try to halt the cutting of Kafa's woodlands and help conservation efforts of the coffee forests, Mesfin has been using these traditional beliefs, trying to bring the somewhat secretive practices more out in the open with public *dejjo* celebrations, and to raise the awareness of the spiritual value of the woodlands. More tangibly, he has also done this with legislation in the biosphere.

During the complicated zoning process for the UNESCO proposal, Mesfin consulted Kafa's *gepetatos* to find out precisely which parts of the forests they deemed most hallowed, and incorporated these into the planning. "I respect his beliefs," he said of Haile Michael, "and added the area that he found sacred to the core zone." Of the seventeen hundred hectares (forty-two hundred acres) around the hot springs that are part of the Kafa biosphere, eleven hundred of them are denoted as core zone. "So it has legal protection," he said, and immunity from being logged. The *gepetato* was pleased, leaving, as a spiritual legacy, the part of the forest most revered by him and his followers. It was now legally, not only spiritually, forbidden to enter.

"The spirits need to be left in peace to be happy," said Mesfin.

In the *gepetato*'s valley, the gathering of wild coffee wound down in January and February, and garden coffee a bit later. The first rains didn't arrive until the beginning of March. On a sloped plot of the *gepetato*'s land some ten days later, two dozen followers goaded pairs of oxen pulling rudimentary wooden plows through the soil with its soft, whiskery stubble of weeds. The rains had softened the ground, and they had begun plowing the fields to prepare for sowing. A rope switch snapped across the bony flank of an ox.

In the wide front room of his mud-walled home, Haile Michael, sitting on a wood ottoman with elegant, curving armrests, returned to the mystery of coffee and its importance in Kafa culture. A *dejjo* sacrifice is done a single time each year for teff, after the harvest around the end of December or early January, he said, and a single time for maize, in July. But coffee is so important that there are three of them.

The first comes when the coffee trees flower. The color of the feathers or coat of the animal sacrificed is important, the *gepetato* said. For the first, it must be white, to symbolically match the blossoms. The previous week he had performed the flowering *dejjo*, sacrificing a white goat and a white hen. A few months later, when small green coffee berries form on the branches, a second offering takes place using a dark or black animal. These first two, as the coffee is maturing, the *gepetato* explained in his unhurried, deep-timbered voice, are in thanks for coffee's arrival, and to ensure that the trees won't be attacked by disease or damaged by misfortune such as hail. The third *dejjo* happens once the coffee berries turn deep crimson and are ready to be harvested. For this, he selects a reddish or orangish-colored animal to match the color of the ripe fruit. He performs this sacrifice to give thanks for the crop.

The only light came from the open door, and the *gepetato*, with a brilliant white shawl wrapped around him, sat at one end of the room mostly obscured in darkness. He had a low, persistent cough, more like a husky sigh; his movements were slightly less sharp than they had been in November. He pulled his dark blue knitted cap down over his ears. As he spoke, an elderly follower crawled toward him to silently kiss his boot before taking a place on one of the wooden benches placed along the wall. From outside came the goading of oxen and the occasional crack of a rope switch.

The sacrifices had a broader purpose, too, one that helped keep harmony in nature and ensure the prosperity of its crops for the year ahead.[16] The prayer offered during the sacrifice not only gives thanks for the coffee, but also to the forest for staying calm and remaining without conflict.

The mood of the forest has always been important. "Even in the time of the last king of Kafa there was a general annual meeting with rulers from the different districts," Mesfin said a few days later in his Bonga office. "And the first question he asked was related to nature: 'Is the forest calm? Are the bees flying? Are wild animals playing, jumping? If bees are flying and moving, if wild animals are jumping, playing, then we are good, we are satisfied. If no bees are flying, no wild animals are jumping, playing, if you don't see a wild animal, then there is a danger coming.'" Nature was not only a reflection of what had happened in the past, but also portended the future.

After an hour or so, the *gepetato* stood up and moved to the doorway, blinking in the midday glare, framed like a priest in the one of the ancient rock-hewn churches of Lalibela. His regal bearing made him appear taller than his height of five feet eight or so. When he stepped out onto the terrace, his assistant, a short man in his fifties wearing rubber boots that reached his knees and a yellow shawl, followed him with a cushion. The *gepetato* held a large wooden staff jacketed with a metal tip. Across the narrow valley was the knoll topped by the juniper tree, another piece of his land.

Haile Michael's eldest son, a young man in a striped polo shirt, sandals, and with the same deep furrow between the eyebrows as his father, stood nearby. He would most likely follow his father to become the fourteenth *gepetato* in the family. Succession wasn't automatic, though. Haile Michael, sometime before his own father died, had disappeared into the forest. No one knew where he went. Once the father passed away, the followers found Haile Michael and brought him back into the community as their spiritual leader.

His eldest son headed down the hill toward the hamlet. In November, the local coffee cooperative along the road had been busy; now, the harvest over, the compound was locked, and the tiered rows of bamboo drying beds were empty. The coffee beans from local gardens were in sixty-kilogram jute sacks. Some sat stacked in warehouses; others had already been loaded onto cargo ships and were making their way toward Oakland, Antwerp, or Busan, South Korea, where high-end roasters were eagerly awaiting the arrival of the new crop.

Up on the knoll, Haile Michael had gone back inside the house. His wife was starting to prepare coffee. Aromatic blue smoke would soon fill the front room as she roasted the beans.

Coffee's importance in Kafa is distinguished in uniquely celebrating each step of its growth from flower to ripe fruit. It is there, too, at the end, before drinking. Sometimes, before taking a drink, the *gepetato* sprinkles a bit from his cup at the entrance of the house as a small offering to Showe Kollo. "Preparing coffee," he said, "is a like a form of praying."

Among the wild groves, coffee has never been simply a drink or a mere forest product. After all these years, its mystique has not vanished. That is what will perhaps ultimately sustain it in the years to come, both in the forests of Kafa and in coffee cups around the globe, where it hasn't lost any of its romance, allure, or magic, either.

Acknowledgments

During the travels, research, and writing of this book, I accrued a lengthy list of people to thank for their insight, information, and generosity.

In Ethiopia, particular thanks goes to the following. In Kafa: Mesfin Tekle, Asaye Alemayehu, Alemayu Haile, Gepetato Haile Michael and family, Sheki Kedir Sedik, Woldegiorgis Shawo, Frehiwet Getahun, Tamirat Haile, Muluken Mekuria, Bereket Kochito, Alemayehu Haile, Mitiku Gebre Mariam, Tetera Mekonen Yemer, Alemayu Gabrielmicheal, Kero Misho, and the staffs at the Kafa Guesthouse and Coffeeland Hotel in Bonga. In Addis Ababa: Haddis Teka Gebremariam, Fish Luke, Fiseha Getachew, Mulugeta Lemenih, Heleanna Georgalis, Aman Adinew, and Jacques Dubois. In Harar: Admasu Temare, Mignot Solomon, Ali Yusef, and Abdela Mume. In Sidamo: Lemlem Dubale. A special thanks to my steadfast driver, Ashanafi Fekadu, for nearly six thousand safe kilometers on some of the country's most challenging roads. As well, many thanks to those whose names I never learned, including various coffee collectors in Kafa, market vendors in Bonga and Harar, and the many who prepared my coffee with patience and virtuosity.

Elsewhere, I owe the deepest gratitude to, in London, Aaron Davis, Surendra Kotecha, the librarians and archivists at Royal Botanic Gardens, Kew, Elaine Charwat and the Linnean Society, Vicente Partida, Libby Plumb, and Kirstin and Jani Peltonen; in Montpellier, France, Benoît Bertrand, Jean-Pierre Labouisse, Philippe Lashermes, and Pierre Charmetant; in Haarlem and Amsterdam, Menno Simons, the staff at Hartekamp, Wytske Feddema, Rob de Ree, and Nynke Feddema; in Germany, Svane Bender, Bianca Schlegel, Eva Danulat, and Ines Possemeyer; in Vienna,

Klaus Bieber; in Barcelona, Matt Goulding, Salvador Sans, Alexandra Witty, Cássia Martinez de Carvalho, Pau Valverde, and Ursula Schläffer; in the USA, Ted Stachura, Timothy Schilling, Thompson Owen, Victor Albert, David Griswold, Keith Eckert, the librarians at the University of Washington's Suzzallo and Allen Libraries, Tod Nelson, Tod Marshall, Jim Finley and Kathleen Sieler, and Bill and Joanne Koehler; in Guatemala, Pablo González, Cristina González, and family, Josué Morales, Manuel Arriola, and Tito and Gerson Otzoyat; in Costa Rica, William Solano; in Panama, Daniel and Rachel Peterson; in Tanzania, Deusdedit Kilambo; and, in Yemen, Amin Al Hakimi and Andrew Nicholson.

As well, I want to express my deep gratitude to the bevy of writers, historians, and scientific researchers whose works fill the bibliography.

I was fortunate to have George Gibson as editor at Bloomsbury. Deep thanks also to Lea Beresford, Laura Phillips, Tara Kennedy, and those in Bloomsbury's New York office, and to copy editor Steve Boldt. Thanks also to Michael Fishwick, Marigold Atkey, Rebecca Thorne, Vicky Beddow, and Alexandra Pringle at Bloomsbury UK; Faiza Khan and Sumika Rajput at Bloomsbury India; and the office of Bloomsbury Australia.

Deep appreciation, too, to my longtime agent, Doe Coover, as well as Frances Kennedy.

As always, my deepest thanks go closest to home—to Eva, Alba, and Maia.

Notes

COFFEE IS OUR BREAD

1. Mesfin Tekle.
2. Lange, *History of the Southern Gonga*, 5.
3. Cramer, *Review of Literature of Coffee Research*, 177.

CHAPTER 1: SOWN BY THE BIRDS

1. Chernet, "Land Resources and Socio-Economic Report," 31.
2. Aerts, "Semi-Forest Coffee Cultivation"; Berecha, "Effects of Forest Management."
3. Schmitt, *Montane Rainforest with Wild* Coffea arabica, 56; Sylvain, "Ethiopian Coffee," 117; Sylvain, "Some Observations on *Coffea arabica*," 41.
4. Senbeta Wakjira, *Biodiversity and Ecology of Afromontane Rainforests*, 28.
5. Schmitt, *Montane Rainforest with Wild* Coffea arabica, 60.
6. Orent, "Lineage Structure and the Supernatural."

CHAPTER 2: ISLAND ETHIOPIA

1. On expedition in East Africa in the early 1890s, Prince Eugenio Ruspoli, son of Rome's mayor and scion to the noble family, reached the Omo River, where he was trampled by an elephant. His collecting bag contained the skin of an extraordinary but unknown bird that would bear his name. About the size of a pheasant, it had emerald and crimson plumage, a punky white crest, and long bluish tail. But there was no information about where Ruspoli collected it. For fifty years it remained a mystery, until one was spotted near the southern Ethiopian village of Negele. With a range limited to some scrubby local woodlands, this rare endemic that graces the cover of the *Birds of Ethiopia and Eritrea* is the most sought-after sighting among bird-watchers in the Horn of Africa.
2. Riechmann, "Literature Survey on Biological Data."
3. Schmitt, *Montane Rainforest with Wild* Coffea arabica, 23.

4. Grühl, *Citadel of Ethiopia*, 169.
5. Lange, *History of the Southern Gonga*, 286.
6. Homer, *Odyssey*, 78.
7. Grühl, *Citadel of Ethiopia*, 170.
8. Pankhurst, *Ethiopians*, 79.
9. Ibid., 97.
10. Shinn and Ofcansky, *Historical Dictionary of Ethiopia*, 328.
11. Love, "French Physician at the Court of Gondar."
12. Pankhurst, *Introduction to the Economic History of Ethiopia*, 211.
13. Bruce, *Travels to Discover*, 333.
14. Bruce, *Travels, Through Part of Africa*, 165.
15. *Portuguese Expedition to Abyssinia*, 234.
16. Bredin, *Pale Abyssinian*, 254.
17. Bruce, *Travels to Discover*, 411.
18. Shinn and Ofcansky, *Historical Dictionary of Ethiopia*, 87.
19. Ibid.
20. Zewde, *History of Modern Ethiopia*, 25.
21. Underhill, "Abyssinia Under Menelik and After," 33.
22. Marcus, *History of Ethiopia*, 104.
23. Underhill, "Abyssinia Under Menelik and After," 36.
24. Markakis, *Ethiopia*, 95.
25. Ibid.
26. Ibid.
27. Woldemariam, *History of the Kingdom of Kaffa*, 139, 250.
28. Marcus, *Life and Times of Menelik II*, 194.
29. Markakis, *Ethiopia*, 97.
30. Fernyhough, "Women, Gender History, and Slavery," 221.
31. Tibebu, *Making of Modern Ethiopia*, 43.
32. Pankhurst, *Ethiopians*, 179.
33. Underhill, "Abyssinia Under Menelik and After," 36.
34. Marcus, *History of Ethiopia*, 99.
35. Pankhurst, *Ethiopians*, 193.
36. Jonas, *Battle of Adwa*, 333.

CHAPTER 3: THE KINGDOM OF KAFA

1. Woldemariam, *History of the Kingdom of Kaffa*, 216.
2. Grühl, *Citadel of Ethiopia*, 278.
3. Lange, *History of the Southern Gonga*, 197.
4. Orent, "Refocusing on the History of Kafa."
5. Zewde, *History of Modern Ethiopia*, 16.
6. Grühl, *Citadel of Ethiopia*, 169.
7. Woldemariam, *History of the Kingdom of Kaffa*, 12.
8. Orent, "Lineage Structure and the Supernatural," 57.
9. Sylvain, "Ethiopian Coffee," 113.
10. Naipaul, *Masque of Africa*, 23.

11. Álvarez, *Narrative of the Portuguese Embassy to Abyssinia*, 349–50.
12. *Portuguese Expedition to Abyssinia*, 233.
13. Grühl, *Citadel of Ethiopia*, 173.
14. Ibid.
15. Lange, *History of the Southern Gonga*, 306.
16. Pankhurst, *Ethiopians*, 179.
17. Grühl, *Citadel of Ethiopia*, 174.
18. Huntingford, *Galla of Ethiopia*, 111.
19. Lange, *History of the Southern Gonga*, 215.
20. Huntingford, *Galla of Ethiopia*, 125.
21. Lange, *History of the Southern Gonga*, 272.
22. Bieber, *Geheimnisvolles Kaffa*, 124.
23. Hassen, *Oromo of Ethiopia*, 92.
24. Woldemariam, *History of the Kingdom of Kaffa*, 85.
25. Skinner, *Abyssinia of To-Day*, 141.
26. Huntingford, *Galla of Ethiopia*, 117.
27. Bulatovich, *Ethiopia Through Russian Eyes*, 212.
28. Woldemariam, *History of the Kingdom of Kaffa*, 232.
29. Hassen, *Oromo of Ethiopia*, 92.
30. Woldemariam, *History of the Kingdom of Kaffa*, 151.
31. Lange, *History of the Southern Gonga*, 277.
32. Ibid., 264.
33. Ibid., 9.
34. Ibid., 8.
35. Chernet, "Land Resources and Socio-Economic Report."
36. Lange, *History of the Southern Gonga*, 267.
37. Zewde, *History of Modern Ethiopia*, 21; Schmitt, *Montane Rainforest with Wild Coffea arabica*.
38. Zewde, *History of Modern Ethiopia*, 21.
39. Huntingford, *Galla of Ethiopia*, 106.
40. Fernyhough, "Slavery and the Slave Trade," 106; Fernyhough, "Women, Gender History, and Slavery," 219.
41. Huntingford, *Galla of Ethiopia*, 126.
42. Lange, *History of the Southern Gonga*, 268.
43. Tibebu, *Making of Modern Ethiopia*, 65.
44. Huntingford, *Galla of Ethiopia*, 111.
45. Ito, "Local Honey Production."
46. Bieber, *Geheimnisvolles Kaffa*, 120.
47. Zewde, *History of Modern Ethiopia*, 22.
48. Ibid., 97.
49. Lange, *History of the Southern Gonga*, 119.
50. Huntingford, *Galla of Ethiopia*, 119.
51. "Gaki Sherocho," 410.
52. Huntingford, *Galla of Ethiopia*, 282.
53. Ibid., 119.
54. Ibid., 282.

55. Ibid., 119.
56. Ibid.
57. Ibid.
58. Bulatovich, *Ethiopia Through Russian Eyes*, 215.
59. Huntingford, *Galla of Ethiopia*, 119.
60. Lange, *History of the Southern Gonga*, 283.

CHAPTER 4: THE LAST KING OF KAFA

1. Prouty and Rosenfeld, *Historical Dictionary*, 133.
2. Woldemariam, *History of the Kingdom of Kaffa*, 253–54.
3. Marcus, *Life and Times of Menelik II*, 185.
4. Bulatovich, *Ethiopia Through Russian Eyes*, 220.
5. Woldemariam, *History of the Kingdom of Kaffa*, 262.
6. Marcus, *Life and Times of Menelik II*, 185.
7. Bulatovich, *Ethiopia Through Russian Eyes*, 221.
8. Ibid., 220.
9. Zewde, *History of Modern Ethiopia*, 4.
10. Markakis, *Ethiopia*, 95.
11. Woldemariam, *History of the Kingdom of Kaffa*, 237–38.
12. Ibid., 238.
13. Bulatovich, *Ethiopia Through Russian Eyes*, 70.
14. Bruce, *Travels to Discover*, 218.
15. Woldemariam, *History of the Kingdom of Kaffa*, 241.
16. Huntingford, *Galla of Ethiopia*, 127.
17. Lange, *History of the Southern Gonga*, 281.
18. Marcus, *Life and Times of Menelik II*, 186.
19. Fernyhough, "Slavery and the Slave Trade," 117.
20. Bulatovich, *Ethiopia Through Russian Eyes*, 122.
21. Ibid., 222.
22. Ibid., 223.
23. Marcus, *Life and Times of Menelik II*, 186.
24. Bulatovich, *Ethiopia Through Russian Eyes*, 223.
25. Ibid.
26. Ibid.
27. Woldemariam, *History of the Kingdom of Kaffa*, 264.
28. Marcus, *Life and Times of Menelik II*, 185–86.
29. Grühl, *Citadel of Ethiopia*, 325.
30. Marcus, *Life and Times of Menelik II*, 186.
31. Ibid.
32. Skinner, *Abyssinia of To-Day*, 142.
33. Marcus, *Life and Times of Menelik II*, 186.
34. Marcus, *Life and Times of Menelik II*, 186.
35. Bulatovich, *Ethiopia Through Russian Eyes*, 206.
36. Ibid.
37. Ibid., 204.

38. Ibid., 226.
39. Ibid., 255.
40. Schmitt, *Montane Rainforest with Wild* Coffea arabica, 7.
41. Lange, *History of the Southern Gonga*, 5.
42. Markakis, *Ethiopia*, 97.
43. Bulatovich, *Ethiopia Through Russian Eyes*, 348.
44. Ibid., 341.
45. Grühl, *Citadel of Ethiopia*, 184.
46. Bulatovich, *Ethiopia Through Russian Eyes*, 220.
47. Grühl, *Citadel of Ethiopia*, 223.
48. Bulatovich, *Ethiopia Through Russian Eyes*, 212.
49. Grühl, *Citadel of Ethiopia*, 225.
50. Bieber, "African Fascination of the Bieber Family."

CHAPTER 5: ORIGINS

1. Ukers, *All About Coffee*, 16.
2. Bieber, *Geheimnisvolles Kaffa*, 119.
3. Ibid., 120.
4. Hildebran, Bradt, and Lesur-Gebremariam, "Holocene Archaeology of Southwest Ethiopia."
5. Woldemariam, *History of the Kingdom of Kaffa*, 54.
6. Ibid., 207.
7. Deffar, "Non-Wood Forest Products in Ethiopia."
8. Pankhurst, "Coffee Ceremony," 519.
9. Woldemariam, *History of the Kingdom of Kaffa*, 54–55.
10. Grühl, *Citadel of Ethiopia*, 237.
11. Ibid., 243.
12. Bieber, *Geheimnisvolles Kaffa*, 120.
13. Bruce, *Travels to Discover*, 246.
14. Bulatovich, *Ethiopia Through Russian Eyes*, 214.
15. Bieber, *Kaffa*, 254.
16. Woldemariam, *History of the Kingdom of Kaffa*, 43.
17. Orent, "Dual Organizations in Southern Ethiopia."

CHAPTER 6: GIFT FOR KING AND COUNTRY

1. Pankhurst, "Coffee Ceremony."
2. Pankhurst, *Economic History of Ethiopia*, 199.
3. Woldemariam, *History of the Kingdom of Kaffa*, 55.
4. Huntingford, *Galla of Ethiopia*, 108.
5. *FAO Coffee Mission to Ethiopia*, 4.
6. Fernyhough, "Slavery and the Slave Trade," 112.
7. Burton, *First Footsteps in East Africa*, 2:109.
8. Markakis, *Ethiopia*, 97.
9. McClellan, "Coffee in Center."
10. Markakis, *Ethiopia*, 97.

11. Grühl, *Citadel of Ethiopia*, 200.
12. Miers, *Slavery in the Twentieth Century*, 177.
13. Fernyhough, "Slavery and the Slave Trade."
14. Rourk, *Coffee Production in Africa*, 5.
15. USDA Foreign Agricultural Services, *GAIN Report*, 2016.
16. Bagersh and Bagersh, "History of the Coffee Sector in Ethiopia."
17. *FAO Statistical Pocketbook, 2015—Coffee*, 74.
18. Burton, *First Footsteps in East Africa*, 1:12.
19. Pankhurst, *Resettlement and Famine in Ethiopia*, 175.
20. McCann, *People of the Plow*, 158.

CHAPTER 7: *COFFEA AETHIOPICA*

1. Blunt, *Compleat Naturalist*, 97.
2. George Clifford Herbarium website, "Clifford."
3. Griffiths, "Clifford's Banana," 22.
4. Blunt, *Compleat Naturalist*, 104, 116.
5. Griffiths, "Clifford's Banana," 22.
6. Krol, "Linnaeus op de Hartekamp."
7. Wellman, *Coffee*, 19.
8. Ibid.
9. Linnaeo, *Hortus Cliffortianus*, 59.
10. Ibid.
11. "Original Journal of a Voyage into the Red Sea," 10.
12. Lorenzetti, *Birth of Coffee*, 40.
13. Naval Intelligence Division, *Western Arabia & the Red Sea*, 264
14. Um, *Merchant Houses of Mocha*, 41.
15. Ibid., 31.
16. Wild, *Coffee*, 73.
17. Hattox, *Coffee and Coffeehouses*, 72.
18. Friis, "Coffee and Qat," 3.
19. Naval Intelligence Division, *Western Arabia & the Red Sea*, 264.
20. de Vries, "Understanding Eurasian Trade," 28.
21. Menassa, "Yemen's Coffee Revival."
22. Rimbaud, *I Promise to Be Good*, 214.
23. Baghdiantz McCabe, *Orientalism in Early Modern France*, 165.
24. Wild, *Coffee*, 73.
25. Robinson, *Coffee in Yemen*, 11. The World Bank's last measurement of arable land in Yemen (2012) was just 2.2 percent.
26. Friis, "Coffee and Qat," 4.
27. Linnaei, *Potus Coffea*, 3.
28. It was published around 1558 and translated in part into French from Arabic in 1699 by Antoine Galland.
29. It was published in the late 1500s and translated into English from Arabic by Henry Hall in 1659.
30. Wellman, *Coffee*, 28.

31. Friis, "Coffee and Qat," 5.
32. Bruce, *Travels to Discover*, 411.
33. Sylvain, "Ethiopian Coffee," 112.
34. Haarer, *Modern Coffee Production*, 328–29.
35. Ibid., 2.
36. Wellman, *Coffee*, 71.
37. Ibid.
38. Milos, "Coffee's Mysterious Origins."
39. Ukers, *All About Coffee*, 11.
40. Anthony et al., "Origin of Cultivated *Coffea arabica* L.," 898.
41. Pankhurst, *Ethiopians*, 33.
42. Ibid.
43. Wellman, *Coffee*, 32.
44. *National Coffee Board of Ethiopia (1957–1972)*.
45. Anthony et al., "Origin of Cultivated *Coffea arabica* L.," 898.
46. Engelmann et al., "Complementary Strategies for *Ex Situ* Conservation," 4.
47. Friis, "Coffee and Qat," 2.
48. Bieber, *Kaffa*, 380.
49. Bieber, *Geheimnisvolles Kaffa*, 120.
50. Grühl, *Citadel of Ethiopia*, 172.
51. Huntingford, *Galla of Ethiopia*, 134.
52. Lashermes et al., "Origin and Genetic Diversity of *Coffea arabica*."

CHAPTER 8: CITY OF SAINTS

1. Barker, "Extract Report on the Probable Geographical Position of Harrar," 241.
2. Vân and Guleid, *Harar*, 2.
3. "Harar Jugol," UNESCO website.
4. Pankhurst, *Economic History of Ethiopia*, 201.
5. "Harar Jugol," UNESCO website.
6. Burton, *First Footsteps in East Africa*, 1:2.
7. Ibid., 2:26.
8. Ibid., 2:27.
9. Ibid., 2:42–43.
10. Nicholl, *Somebody Else*, 95.
11. Rimbaud, *I Promise to Be Good*, 111.
12. Ibid., 211.
13. Ibid., 191.
14. Ibid., 211.
15. Ibid., 214.
16. Ibid., 222.
17. Ibid., 259.
18. I have never experienced such withering heat or lethargy as during a week marooned in Djibouti waiting to cross to Yemen. There was little to do but wait, like much of the town, for the afternoon arrival in the market of khat flown in from Ethiopia, and then retire behind wooden shutters to slowly chew the

bundle of tender, mildly narcotic leaves until the stupefying heat faded enough to venture back outside.

19. Nicholl, *Somebody Else*, 211.
20. Ibid., 212.
21. Rimbaud, *I Promise to Be Good*, 255.
22. Nicholl, *Somebody Else*, 223.
23. Menelik also complained about Rimbaud, an unknown Frenchman "who had no regards to his royal highness, who didn't deign to give the smallest present to the Empress Taitu." Vân and Guleid, *Harar*, 28.
24. Rimbaud, *I Promise to Be Good*, 256.
25. Pankhurst, *Economic History of Ethiopia*, 201.
26. Rimbaud, *I Promise to Be Good*, 324.
27. Nicholl, *Somebody Else*, 266.
28. Ibid., 247.
29. Downing, "A Decade in Hell."
30. Rimbaud, *I Promise to Be Good*, 275.
31. Ibid., 304–5.
32. Ibid., 333.
33. Labouisse et al., "Current Status of Coffee," 1084.
34. Pankhurst, "Coffee Ceremony," 520.
35. Ibid., 520.
36. Sylvain, "Ethiopian Coffee," 121.
37. Ibid.
38. Barker, "Extract Report on the Probable Geographical Position of Harrar."
39. Skinner, *Abyssinia of To-Day*, 190.
40. Krapf, *Travels, Researches, and Missionary Labors*, 461.

CHAPTER 9: OUT OF ARABIA

1. Hattox, *Coffee and Coffeehouses*, 26.
2. Ibid., 77.
3. Ibid., 60.
4. Ibid., 81.
5. Bennett and Bealer, *World of Caffeine*, 19.
6. McHugo, "Coffee and Qahwa."
7. Hattox, *Coffee and Coffeehouses*, 60.
8. de la Roque, *Voyage to Arabia Felix*, 313.
9. Ibid., 321.
10. Hattox, *Coffee and Coffeehouses*, 10.
11. Ukers, *All About Coffee*, 26.
12. Spary, *Eating and Enlightenment*, 94.
13. Bennett and Bealer, *World of Caffeine*, 151
14. Spary, *Eating and Enlightenment*, 52.
15. Baghdiantz McCabe, *Orientalism in Early Modern France*, 189–90.
16. Wellman, *Coffee*, 25.
17. Luttinger and Dicum, *Coffee Book*.

18. Hoffmann, *World Atlas of Coffee*, 154.
19. de Vries, "Understanding Eurasian Trade," 28.
20. Pendergrast, *Uncommon Grounds*, 17.
21. Cramer, *Review of Literature of Coffee Research in Indonesia*, 5.
22. Ibid., xiii.
23. Wellman, *Coffee*, 18.
24. "Coffee–*Coffea arabica*," Hortus Botanicus Amsterdam website.
25. Cramer, *Review of Literature of Coffee Research in Indonesia*, 5.
26. Ibid. Haarer (*Modern Coffee Production*, 380) claims a year earlier.
27. Wellman, *Coffee*, 33.
28. Cramer, *Review of Literature of Coffee Research in Indonesia*, 5.
29. Haarer, *Modern Coffee Production*, 380.
30. Cramer, *Review of Literature of Coffee Research in Indonesia*, 5.
31. de Vries, "Understanding Eurasian Trade," 28.
32. Cramer, *Review of Literature of Coffee Research in Indonesia*, 5.
33. *Plants in the Spotlight*, 131.
34. "Coffee–*Coffea arabica*," Hortus Botanicus Amsterdam website.
35. Bradley, *Short Historical Account*, 7–8. Bradley used a folding plate with an illustration of the tree in his book *The Virtue and Use of Coffee, with Regard to the Plague and Other Infectious Distempers*.
36. Wellman, *Coffee*, 34.
37. Ukers, *All About Coffee*, 6.
38. Ellis, *Historical Account of Coffee*, 16.
39. Wellman, *Coffee*, 19.
40. Baghdiantz McCabe, *Orientalism in Early Modern France*, 208.
41. Ibid., 206.
42. Wellman, *Coffee*, 34.
43. Ibid.
44. Ukers, *All About Coffee*, 44.
45. Pendergrast, *Uncommon Grounds*, 16.
46. Haarer, *Modern Coffee Production*, 6.
47. Mureithi, "Coffee in Kenya."
48. Spary, *Eating and Enlightenment*, 87.
49. Ibid., 87.
50. Kieran, "Origins of Commercial Arabica Coffee Production in East Africa," 57.
51. Ibid., 61.
52. Ibid.
53. Blixen, *Out of Africa*, 31.
54. Gogan, *Holy Ghost Missions*, 25.
55. Ibid.
56. Kieran, "Origins of Commercial Arabica Coffee Production in East Africa," 63.
57. Gogan, *Holy Ghost Missions*, 24.
58. Kieran, "Origins of Commercial Arabica Coffee Production in East Africa," 63.
59. "Karen Blixen," National Museums of Kenya website.
60. Blixen, *Out of Africa*, 31.

61. Ibid., 32.
62. "Karen Blixen," National Museums of Kenya website.
63. Blixen, *Out of Africa*, 32.
64. Ibid., 17.
65. Thurman, *Isak Dinesen*, 240.
66. Blixen, *Out of Africa*, 247.
67. Thurman, *Isak Dinesen*, 243.
68. Blixen, *Out of Africa*, 15.

CHAPTER 10: BEYOND WAVES

1. "Blue Bottle—WC Morse," Dialogue Design Build website.
2. Siddle and Venema, "Saving Coffee from Extinction."
3. Kaplan, "Mr. Coffee Creator Vincent Marotta Sr."
4. McGregor, "Starbucks Brought Italian Café Style to America."
5. Schultz and Yang, *Pour Your Heart into It*, 52.
6. Ibid.
7. Ibid., 77.
8. Ibid., 5.
9. Fabricant, "Americans Wake Up and Smell the Coffee."
10. Ibid.
11. "Is Starbucks Really Always Two Blocks Away?"
12. Fabricant, "Americans Wake Up and Smell the Coffee."
13. *Frasier*.
14. Schultz and Yang, *Pour Your Heart into It*, 52.
15. Oremus, "Genius Barista."
16. Yang, "Fewer Cups."
17. Raine, "Alfred Peet."
18. Freeman, Talk at the Commonwealth Club.
19. Kokalitcheva, "Blue Bottle Raises $70 Million."
20. "Stepping Away from Wholesale," Blue Bottle website.
21. Strand, "Seductive Cup."
22. Carmichael, "End of Stumptown."
23. Geller, "Nestlé on 'High Alert.'"
24. "Open Letter," Intelligentsia Coffee website.
25. Oremus, "Genius Barista."
26. Cohen, "Exclusive: Keurig Deal Gives Coffee Traders Jitters."
27. Ibid.
28. "Open Letter," Intelligentsia Coffee website.
29. Perez, "Coffee-Loving Millennials Push Demand to a Record."
30. "Orphan Crop."

CHAPTER 11: *LA ROYA*

1. "Guatemala Antigua Finca El Valle," Batdorf & Bronson website.
2. "Guatemala Finca El Valle by PT's Coffee Roasting Co."

3. McCook, "Global Rust Belt," 179.
4. Ayres, *Harry Marshall Ward*, 10.
5. McCook, "Global Rust Belt," 179.
6. Ibid.
7. Ibid.
8. Haarer, *Modern Coffee Production*, 6.
9. McCook, "Global Rust Belt," 182.
10. Wellman, *Coffee*, 251.
11. Ibid., 54; Ayres, *Harry Marshall Ward*, 4.
12. Ukers, *All About Coffee*, 237.
13. McCook, "Global Rust Belt."
14. Ibid., 180; Ayres, *Harry Marshall Ward*, 10–11.
15. Wellman, *Coffee*, 257.
16. McCook, "Global Rust Belt."
17. Ibid.
18. Wellman, *Coffee*, 257.
19. McCook, "Global Rust Belt," 182.
20. Ayres, *Harry Marshall Ward*, 5.
21. Wellman, *Coffee*, 258.
22. McCook, "Global Rust Belt," 185.
23. Ibid., 184.
24. Kushalappa and Eskes, *Coffee Rust*, 2.
25. Ibid.
26. McCook, "Global Rust Belt," 189–90.
27. Ibid., 190–91.
28. Ibid., 191.
29. Kushalappa and Eskes, *Coffee Rust*, 5.
30. Ibid.
31. Avelino et al., "Coffee Rust Crises."
32. Drapkin, "What Is Coffee Rust?"
33. Ibid.
34. "Unaccompanied Alien Children."
35. Avelino et al., "Coffee Rust Crises."
36. Partlow, "Why El Salvador Became the Hemisphere's Murder Capital."
37. "Unaccompanied Alien Children."
38. Partlow, "Why El Salvador Became the Hemisphere's Murder Capital."
39. "Unaccompanied Alien Children."
40. Drapkin, "Central American Coffee Plague."
41. USDA Foreign Agricultural Services, *GAIN Report*, 2016.
42. Sage, "Some Insights on Coffee Leaf Rust."
43. Ibid.
44. Allegro Coffee Company Facebook post, October 15, 2014.
45. Blixen, *Out of Africa*, 17.

CHAPTER 12: IMPOVERISHED

1. Kushalappa and Eskes, *Coffee Rust*, 178.
2. Kubota, "Introduction to *Coffea* Genetics."
3. Lashermes, Bertrand, and Etienne, "Breeding Coffee," 526.
4. Ibid.
5. USDA Foreign Agricultural Services, *GAIN Report*, 2017.
6. Wellman, *Coffee*, 39.
7. Ibid., 258.
8. Cramer, *Review of Literature of Coffee Research in Indonesia*, xiv.
9. Zimmer, "How Caffeine Evolved."
10. Nealon, "Coffee Genome Sheds Light on the Evolution of Caffeine."
11. Zimmer, "How Caffeine Evolved."
12. Summers, "How Vietnam Became a Coffee Giant."
13. From 1912 to 1960. Pendergrast, *Uncommon Grounds*, 142, 239.
14. "Varieties," Stumptown Coffee website.
15. Meister, "Coffee Varieties."
16. Sheridan, "Origins of the Castillo Cultivar."
17. Ibid.
18. Ibid.
19. Drapkin, "What Is Coffee Rust?"
20. Ibid.
21. Avelino et al., "Coffee Rust Crises."
22. Sheridan, "Castillo or Caturra?"
23. Kotecha, "Arabicas from the Garden of Eden."
24. Zamir, "Wake-up Call with Coffee."
25. Ibid.
26. Kotecha, "Arabicas from the Garden of Eden."
27. Davis, "Arabica."
28. "Kew Gardens."
29. Charles, "Exploring Coffee's Past to Rescue Its Future."

CHAPTER 13: COLLECTING

1. Poncet, *Voyage to Aethiopia*, 119.
2. Meyer, "Notes on Wild *Coffea arabica*," 142.
3. Bredin, *Pale Abyssinian*, 42.
4. Fry, *Plant Hunters*, 6.
5. *Georg Wilhelm Schimper—in Abyssinia*.
6. Bridson and Forman, *Herbarium Handbook*, 2.
7. Ukers, *All About Coffee*, 228–29.
8. Meyer, "Notes on Wild *Coffea arabica*," 136.
9. *FAO Coffee Mission to Ethiopia*, viii.
10. Dulloo et al., "Conservation of Coffee Genetic Resources," 3.
11. Sylvain, "Ethiopian Coffee," 133.
12. Sylvain, "Some Observations on *Coffea arabica*."
13. Wellman, *Coffee*, 39.

14. Engelmann et al., *Conserving Coffee Genetic Resources*, 35.
15. Meyer, "Notes on Wild *Coffea arabica*," 136.
16. Meyer, "Recent Introductions of Wild Arabica Coffee Germ Plasm," 123.
17. *FAO Coffee Mission to Ethiopia*, 22.
18. Meyer, "Recent Introductions of Wild Arabica Coffee Germ Plasm," 124.
19. Sullivan, "Frederick Meyer."
20. Meyer, "Recent Introductions of Wild Arabica Coffee Germ Plasm," 120.
21. Vega, Ebert, and Ming, "Coffee Germplasm Resources," 420.
22. Jean-Pierre Labouisse.

CHAPTER 14: EX SITU

1. Dulloo et al., "Conservation of Genetic Coffee Resources," 4.
2. Labouisse et al., "Current Status of Coffee," 1085–86.
3. Rourk, *Coffee Production in Africa*, 5.
4. Jean-Pierre Labouisse.
5. *National Coffee Board of Ethiopia (1957–1972)*.
6. Kufa, "Overview of Coffee Research in Ethiopia," 230.
7. "Biodiversity-Related Conventions," Convention on Biological Diversity website.
8. Anthony et al., "Conservation of Coffee Genetic Resources," 24.
9. Labouisse et al., "Current Status of Coffee," 1087.
10. Siddle and Venema, "Saving Coffee from Extinction."
11. Minet, "Aux Sources de l'Arabica."
12. Kufa, "Coffee Research in Ethiopia."

CHAPTER 15: GEISHA

1. Haarer, *Modern Coffee Production*, 406.
2. Watts, "Geisha Trilogy."
3. Boot, "Exploring the Holy Grail."
4. Boot, "Variety Is the Spice of Coffee."
5. "Hacienda La Esmeralda."
6. Ibid.
7. Ibid.
8. "Jaramillo Coffee from Hacienda La Esmeralda," Sweet Maria's website.
9. Ibid.
10. "Daniel Peterson, Hacienda Esmeralda."
11. "Jaramillo Coffee from Hacienda La Esmeralda," Sweet Maria's website.
12. Ibid.
13. Salvadori, *Slaves and Ivory Continued*, 13.
14. Ibid., 14.
15. Ibid., 120.
16. Millor, "Inventory of the Coffee Varieties," 1.
17. Salvadori, *Slaves and Ivory Continued*, 317.
18. Kotecha, "Arabicas from the Garden of Eden."
19. "News and Notes," *Coffee and Cacao Technical Services*, 59.

20. Millor, "Inventory of the Coffee Varieties," 1.
21. "Panama Hacienda La Esmeralda Gesha," Sweet Maria's website.
22. Weissman, *God in a Cup*, 36.
23. "Raising Coffee Consciousness."
24. Pendergrast, "Tastes."
25. "Hacienda La Esmeralda."
26. "Esmeralda Special," Hacienda La Esmeralda website.
27. Watts, "Geisha Trilogy."
28. "Best of Panama 2013," Stoneworks Specialty Coffee Auction website.
29. Millor, "Inventory of the Coffee Varieties," 1.
30. *FAO Coffee Mission to Ethiopia*, 18.
31. Blore, "Arabica Coffee Selection," 39.

CHAPTER 16: A MATTER OF DEGREES

1. Davis, "Arabica."
2. Davis et al., "Impact of Climate Change on Indigenous Arabica Coffee."
3. Davis, "Arabica."
4. Ibid.
5. Thomas, "Wild *Arabica* Coffee on the Boma Plateau."
6. "World Coffee Research Finds Wild Arabica."
7. Cohen and Castro, "As Climate Change Threatens CentAm Coffee."
8. Brown, "Report."
9. Carrington, "How Climate Change Will Brew a Bad-Tasting, Expensive Cup of Coffee."
10. McFerron, "Global Coffee Shortage Looms."
11. Ovalle-Rivera et al., "Projected Shifts in *Coffea arabica* Suitability."
12. Sheridan, "Castillo or Caturra?"
13. Davis, "Building a Climate Resilient Coffee Economy for Ethiopia."
14. Davis et al., "Coffee Farming and Climate Change."
15. Davis, "Building a Climate Resilient Coffee Economy for Ethiopia."
16. Davis, "Arabica."

CHAPTER 17: IN SITU

1. Possemeyer, "Wild Coffee."
2. Woldemariam Gole, *Vegetation of the Yayu Forest*, 25.
3. Dulloo et al., "Conservation of Genetic Resources," 7.
4. Tran, "Ethiopia Enlists Help of Forest Communities."
5. Labouisse et al., "Current Status of Coffee," 1084.
6. *FAO Coffee Mission to Ethiopia*, viii.
7. Federal Democratic Republic of Ethiopia Central Statistical Agency, "Population Projection of Ethiopia."
8. Davis et al., "Coffee Farming and Climate Change."
9. "Bebeka Coffee Estate," Horizon Plantations website.
10. *FAO Statistical Pocketbook, 2015—Coffee*, 74.
11. Wallengren, "Ethiopia."

12. Ibid.
13. Maasho, "Saudi Investor's Ethiopian Farms to Raise Coffee, Tea Output."
14. Bieber, *Kaffa*, 1384.
15. Schmitt, *Montane Rainforest with Wild* Coffea arabica, 7.
16. Stellmacher and Eguavoen, "Rules of Hosts and Newcomers," 3.
17. Ibid., 7.
18. Tolera et al., "In-Situ Conservation of Wild Forest Coffee," 2.
19. Gobeze et al., "Participatory Forest Management," 348.
20. Dulloo et al., "Conservation of Coffee Genetic Resources," 6.
21. Strand, "Coffee Is Not Dead."
22. Davis, "Arabica."
23. Strand, "Coffee Is Not Dead."
24. Hein and Gatzweiler, "Economic Value of Coffee."

CHAPTER 18: SACRIFICES

1. Lange, *History of the Southern Gonga*, 283.
2. Ibid., 284.
3. Grühl, *Citadel of Ethiopia*, 177.
4. Lange, *History of the Southern Gonga*, 189.
5. Ibid.
6. Orent, "Lineage Structure and the Supernatural."
7. Lange, *History of the Southern Gonga*, 278–79.
8. Huntingford, *Galla of Ethiopia*, 133.
9. Woldemariam, *History of the Kingdom of Kaffa*, 92.
10. Lange, *History of the Southern Gonga*, 300.
11. Gobeze et al., "Participatory Forest Management," 348.
12. Naipaul, *Masque of Africa*, 161.
13. Riechmann, "Literature Survey on Biological Data," 26.
14. Woldemariam, *History of the Kingdom of Kaffa*, 65.
15. Hari, "Valley of Taboos."
16. Woldemariam, *History of the Kingdom of Kaffa*, 220.

Bibliography

Aerts, Raf, et al. "Semi-Forest Coffee Cultivation and the Conservation of Ethiopian Afromontane Rainforest Fragments." *Forest Ecology and Management*, March 2011.

Ahmad, Abdussamad H. "Ethiopian Slave Exports at Matamma, Massawa and Tajura c. 1830 to 1885." In *The Economics of the Indian Ocean Slave Trade*, edited by William Gervase Clarence-Smith. London: Routledge, 2013.

———. "Priest Planters and Slavers of Zägé (Ethiopia), 1900–1935." *International Journal of African Historical Studies 29*, no. 3 (1996).

Álvarez, Father Francisco. *Narrative of the Portuguese Embassy to Abyssinia During the Years 1520–1527*. Translated from the Portuguese and edited with notes and an introduction by Lord Stanley of Adlerley. London: Hakluyt Society, 1881.

Anthony, Françoise, et al. "Conservation of Coffee Genetic Resources in the CATIE Field Genebank." In *Conserving Coffee Genetic Resources*, edited by F. Engelmann et al. Rome: Bioversity International, 2007.

Anthony, Françoise, et al. "The Origin of Cultivated *Coffea arabica* L. Varieties Revealed by AFLP and SSR Markers." *Theoretical and Applied Genetics 104* (2002): 894–900.

Aregay, Merid W. "The Early History of Ethiopia's Coffee Trade and the Rise of Shawa." *Journal of African Studies 29* (1988): 19–25.

Ash, John, and John Atkins. *Birds of Ethiopia and Eritrea: An Atlas of Distribution*. London: Christopher Helm, 2009.

Avelino, Jacques, et al. "The Coffee Rust Crises in Colombia and Central America (2008–2013): Impacts, Plausible Causes and Proposed Solutions." *Food Security 7*, no. 2 (March 2015): 303–21.

Ayres, P. G. *Harry Marshall Ward and the Fungal Thread of Death*. Saint Paul, MN: American Phytopathological Society, 2005.

Bagersh, Abdullah A., and Omar A. Bagersh. "History of the Coffee Sector in Ethiopia." *Jebena*, November 2013.

Baghdiantz McCabe, Ina. *Orientalism in Early Modern France: Eurasian Trade, Exoticism and the Ancien Régime.* Oxford: Berg, 2008.

Barker, W. C. "Extract Report on the Probable Geographical Position of Harar; with Some Information Relative to the Various Tribes in the Vicinity." *Journal of the Royal Geographical Society of London 12* (1842).

"Bebeka Coffee Estate." Horizon Plantations website. horizonplantations.com/be beka-horizon.html.

Bel, Zenobia. "Ethiopia Builds Coffee Museum." June 16, 2015. www.ethiogrio.com /news/26161-ethiopia-builds-coffee-museum-to-help-brand-its-coffees-in -bonga.html.

Bennett, Alan Weinberg, and Bonnie K. Bealer. *The World of Caffeine: The Science and Culture of the World's Most Popular Drug.* New York: Routledge, 2001.

Berecha, Gezahegn. "Effects of Forest Management on Mating Patterns, Pollen Flow and Intergenerational Transfer of Genetic Diversity in Wild Arabica Coffee (*Coffea arabica* L.) from Afromontane Rainforests." *Biological Journal of the Linnean Society 112*, no. 1 (May 2014).

Bertrand, Benoît, et al. "Performance of *Coffea arabica* F1 Hybrids in Agroforestry and Full-Sun Cropping Systems in Comparison with American Pure Line Cultivars." *Euphytica 181*, no. 2 (September 2011): 147–58.

"Best of Panama 2013." Stoneworks Specialty Coffee Auction website. auction.stone-works.com/PA2013/final_results.html.

Bieber, Friedrich. *Kaffa—ein Altkuschitisches Volkstum in Inner-Afrika.* Vol. 1. Münster, Germany: Aschendroff Verlagsbuchhandlung, 1920.

Bieber, Klaus. "The African Fascination of the Bieber Family." 2014. Bieber Archives at the District Museum Wien-Hietzing.

Bieber, Otto. *Geheimnisvolles Kaffa.* Vienna: Universum, 1948.

"Biodiversity-Related Conventions." Convention on Biological Diversity website. www.cbd.int/brc/.

Blixen, Karen. *Out of Africa.* London: Penguin, 1984.

Blore, T. W. D., "Arabica Coffee Selection and Genetic Improvement in Kenya." *Kenya Coffee 30*, no. 491 (1965): 39.

"Blue Bottle—WC Morse." Dialogue Design Build website. dialoguedesignbuild .com/portfoliointeriorsandfurniturewc-morse.

Blunt, Wilfrid. *The Compleat Naturalist: A Life of Linnaeus.* New York: Viking, 1971.

Bolton, Dan. "The Gesha Legacy." *Stir,* April–May 2015.

Boot, Willem. "Exploring the Holy Grail." *Roast,* May–June 2013.

———. "Variety Is the Spice of Coffee: Geisha and Other Varietals. *Roast,* May–June 2006.

Bradley, Richard. *A Short Historical Account of Coffee.* London: Emanuel Matthews, 1720.

Bredin, Miles. *The Pale Abyssinian: A Life of James Bruce, African Explorer and Adventurer.* London: HarperCollins, 2000.

Bridson, D., and L. Forman, eds. *The Herbarium Handbook.* 3rd ed. Kew, London: Royal Botanic Gardens, 1998.

Briggs, Philip. *Ethiopia.* 6th ed. UK: Chalfont St. Peter, Bradt Travel Guides, 2014.

Brown, Nick. "Report: Climate Change May Cut Available Coffee Growing Land in Half by 2050." *Daily Coffee News by Roast Magazine*, December 18, 2014.

Bruce, James. *Travels to Discover the Source of the Nile in the Years 1768, 1769, 1770, 1771, 1772, and 1773.* Vol. 2. Dublin: P. Wogan et al., 1791.

———. *Travels, Through Part of Africa, Syria, Egypt, and Arabia, into Abyssinia, To Discover the Source of the Nile, Performed Between the Years 1768 and 1773.* Glasgow, Scotland: W. Lange, 1819.

Bulatovich, Alexander. *Ethiopia Through Russian Eyes: Country in Transition, 1896–98.* Translated by Richard Seltzer Lawrenceville, NJ: Red Sea, 2000.

Burton, Richard F. *First Footsteps in East Africa; Or, an Exploration of Harar.* Vols. 1 & 2. New York: Dover, 1987. Unabridged republication of 1894 ed.

Carmichael, Todd. "The End of Stumptown, America's Hippest Coffee Brand." *Eat Like a Man* blog, www.esquire.com/food-drink/drinks/a10027/stumptown-sold-out-5839692/.

Carrington, Damian. "How Climate Change Will Brew a Bad-Tasting, Expensive Cup of Coffee." *Guardian*, March 28, 2014.

Caulk, Richard. *Between the Jaws of Hyenas: A Diplomatic History of Ethiopia (1876–1896).* Wiesbaden, Germany: Otto Harrassowitz, 2002.

Charles, Dan. "Exploring Coffee's Past to Rescue Its Future." NPR, April 26, 2013. www.npr.org/sections/thesalt/2013/04/26/178865467/exploring-coffees-past-to-rescue-its-future.

Charrier, André, and Julien Berthaud. "Botanical Classification of Coffee." In *Coffee: Botany, Biochemistry, and Production of Beans and Beverage*, edited by M. N. Clifford and K. C. Willson. Kent, UK: Croom Helm, 1985.

Chernet, Tezera. "Land Resources and Socio-Economic Report of Bonga, Boginda, Mankira and the Surrounding Areas in Kaffa Zone, SNNPRS, Ethiopia." Addis Ababa, July 2008.

Clay, Jason. *World Agriculture and the Environment: A Commodity-by-Commodity Guide to Impacts and Practices.* Washington, DC: Island, 2004.

Clifford, M. N., and K. C. Willson, eds. *Coffee: Botany, Biochemistry, and Production of Beans and Beverage.* London: Croom Helm, 1985.

"Coffee–*Coffea arabica*." Hortus Botanicus Amsterdam website dehortus.nl/en/Coffee.

Cohen, Luc. "Exclusive: Keurig Deal Gives Coffee Traders Jitters About Payments." Reuters, December 9, 2015.

Cohen, Luc, and Ivan Castro. "As Climate Change Threatens CentAm Coffee, a Cocoa Boom Is Born." Reuters, January 18, 2016.

Cramer, P. J. S. *A Review of Literature of Coffee Research in Indonesia.* Edited by Frederick L. Wellman. Turrialba, Costa Rica: SIC (Inter-American Institute of Agricultural Sciences), 1957.

Dagnew, Tesfaye, and Mesfin Wodajo. "The Socio-Cultural Functions of Kafa Proverbs." *African Journal of History and Culture* 6 (2014): 94–99.

"Daniel Peterson, Hacienda Esmeralda, Panama, Pioneering Geisha." Talk at Le Carnaval du Café, Paris, 2012. vimeo.com/52604159.

Davis, Aaron. "Arabica—from Origin to Extinction." Talk at Re:co: The Specialty Coffee Symposium. Boston, 2013.

————. "Building a Climate Resilient Coffee Economy for Ethiopia." Kew Gardens' website blog. August 2014.

Davis, Aaron, et al. "Coffee Farming and Climate Change in Ethiopia: Impact, Forecasts, Resilience and Opportunities." London: Kew, 2016.

Davis, Aaron, et al. "The Impact of Climate Change on Indigenous Arabica Coffee (*Coffea arabica*): Predicting Future Trends and Identifying Priorities." *PLoS ONE 7*, no. 11 (2012).

Deffar, Girma. "Non-Wood Forest Products in Ethiopia." Addis Ababa: FAO, December 1998.

de Vries, Jan. "Understanding Eurasian Trade in the Era of the Trading Companies." In *Goods from the East, 1600–1800: Trading Eurasia*, edited by Maxine Berg. London: Palgrave Macmillan, 2015.

Dinesen, Isak. *Letters from Africa: 1914–1931*. Edited by Frans Lasson. Translated by Anne Born. London: Picador, 1983.

Dire Dawa. Addis Ababa: Shama, 2013.

Downing, Ben. "A Decade in Hell." Review of *Somebody Else: Arthur Rimbaud in Africa, 1880–1991*, by Charles Nicholl. *New Yorker*, October 24, 1999.

Drapkin, Julia Kumari. "Central American Coffee Plague Behind Recent Wave of Immigrants to Metro New Orleans, Elsewhere." *Times-Picayune*, August 21, 2014.

————. "What Is Coffee Rust and Why Is It Pushing People to the U.S. Border?" *Times-Picayune*, August 21, 2014.

Dulloo, M. E., et al. "Conservation of Coffee Genetic Resources: Constraints and Opportunities." 19th ASIC Coffee Conference, May 14–18, 2001.

Ebert, Andrea W., et al. "Securing Our Future: CATIE's Germplasm Collections." Technical Series Bulletin no. 26. 2007.

Edwards, S. *Some Wild Flowering Plants of Ethiopia*. Addis Ababa: University, 1976.

Ellis, John. *A Historical Account of Coffee*. Cambridge: Cambridge, 2013. Facsimile of the 1774 ed.

Engelmann F., et al., eds. "Complementary Strategies for *Ex Situ* Conservation of Coffee (*Coffea arabica* L.) Genetic Resources. A Case Study in CATIE, Costa Rica." Topical Reviews in Agricultural Biodiversity. Rome: Bioversity International, 2007.

Engelmann F., et al., eds. *Conserving Coffee Genetic Resources*. Rome: Bioversity International, 2007.

Estes, Richard D. *The Safari Companion*. Rev. White River Junction, VT: Chelsea Green, 1999.

Ethiopia: The Handbook for Ethiopia. Nairobi: University Press of Africa, 1969.

Ethiopia's Central and Southern Rift Valley. Informative map. Washington, D.C.: National Geographic Society, 2011.

Fabricant, Florence. "Americans Wake Up and Smell the Coffee." *New York Times*, September 2, 1992.

FAO Coffee Mission to Ethiopia, 1964–65. Rome: FAO, 1968.

FAO Statistical Pocketbook, 2015—Coffee. Rome: FAO, 2015.

"A Feasibility Study of Public Private Partnership in Sustainable Ethiopia's Coffee Quality Improvement Programme." *International Multi-Disciplinary Journal, Ethiopia 3*, no. 2 (January 2009).

Federal Democratic Republic of Ethiopia Central Statistical Agency. "Population Projection of Ethiopia for All Regions at Wereda Level from 2014–2017." Addis Ababa. August 2013.

Fernyhough, Timothy. "Slavery and the Slave Trade in Southern Ethiopia in the 19th Century." In *The Economics of the Indian Ocean Slave Trade*, edited by William Gervase Clarence-Smith. London: Routledge, 2013.

———. "Women, Gender History, and Slavery in Nineteenth-Century Ethiopia." In *Women and Slavery*, Vol. 2: *The Modern Atlantic*. Athens: Ohio University, 2007.

"Food Security Crisis Likely Due to Coffee Rust and Drought." Central, America FoodSecurity Alert. August 13, 2014. www.fews.net/central-america-and-carib bean/alert/august-12-2014.

Frasier. Season 10, Episode 20, "Farewell, Nervosa," written by Eric Zicklin, 2003.

Freeman, D., and A. Pankhurst. *Peripheral People: The Excluded Minorities of Ethiopia*. London: Hurst, 2003.

Freeman, James. Talk at the Commonwealth Club in San Francisco, June 2, 2016. audio.commonwealthclub.org/audio/podcast/cc_20160602_Perfect_Brew.mp3.

Friedrich Julius Bieber: An Africa Explorer Who Was Living in Vienna, 1873–1924. District Museum Hietzing, n.d.

Friis, Ib. "Coffee and Qat on the Royal Danish Expedition to Arabia—Botanical, Ethnobotanical and Commercial Observations Made in Yemen, 1762–1763." *Archives of Natural History 41*, no. 1 (2015) 101–12.

———. *Forests & Forest Trees of Tropical Africa*. London: HMSO, 1992.

———. "Travelling Among Fellow Christians (1768–1833): James Bruce, Henry Salt and Eduard Rüppell in Abyssinia." *Scientia Danica*, Series H, *Humanistica*, January 2013, 4:161–94.

Fry, Carolyn. *The Plant Hunters*. London: Andre Deutsch, 2012.

"Gaki Sherocho," *Dictionary of African Biography 6*. New York: Oxford, 2012.

Geller, Martinne. "Nestlé on 'High Alert' After JAB's Spate of Coffee Deals." Reuters, February 18, 2016.

George Clifford Herbarium website. "Clifford." www.george-clifford.nl/UK/clifford _UK.htm.

———. "*Hortus Cliffortianus*." www.george-clifford.nl/UK/hc_UK.htm.

———. "Ornaments." www.george-clifford.nl/UK/ornaments.htm.

Georg Wilhelm Schimper—in Abyssinia. Edited by Andreas Gestrich and Dorothea McEwan in collaboration with Stefan Hanß. Critical online edition, 2015. www.ghil.ac.uk/Schimper.

Getahun, Solomon Addis, and Wudu Tafete Kassu. *Culture and Customs of Ethiopia*. Santa Barbara, CA: Greenwood, 2014.

Gibb, Camilla. *Sweetness in the Belly*. New York: Picador, 2000.

Githae, Eunice, Charles Gachene, and David W. Odee. "Implication for *In Situ* Conservation of Indigenous Species with Special Reference to Wild *Coffea arabica* L. Population in Mount Marsabit Forest, Kenya." *Tropical and Subtropical Agroecosystems 14* (2011): 715–22.

Gobeze, T., et al. "Participatory Forest Management and Its Impacts on Livelihoods and Forest Status: The Case of Bonga Forest in Ethiopia." *International Forestry Review 11* no. 3 (2009).

Gogan, Cothrai. *Holy Ghost Missions: The Spiritians in Nairobi, 1899–1999.* Nairobi: Spiritus, 1998.

Grant, James Augustus. *A Walk Across Africa or Domestic Scenes From My Nile Journal.* Edinburgh and London: William Blackwood and Sons, 1864.

Griffiths, Mark. "Clifford's Banana: How Natural History Was Made in a Garden." *Linnean Special Issue No. 7: The Linnaean Collections,* edited by B. Gardiner and M. Morris. Oxford: Wiley-Blackwell, 2007.

Grühl, Max. *The Citadel of Ethiopia: The Empire of the Divine Emperor.* London: Jonathan Cape, 1932.

"Guatemala Antigua Finca El Valle." Batdorf & Bronson, website. www.batdorfcof fee.com/guatemala-antigua-finca-el-valle.html.

"Guatemala Finca El Valle by PT's Coffee Roasting Co. (Topeka, Kansas)—92 Points." *Coffee Review,* October 12, 2012.

"Guatemala Volcano Eruption Forces Evacuations." Reuters, February 8, 2015.

Guide Book of Ethiopia. Addis Ababa: Chamber of Commerce, 1954.

Haarer, A. E. *Modern Coffee Production.* London: Leonard Hill, 1956.

"Hacienda La Esmeralda." Coffee Awesome podcast. May 21, 2014. www.coffeeawe some.net/?p=18.

Hämäläinen, Pertti. *Yemen: A Travel Survival Kit.* Berkeley: Lonely Planet, 1991.

"Harar Jugol, the Fortified Historic Town." World Heritage List. UNESCO website. whc.unesco.org/en/list/1189.

Hari, Johann. "The Valley of Taboos: V. S. Naipaul Dares to Discuss Africa's Indigenous Beliefs." Review of *The Masque of Africa,* by V. S. Naipaul. *Slate,* October 25, 2010.

Hassen, Mohammed. *The Oromo of Ethiopia: A History, 1570–1860.* Trenton, NJ: Red Sea, 1994.

Hattox, Ralph S. *Coffee and Coffeehouses: The Origins of a Social Beverage in the Medieval Near East.* Seattle: University of Washington, 1985.

Hein, Lars, and Franz Gatzweiler. "Economic Value of Coffee (*Coffea arabica*) Genetic Resources." *Ecological Economics 60,* no. 1 (November 2006): 176–85.

Hibbert, Christopher. *Africa Explored: Europeans in the Dark Continent, 1767–1889.* London: Penguin, 1984.

Hildebrand, Elisabeth, Steven Bradt, and Joséphine Lesur-Gebremariam. "The Holocene Archaeology of Southwestern Ethiopia: New Insights from the Kafa Archaeology Project." *African Archaeology Review 27* (2010): 255–89.

Hoffman, James. *The World Atlas of Coffee: From Beans to Brewing.* London: Mitchell Beazley, 2014.

Homer. *The Odyssey.* Translated by Robert Fagles. London: Penguin, 1996.

Howard, Sarah. *Ethiopia–Culture Smart!* Rev. London: Kuperard, 2013.

Huntingford, G. W. B. *The Galla of Ethiopia: The Kingdoms of Kafa and Janjero.* London: International African Institute, 1955.

Hylander, Kristoffer, et al. *Nature, People and Agriculture in Southwestern Ethiopia.* Stockholm: Stockholm University, 2014.

"International Coffee Day: A Devastating Plague of Coffee Rust That Is Leaving Communities Hungry and Desperate." *Save the Children* blog. September 29, 2014. blogs.savethechildren.org.uk/2014/09/international-coffee-day-a-devas tating-plague-of-coffee-rust-that-is-leaving-communities-hungry-and-desperate/.

"Is Starbucks Really Always Two Blocks Away?" Aleksey Bilogur website. www.resi dentmar.io/2016/02/09/average-chain-distance.html.

Ito, Yoshimasa. "Local Honey Production Activities and Their Significance for Local People: A Case of Mountain Forest Area of Southwestern Ethiopia." *African Study Monographs*, March 2014.

"Jaramillo Coffee from Hacienda La Esmeralda." Sweet Maria's website. www.sweet marias.com/travelogues/panama-Jaramillo.html.

Jeffrey, James. "Arabica in Addis Ababa: Climbing the Coffee Ladder in Ethiopia." Al Jazeera America, October 20, 2014.

———. "Boom Times for Ethiopia's Coffee Shops." BBC News, October 16, 2014. www.bbc.com/news/business-29541768.

Jonas, Raymond. *The Battle of Adwa: African Victory in the Age of Empire*. Cambridge, MA: Belknap, 2011.

Kaplan, Sarah. "Mr. Coffee Creator Vincent Marotta Sr., Who Revolutionized the Way We Caffeinate, Dies at 91." *Washington Post*, August 4, 2015.

"Karen Blixen. Location and Historical Background." National Museums of Kenya website. www.museums.or.ke/content/blogcategory/13/19/.

Kassahun, Tesfaye Geletu. "Genetic Diversity of Wild *Coffea arabica* Populations in Ethiopia as a Contribution to Conservation and Use Planning." Ecology and Development Series No. 44, 2006.

Kathurima, C. W., et al. "Genetic Diversity Among Commercial Coffee Varieties, Advanced Selections and Museum Collections in Kenya Using Molecular Markers." *International Journal of Biodiversity and Conservation 4*, no. 2 (2012): 39–46.

Keay, John. *The Honourable Company: History of the English East India Company*. London: HarperCollins, 1993.

"Kew Gardens—Beyond the Gardens: The Forgotten Home of Coffee." vimeo. com/67890000.

Kieran, J. A. "The Origins of Commercial Arabica Coffee Production in East Africa." *African Historical Studies 2*, no. 1 (1969): 51–67.

Kingdon, Jonathan. *Island Africa: The Evolution of Africa's Rare Animals and Plants*. London: Collins, 1990.

Kokalitcheva, Kia. "Blue Bottle Raises $70 Million for an Artisanal Coffee Empire." *Fortune*, June 4, 2015.

Kotecha, Surendra. "Arabicas from the Garden of Eden—*Coffea aethiopica*." *Café Europe: Voice of the Specialty Coffee Association of Europe 31* (2007).

Kraft, Kraig. "Coffee Hybrids and a Frank Talk About Breeding Coffee." Coffeeland website. May 25, 2015. coffeelands.crs.org/2015/05/coffee-hybrids-and-a-frank -talk-about-breeding-coffee/.

Krapf, Ludwig. *Travels, Researches, and Missionary Labours, During an Eighteen Years' Residence in Eastern Africa*. London: Trüber, 1860.

Krishnan, Sarada, and Tom A. Ranker. "Coffee Genomics." In *Omics Technologies: Tools for Food Science*. Boca Raton, FL: CRC, 2012.

Krol, Hans. "Linnaeus op de Hartekamp (1735–1737)." January 3, 2012. ilibrariana .wordpress.com/2012/01/02/linnaeus-op-de-hartekamp-1735-1737/.

Kubota, Lily. "An Introduction to *Coffea* Genetics." *Specialty Coffee Chronicle*, January 8, 2013.

Kufa, Taye. "Coffee Research in Ethiopia." *Jebena*, November 2013.
———. "An Overview of Coffee Research in Ethiopia." Slideshow. September 15, 2015.
Kushalappa, Ajjamada C., and Albertus B. Eskes. *Coffee Rust: Epidemiology, Resistance, and Management.* Boca Raton, FL: CRC, 1989.
Labouisse, Jean-Pierre, et al. "Current Status of Coffee (*Coffea arabica* L.) Genetic Resources in Ethiopia: Implications for Conservation." *Genetic Resources and Crop Evolution 55* (July 2008): 1079.
Lamb, David. *The Africans.* New York: Vintage, 1987.
Lange, Werner J. *History of the Southern Gonga (Southwestern Ethiopia).* Wiesbaden, Germany: Franz Steiner Verlag, 1982.
Lashermes, Philippe, Benoît Bertrand, and Hervé Etienne. "Breeding Coffee (*Coffea arabica*) for Sustainable Production." In *Breeding Plantation Tree Crops: Tropical Species*, edited by Shri Mohan Jain and P. M. Priyadarshan. New York: Springer, 2009.
Lashermes, Philippe, et al. "Genetic Diversity for RAPD Markers Between Cultivated and Wild Accessions of *Coffea arabica*." *Euphytica 87*, no. 1 (January 1996).
Lashermes, Philippe, et al. "Origin and Genetic Diversity of *Coffea arabica*." Association Scientifique Internationale pour le Café (ASIC). 16th Scientific Colloquium on Coffee, Kyoto, 1995.
Lasson, Frans, and Anne Born. *Isak Dinesen, Letters from Africa, 1914–1931.* Chicago: University of Chicago, 1981.
Last, Jill. *Ethiopians and the Houses They Live In.* Ethiopian Tourist Commission.
The Legend of Ethiopian Coffee. Africa Rikai Project. Addis Ababa: Gudina Tumsa, 2012.
Levine, Donald N. *Greater Ethiopia: The Evolution of a Multiethnic Society.* Chicago: University of Chicago Press, 1974.
Linnaei, Caroli. *Potus Coffea.* Upsaliae [Upsala], Sweden, 1761.
Linnaeo, Carolo. *Hortus Cliffortianus.* Amsterdam, 1737.
Lorenzetti, Linda Rice. *The Birth of Coffee.* New York: Clarkson Potter, 2000.
Love, Ronald S. "A French Physician at the Court of Gondar: Poncet's Ethiopia in the 1690s." *Proceedings of the Western Society for French History* 31 (2003).
Luttinger, Nina, and Gregory Dicum. *The Coffee Book: Anatomy of an Industry from Crop to the Last Drop.* 2nd ed. New York: New Press, 2006.
Luxner, Larry. "Ethiopian Coffee Industry: Overcoming Difficulties." *Tea & Coffee Trade Journal 174*, no. 2 (February–March 2001).
Maasho, Aaron. "Saudi Investor's Ethiopian Farms to Raise Coffee, Tea Output." Reuters, June 25, 2015.
Marcus, Harold G. *A History of Ethiopia.* Updated ed. Berkeley: University of California, 2002.
———. *The Life and Times of Menelik II: Ethiopia, 1844–1913.* Oxford: Clarendon, 1975.
Markakis, John. *Ethiopia: The Last Two Frontiers.* Suffolk, UK: James Currey, 2011.
McCann, James. *People of the Plow: An Agricultural History of Ethiopia.* Madison: University of Wisconsin, 1995.

McClellan, Charles W. "Coffee in Center—Periphery Relations: Gedo in the Early Twentieth Century." In *The Southern Marches of Imperial Ethiopia: Essays in History and Social Anthropology*, edited by Donald Donham and Wendy James. Cambridge: Cambridge, 1986.

McCook, Stuart. "Global Rust Belt: *Hemileia vastatrix* and the Ecological Integration of World Coffee Production Since 1850." *Journal of Global History 1*, no. 2 (2006): 177–95.

McFerron, Whitney. "Global Coffee Shortage Looms as Market Braces for Climate Change." Bloomberg, October 1, 2015.

McGregor, Jena. "Starbucks Brought Italian Café Style to America. Can It Bring American Coffee to Italy?" *Washington Post*, February 29, 2016.

McHugo, John. "Coffee and Qahwa: How a Drink for Arab Mystics Went Global." *BBC Magazine*, April 18, 2013.

Mdahoma, Sauda. *Kaldi and the Dancing Goats: The Legend of Ethiopian Coffee*. Addis Ababa: Shama, 2002.

Meister, Erin. "Coffee Varieties: Timor Hybrid." *Serious Eats*. drinks.seriouseats .com/2013/06/coffee-varieties-what-is-timor-hybrid-sumatran-coffee-catimor -what-does-it-taste-like-flavor.html.

Menassa, Pascale. "Yemen's Coffee Revival." Translated by Pascale el-Khoury. *Al Monitor*, February 2, 2014.

Mendelsohn, Daniel. "Rebel Rebel: Arthur Rimbaud's Brief Career." *New Yorker*, August 29, 2011.

Meyer, Frederick G. "Notes on Wild *Coffea arabica* from Southwestern Ethiopia, with Some Historical Considerations." *Economic Botany 19*, no. 2 (April–June 1965): 136–51.

———. "Recent Introductions of Wild Arabica Coffee Germ Plasm from Ethiopia for Updating Coffee Research." *Proceedings of the International Symposium on Plant Introduction, Escuela Agricola Panamericana, Tegucigalpa, Honduras, November 30–December 2, 1966*.

Mezlekia, Nega. *Notes from the Hyena's Belly: An Ethiopian Boyhood*. New York: Picador, 2002.

Miers, Suzanne. *Slavery in the Twentieth Century: The Evolution of a Global Problem*. Walnut Creek, CA: AltaMira, 2003.

Milkias, Paulos. *Ethiopia. Africa in Focus*. Santa Barbara, CA: ABC-CLIO, 2011.

Millor, F. "Inventory of the Coffee Varieties and Selections Imported into and Growing Within East-Africa." Unpublished, 1969.

Milos, Giorgio. "Coffee's Mysterious Origins." *Atlantic Monthly*, August 6, 2010.

Minet, Pascaline. "Aux Sources de l'Arabica." *Le Temps*, April 25, 2013. English translation in *Worldcrunch*. www.worldcrunch.com/global-gourmet/seeking-the-true -source-of-arabica-coffee-in-the-ethiopian-forest/c10s11663/.

Moorehead, Alan. *The Blue Nile*. New York: Perennial, 2000.

———. *The White Nile*. New York: Harper & Brothers, 1960.

Morris, Jan. *Farewell the Trumpets: An Imperial Retreat*. London: Faber & Faber, 1998.

Moss, Stephen. "Birdwatch: Prince Ruspoli's Turaco." *Guardian*, November 20, 2011.

Mureithi, Leopold P. "Coffee in Kenya: Some Challenges for Decent Work." Sectoral Activities Programme, Working Paper. Geneva, 2008.

NABU. *Kafa Biosphere Reserve: Your Visitors' Guide.* Edited by Svane Bender-Kaphengst and Daniela Tunger. Berlin: NABU, 2013.

Naipaul, V. S. *The Masque of Africa.* Toronto: Vintage: 2011.

National Coffee Board of Ethiopia (1957–1972). Addis Ababa: National Coffee Board, January 1972.

Naval Intelligence Division. *Western Arabia & the Red Sea.* Repr., London: Kegan Paul, 2005.

Nealon, Cory. "Coffee Genome Sheds Light on the Evolution of Caffeine." Press release. University of Buffalo, September 4, 2014.

"News and Notes." *Coffee and Cacao Technical Services* (Turrialba, Costa Rica) *2*, no. 4 (January–March 1960).

Nicholl, Charles. *Somebody Else: Rimbaud in Africa.* Chicago: University of Chicago, 1997.

Njoku, Raphael Chijioke. *The History of Somalia.* Santa Barbara, CA: Greenwood, ˚2013.

"Open Letter from Doug Zell." Intelligentsia Coffee website. www.intelligentsiacof fee.com/content/open-letter-doug-zell.

Oremus, Will. "Genius Barista." Slate.com, March 24, 2014.

———. "Why Coffee Snobs Shouldn't Be Steamed That Peet's Bought Stumptown." Slate.com, October 7, 2015.

Orent, Amnon. "Dual Organizations in Southern Ethiopia: Anthropological Imagination or Ethnographic Fact." *Ethnology 9*, no. 3 (July 1970): 228–33.

———. "Lineage Structure and the Supernatural: The Kafa of Southwest Ethiopia." Ph.D. diss., Boston University, 1969.

———. "Refocusing on the History of Kafa Prior to 1897: A Discussion of Political Processes." *African Historical Studies 3*, no. 2 (1970): S. 263–93.

"Original Journal of a Voyage into the Red Sea, in the Swift Sloop of War, 1795." *Gentleman's Magazine and Historical Chronicle for the Year MDCCCVI 76*, pt. 1. London: J. Nichols and Son, 1806.

"An Orphan Crop." *Global Coffee Report*, November 2011.

Ovalle-Rivera, Oriana, et al. "Projected Shifts in *Coffea arabica* Suitability Among Major Global Producing Regions due to Climate Change." *PLoS ONE 10*, no. 4 (2015): e0124155.

Pankhurst, Alula. *Resettlement and Famine in Ethiopia: The Villager's Experience.* Manchester: Manchester University, 1992.

Pankhurst, Richard. *Economic History of Ethiopia, 1800–1935.* Addis Ababa: Haile Selassie I University, 1968.

———. *Ethiopian Borderlands: Essays in Regional History from Ancient Times to the End of the 18th Century.* Lawrenceville, NJ: Red Sea Press, 1997.

———. *The Ethiopians: A History.* Malden, MA: Blackwell, 1998.

———. *An Introduction to the Economic History of Ethiopia, from Early Times to 1800.* London: Lalibela House, 1961.

———. "Muslim Commercial Towns, Villages and Markets of Christian Ethiopia Prior to the Rise of Tewodros." *Collectanea Aethiopica*, edited by S. Uhlig and B Tayl, 111–30. Stuttgart: Franz Steiner Verlag, 1998.

Pankhurst, Rita. "Coffee Ceremony and the History of Coffee Consumption in Ethiopia," *Ethiopia in Broader Perspective: Papers of the XIIIth International Conference of Ethiopian Studies, Kyoto, 12–17 December 1997,* 2:516–39.

Partlow, Joshua. "Why El Salvador Became the Hemisphere's Murder Capital." *Washington Post,* January 5, 2016.

Pendergrast, Mark. "Tastes: What Is Coffee Worth?" *Wine Spectator,* November 15, 2006.

———. *Uncommon Grounds: The History of Coffee and How It Transformed Our World.* New York: Basic, 2010.

Perez, Marvin. "Coffee-Loving Millennials Push Demand to a Record." Bloomberg, October 30, 2016.

Plants in the Spotlight: Biodiversity from All over the World in the Heart of Amsterdam. Amsterdam: Hortus Botanicus Amsterdam, 2010.

Poncet, Charles-Jacques. *A Voyage to Aethiopia, Made in the Years 1698, 1699, and 1700. Describing Particularly that Famous Empire; as also the Kingdoms of Dongola, Sennar, Part of Egypt, &c. With the Natural History of Those Parts. By Monsieur Poncet, M.D. Faithfully Translated from the French Original.* London: Printed for W. Lewis at the Dolphin, next Tom's Coffee-House in Russel-Street, Covent-Garden, 1709.

Possemeyer, Ines. "Wild Coffee." *GEO,* February 2012.

The Portuguese Expedition to Abyssinia in 1541–1543, as Narrated by Castanhoso. Translated and edited by R. S. Whiteway. London: Hakluyt Society, 1902.

Prouty, Chris, and Eugene Rosenfeld. *Historical Dictionary of Ethiopia and Eritrea.* 2nd ed. Metuchen, NJ: Scarecrow, 2004.

Raine, George. "Alfred Peet, 1920–2007: Coffee Pioneer Influenced America's Taste." *San Francisco Chronicle,* September 1, 2007.

"Raising Coffee Consciousness: The Cup of Excellence and Green Coffee Competitions." *Coffee Review,* November 3, 2004. www.coffeereview.com/raising-coffee-consciousness-the-cup-of-excellence-and-green-coffee-competitions/.

Redi, Omer. "They Have Become Farmers of Trees." Inter Press Service, November 19, 2010.

Redman, Nigel. *Birds of the Horn of Africa: Ethiopia, Eritrea, Djibouti, Somalia, and Socotra.* 2nd ed. London: Christopher Helm, 2011.

Rice, Edward. *Captain Sir Richard Francis Burton: A Biography.* Boston: Da Capo, 2001.

Rice, Robert. "Sun Versus Shade Coffee: Truth and Consequences." May 27, 1996. www.ico.org/event_pdfs/environment/rice.pdf.

Riechmann, Dennis. "Literature Survey on Biological Data and Research Carried Out in Bonga Area, Kafa, Ethiopia." NABU, unpublished, November 2007.

Rimbaud, Arthur. *I Promise to Be Good: The Letters of Arthur Rimbaud.* Translated and edited by Wyatt Mason. New York: Modern Library, 2003.

———. *Rimbaud: Complete Works.* Translated by Paul Schmidt. New York: Harper & Row, 1975.

Robb, Graham. *Rimbaud.* New York: Norton, 2001.

Robins, Nick. *The Corporation That Changed the World.* Hyderabad, India: Orient Longman, 2006.

Robinson, J. Brian. *Coffee in Yemen: A Practical Guide.* Eschborn, Germany: GT2, 1993.

de la Roque, Jean. *A Voyage to Arabia Felix Through the Eastern Ocean and the Streights of the Red-Sea, Being the First Made by the French in the Years 1708, 1709 and, 1710.* London: E. Symon, 1732.

Rourk, J. Phillip. *Coffee Production in Africa.* Washington, DC: U.S. Department of Agriculture Foreign Agricultural Service, September 1975.

Ryan, Chris. "Volcano Ash Dusts Finca El Valle but Farm Is Safe." Sustainable Harvest website. February 11, 2015. www.sustainableharvest.com/volcano -ash-dusts-finca-el-valle/.

Sadler, Peter. *Regional Development* in *Ethiopia.* Bangor Occasional Papers in Economics. Cardiff: University of Wales, 1976.

Sage, Emma. "Coffee Plants for the Future: Update on the World Coffee Research Breeding Program." *Specialty Coffee Chronicle,* April 6, 2015.

———. "Some Insights on Coffee Leaf Rust (Hemileia vastatrix)." *Specialty Coffee Chronicle,* February 15, 2015.

Salvadori, Cynthia. *Slaves and Ivory Continued: Letters of R .C. R. Whalley, British Consul, Maji, SW Ethiopia, 1930–1935.* Addis Ababa: Sharma, 2010.

Sardar, Ziauddin. *Mecca: The Sacred City.* Delhi: Bloomsbury, 2014.

Schmitt, Christine B. *Montane Rainforest with Wild* Coffea arabica *in the Bonga Region (SW Ethiopia): Plant Diversity, Wild Coffee Management and Implications for Conservation.* Ecology and Development Series no. 47, 2006.

Schmitt, Christine B., et al. "Wild Coffee Management and Plant Diversity in the Montane Rainforest of Southwestern Ethiopia." *African Journal of Ecology 48,* no. 1 (March 2010).

Schultz, Howard, and Dori Jones Yang. *Pour Your Heart into It.* New York: Hyperion, 1997.

Senbeta, Wakjira Feyera. *Biodiversity and Ecology of Afromontane Rainforests with Wild* Coffea arabica *L. Populations in Ethiopia.* Ecology and Development Series no. 38. Göttingen, Germany: Cuvillier Verlag, 2006.

Sheridan, Michael. "Castillo or Caturra? A Simple Question." *Specialty Coffee Chronicle,* August 4, 2015. www.scaa.org/chronicle/2015/08/04/castillo-or-caturra -a-simple-question/.

———. "The Origins of the Castillo Cultivar." *Coffeelands* (blog). coffeelands.crs .org/2013/01/the-origins-of-the-castillo-cultivar/.

Shinn, David H., and Thomas P. Ofcansky. *Historical Dictionary of Ethiopia.* 2nd ed. Plymouth, UK: Scarecrow, 2013.

Siddle, Julian, and Vibeke Venema. "Saving Coffee from Extinction." *BBC Magazine,* May 24, 2015. www.bbc.com/news/magazine-32736366.

Sinclair, I., and P. Ryan. *Birds of Africa: South of the Sahara.* Princeton, NJ: Princeton University, 2003.

Skinner, Robert P. *Abyssinia of To-Day: An Account of the First Mission Sent by the American Government to the Court of the King of Kings (1903–1904).* New York: Longmans, Green, 1906.

Spary, E. C. *Eating and Enlightenment.* Chicago: University of Chicago Press, 2012.

Stellmacher, Till, and Irit Eguavoen. "The Rules of Hosts and Newcomers. Local Forest Management After Resettlement in Ethiopia." European Conference of African Studies, Uppsala, 2011.

"Stepping Away from Wholesale." Blue Bottle website. June 22, 2015. bluebottle coffee.com/frequency/stepping-away-from-wholesale.

Strand, Oliver. "Coffee Is Not Dead—but It Is Losing Its Wild Side." *Guardian*, November 13, 2012.

———. "A Seductive Cup." *New York Times*, September 15, 2009.

Sullivan, Patricia. "Frederick Meyer, 88; Taxonomist at National Arboretum and Author." *Washington Post*, November 14, 2006.

Summers, Chris. "How Vietnam Became a Coffee Giant." *BBC Magazine*, January 25, 2014. www.bbc.com/news/magazine-25811724.

Sylvain, Pierre G. "Ethiopian Coffee: Its Significance to World Coffee Problems." *Economic Botany 12*, no. 2 (1958): 111–39.

———. "Some Observations on *Coffea arabica* in Ethiopia." *Turrialba 5* (1955): 37–53.

Tadesse, Kebede. *Trees of Ethiopia*. Addis Ababa: Washera, 2004.

Tadesse, M. *Some Endemic Plants of Ethiopia*. Addis Ababa: Ethiopian Tourism Commission, 1991.

Taye Kufa Obso. "Ecophysiological Diversity of Wild Arabica Coffee Populations in Ethiopia: Growth, Water Relations and Hydraulic Characteristics Along a Climatic Gradient." Ecology and Development Series no. 46, 2006.

Tefferi, Fetlework. *Ethiopian Pepper & Spice*. Addis Ababa: Shama, 2014.

Thomas, A. S. "The Wild *Arabica* Coffee on the Boma Plateau, Anglo-Egyptian Sudan." *Empire Journal of Experimental Agriculture 10* (1942).

Thurman, Judith. *Isak Dinesen: The Life of a Storyteller*. New York: Picador, 1982.

Tibebu, Teshale. *The Making of Modern Ethiopia, 1896–1974*. Trenton, NJ: Red Sea, 1995.

Tolera, Motuma, et al. "In-Situ Conservation of Wild Forest Coffee—Exploring the Potential of Participatory Forest Management in South West Ethiopia." WFC2015—XIV World Forestry Congress, September 7–11, 2015, Durban, South Africa.

Tran, Mark. "Ethiopia Enlists Help of Forest Communities to Reverse Deforestation." *Guardian*, April 15, 2013.

Ukers, William. *All About Coffee*. New York: Tea and Coffee Trade Journal, 1922.

Ullendorff, Edward. *The Ethiopians: An Introduction to the Country and People*. London: Oxford, 1960.

Um, Nancy. *The Merchant Houses of Mocha: Trade and Architecture in an Indian Ocean Port*. Seattle: University of Washington, 2009.

"Unaccompanied Alien Children. Improved Evaluation Efforts Could Enhance Agency Programs to Reduce Migration from Central America." Statement of Kimberly Gianopoulos, Director, International Affairs and Trade. Testimony before the Committee on Homeland Security and Governmental Affairs, U.S. Senate, October 21, 2015.

Underhill, G. E. "Abyssinia Under Menelik and After." *Quarterly Review* (London) *470* (January 1922).

USDA Foreign Agricultural Services. *GAIN Report*. June 13, 2016. gain.fas.usda.gov /Recent%20GAIN%20Publications/Coffee%20Annual_Addis%20Ababa _Ethiopia_6-13-2016.pdf.

USDA Foreign Agricultural Services. *GAIN Report.* May 15, 2017. gain.fas.usda
  .gov/Recent%20GAIN%20Publications/Coffee%20Annual_Bogota_Colom
  bia_5-15-2017.pdf.

Vân, David Vô, and Mohammed Jami Guleid. *Harar: A Cultural Guide.* Addis
  Ababa: Shama, 2007.

"Varieties." Stumptown Coffee website. www.stumptowncoffee.com/varieties/.

Vega, Fernando E., Andreas W. Ebert, and Ray Ming. "Coffee Germplasm Resources,
  Genomics, and Breeding." *Plant Breeding Reviews 30.* Edited by Jules Janick.
  Hoboken, NJ: John Wiley & Sons, 2008.

Visit Sidama: Tour Guide Book. Vol. 2. Hawassa, Ethiopia: Sidama Zone Culture,
  Tourism and Government Affairs Department, 2014.

Vivero, Pol J. L. *A Guide to Endemic Birds of Ethiopia and Eritrea.* Addis Ababa:
  Shama, 2006.

Wallengren, Maja. "Ethiopia: Production Is Growing Again in the Birthplace of
  Coffee." *Tea & Coffee Trade Journal,* January 2015.

Watts, Geoff. "Geisha Trilogy." Intelligentsia Coffee newsletter, August 2015.

Watts, Jonathan. "Driven by Fear: The Salvadorean Children Sent on the Perilous
  Journey to the US." *Guardian,* August 29, 2015.

Waugh, Evelyn. *Remote People.* London: Duckworth, 1931.

———. *Waugh in Abyssinia.* London: Penguin, 1984.

Weissman, Michaele. *God in a Cup: The Obsessive Quest for the Perfect Coffee.* Hoboken,
  NJ: John Wiley & Sons, 2008.

Wellman, Frederick L. *Coffee.* World Crop Series. London: Leonard Hill, 1961.

"What People Have Said About Linnaeus." Uppsala University website on Carl
  Linnaeus. www.linnaeus.uu.se/online/life/8_3.html.

Wheeler, Sara. *Too Close to the Sun: The Life and Times of Denys Finch Hatton.* New
  York: Random House, 2009.

Wild, Antony. *Coffee: A Dark History.* New York: W. W. Norton, 2004.

Woldemariam, Bekele. *The History of the Kingdom of Kaffa: The Birth Place of Coffee:
  1390–1935.* Hawassa, Ethiopia: Association for Research and Conservation of
  Culture, Indigenous Knowledge and Cultural Landscape, 2010.

Woldemariam, Gole Tadesse. *Vegetation of the Yayu Forest in SW Ethiopia: Impacts
  of Human Use and Implications for In Situ Conservation of Wild Coffea* arabica
  L. Populations. Ecology and Development Series no. 10, 2003.

World Coffee Research. *Sensory Lexicon.* College Station, TX: World Coffee
  Research, 2016.

"World Coffee Research Finds Wild Arabica in South Sudanese Forest." World Coffee
  Research press release, May 16, 2012.

Yang, Dori Jones. "Fewer Cups, but a Much Richer Brew." Bloomberg, November
  18, 1991.

Yoseph, Metasebia. *A Culture of Coffee.* New York: Muse Collective, 2013.

Zamir, Dani. "A Wake-up Call with Coffee." *Science,* September 5, 2014.

Zewde, Bahru. *A History of Modern Ethiopia: 1855–1991.* 2nd ed. Addis Ababa: Addis
  Ababa University, 2002.

Zimmer, Carl. "How Caffeine Evolved to Help Plants Survive and Help People Wake
  Up." *New York Times,* September 4, 2014.

Index

Note: page numbers in italics refer to images; those followed by n refer to footnotes.

A Note on the Author

Jeff Koehler is an American writer, photographer, traveler, and cook. His most recent book, *Darjeeling: The Colorful History and Precarious Fate of the World's Greatest Tea*, won the 2016 IACP award for literary food writing and the Gourmand Award for Best in the World for a tea book. Other titles include *Spain: Recipes and Traditions*, named one of 2013's top cookbooks by numerous publications, including the *New York Times*; *Morocco: A Culinary Journey with Recipes*; and *La Paella*. His work has appeared in *Saveur, Food & Wine*, NPR.org, NationalGeographic.com, the *Washington Post*, the *Independent, Afar, Fine Cooking, Tin House*, and the Best Food Writing series. After graduating from Gonzaga University, he spent four years in Africa and Asia before doing postgraduate work at King's College, London. Since 1996 he has lived in Barcelona.

www.jeff-koehler.com
Twitter: @koehlercooks
Instagram: jeff_koehler